Don't Be Trapped in the Cities!! Get Out <u>Now!</u>

Are You Ready and Prepared for What's Coming?

by Linda Clore

World rights reserved. This book or any portion thereof may not be copied or reproduced in any form or manner whatever, except as provided by law, without the written permission of the publisher, except by a reviewer who may quote brief passages in a review.

The author assumes full responsibility for the accuracy of all facts and quotations as cited in this book. The opinions expressed in this book are the author's personal views and interpretations, and do not necessarily reflect those of the publisher.

This book is provided with the understanding that the publisher is not engaged in giving spiritual, legal, medical, or other professional advice. If authoritative advice is needed, the reader should seek the counsel of a competent professional.

Copyright © 2016 ASPECT Books, Inc.

ISBN-13: 978-1-4796-0690-0 (Paperback)

ISBN-13: 978-1-4796-0691-7 (ePub)

ISBN-13: 978-1-4796-0692-4 (Mobi)

Library of Congress Control Number: 2016909817

All scripture quotations, are taken from the King James Version. Public domain.

"Words From the Lord"

While writing on my book, ***Don't Be Trapped in the Cities!! Get Out* <u>Now!</u>** the Lord impressed me how to design the cover of my book, as I kept praying for wisdom and knowledge from the Lord to write the things the Lord wanted me to say for Him to His people. I knew I wanted to have a Spirit of Prophecy quotation on the cover of the book, but which quote did the Lord want? I prayed and asked the Lord to please let me know what quote He wanted to appear on the cover of the book He was impressing me to write. That night, in a dream, the Lord showed me this quote: "If God abhors one sin above another, of which His people are guilty, it is doing nothing in case of an emergency. Indifference and neutrality in a religious crisis is regarded of God as a grievous crime and equal to the very worst type of hostility against God." *Testimonies for the Church,* vol. 3, p. 281, by Ellen G. White.

The Lord has been impressing me to hurry and get this information out to His people before it's too late!

Dedication

I dedicate this book, **Don't Be Trapped in the Cities!! Get Out** <u>Now!</u>, to my dear and precious husband, David, for his tremendous encouragement and prayers for me to keep on writing this book that God wanted written for His people, "...for such a time as this," Esther 4:14. "Thank you, honey, for your support, your love and patience and kindness and being so understanding as I had to spend so much time in compiling and researching for this book. What a blessing you have been to me and I appreciate it all so much! God bless you! I Love you!

I, also, want to dedicate this book to my precious son, Jonathan, for the part he has had in the writing of this book, by allowing me to share some of his life experiences in his journey back to God. Although Jonathan has not yet experienced total conversion in the writing of this book, he has certainly come a long way in his experience with God, as we continue to claim the promise in Prov. 22:6, "Train up a child in the way he should go: and when he is old, he will not depart from it." "Thank you Jonathan for remaining home with Mom and Dad, as we continue to encourage you in your walk back to God. We love you and continue to pray for you and your salvation. God bless you! God has a plan for your life! Jesus loves you! John 3:16; Jer. 29:11–14; Jer. 31:15–17.

Jonathan, Dad and I prayed for a child we could raise for the Lord, and God blessed us with you. Your name, Jonathan Paul means: "Little Gift of God." We dedicated you to the Lord before you were even born and then soon after you were born, too. You belong to Jesus. We raised and trained you for the Lord. By the time you were 3 years old, you had memorized over 500 Bible verses and where they were found in the King James Version of the Bible. At 3 years old you said, "I want to be a preacher!" Back when you were 3 years old, when we were talking to Evangelist Fordyce Detamore at his evangelistic meetings in Kansas City, back in 1973, I remarked to Fordyce Detamore that our son Jonathan was 3 years old and he said he wanted to be a preacher. Fordyce Detamore said, "That's when I decided I wanted to be a preacher, too!" When you were 8 years old you were baptized and preached your 1st sermon to me and my mom, your grandma Gladys. Jonathan, we want to enjoy heaven with you. We pray you'll soon surrender all to Jesus and put Him 1st in your life. Matt. 6:33; Phil 4:13; Luke 9:23. Jonathan, you have a lot of people all over praying for your conversion. We have the promise of the Lord, given to His prophet, Sister White, where she wrote in *Testimonies for the Church*, vol. 6, p. 401, "Self-denying efforts will be put forth to save the lost, and many who have strayed from the fold will come back to follow the great Shepherd."

Hang in there, Jonathan! Never give up! Jesus is soon to come and take His children Home. Let's be ready and help others be ready. Matt. 5:16; Gal. 6:9.

Jonathan, Dad and I love you and are proud of how well you're doing! Keep on keepin' on for Jesus!

I, also would like to dedicate this book to God's people who read this book and have the courage and the faith and the trust in Jesus to step out of their comfort zone and follow God's counsel to move out of the large wicked cities as soon as possible and follow the counsel of Sister White found in *Country Living,* pp. 22–28 where she says, "Remember that God has given to every man his work. Choose some locality where you will have opportunity to let your light shine forth amid the moral darkness… and let everyone connected with the office hold himself in readiness to leave, if God shall call him to some new place…I think how the angels must feel seeing the end approaching, and those who claim to have the knowledge of God and Jesus Christ whom He hath sent, huddle together, colonize, and attend meetings, and feel discouraged and dissatisfied if there is not much preaching to benefit their souls and strengthen the church, while they are doing literally nothing…

Go out and establish centers of influence in places where nothing, or next to nothing, has been done. Break up your consolidated mass; diffuse the saving beams of light, and shed light into the darkened corners of the earth…

More and more, as time advances, our people will have to leave the cities. For years we have been instructed that our brethren and sisters, and especially families with children, should plan to leave the cities as the way opens before them to do so. Many will have to labor earnestly to help open the way. But until it is possible for them to leave, so long as they remain, they should be most active in doing missionary work, however limited their sphere of influence may be…

Your letter tells me, my brother, that there are many who are stirred deeply to move out of Battle Creek. There is need, great need, of this work being done, and now. Those who have felt at last to make a move, let it not be in a rush, in an excitement, or in a rash manner, or in a way that hereafter they will deeply regret that they did move…

Take heed that there shall be no rash movements made in heeding the counsel in moving from Battle Creek. Do nothing without seeking wisdom of God, who hath promised to give liberally to all who ask and who upbraideth not. All that anyone can do is to advise and counsel, and then leave those who are convicted in regard to duty to move under divine guidance, and with their whole hearts open to learn and obey God…

Let everyone take time to consider carefully; and not be like the man in the parable who began to build, and was not able to finish. Not a move should be made but that movement and all that it portends are carefully considered — everything weighed…. To every man was given his work according to his several ability. Then let him not move hesitatingly, but firmly, and yet humbly trusting in God.

There may be individuals who will make a rush to do something, and enter into some business they know nothing about. This God does not require. Think candidly, prayerfully, studying the Word with all carefulness and prayerfulness, with mind and heart awake to hear the voice of God… To understand the will of God is a great thing… Let there be much praying done, and even with fasting, that not one shall move in darkness, but move in the light as God is in the light… Let there be wise generalship in this matter, and all move under the guidance of a wise, unseen Counselor, which is God… Now I plead with every soul to look not too strongly and confidently to human counselors, but look most earnestly to God, the one wise in counsel. Submit all your ways and your will to God's ways and to God's will…

If everyone will come to Jesus in a teachable spirit, with contrition of heart, then he is in a condition of mind to be instructed and to learn of Jesus and obey His orders…

We cannot have a weak faith now, we cannot be safe in a listless, indolent, slothful attitude. Every jot of ability is to be used, and sharp, calm, deep thinking is to be done. The wisdom of any human agent is not sufficient for the planning and devising in this time. Spread every plan before God with fasting, [and] with the humbling of the soul before the Lord Jesus, and commit thy ways unto the Lord. The sure promise is, He will direct thy paths. He is infinite in resources. The Holy One of Israel, who calls the host of heaven by name, and holds the stars of heaven in position, has you individually in His keeping…

I would that all could realize what possibilities and probabilities there are for all who make Christ their sufficiency and their trust. The life hid with Christ in God ever has a refuge; he can say, 'I can do all things through Christ, which strengtheneth me.'

I leave this matter with you; for I have been worried

and troubled in regard to the dangers that assail all in Battle Creek, lest they shall move indiscreetly and give the enemy advantage. This need not be, for if we walk humbly with God, we shall walk safely." Read: Prov. 3:5–8; Ps. 32:8; Ps. 37:3–7; Prov. 11:14. You can do it! I'll be praying for you!

I, also, write this book, with its dreams and counsel and advice and warnings to you, my dear Christian reader, and may this information, I've shared with you, be a source of encouragement and help to you as you pray and follow God's plans in your life. And take that "step of faith," trusting God's promises, and follow God's guidance in your life and determine to let the Lord lead in your plans and decisions for the crisis ahead of us all!

Remember what Sister White writes in her *Desire of Ages* book, pp. 250-251, "In the apostles of our Lord there was nothing to bring glory to themselves. It was evident that the success of their labors were due only to God. The lives of these men, the character they developed, and the mighty work that God wrought through them, are a testimony to what He will do for all who are teachable and obedient.

He who loves Christ the most will do the greatest amount of good. There is no limit to the usefulness of one who, putting self aside, makes room for the working of the Holy Spirit upon his heart, and lives a life wholly consecrated to God. If men will endure the necessary discipline, without complaining or fainting by the way, God will teach them hour by hour, and day by day. He longs to reveal His grace. If His people will remove the obstructions, He will pour forth the waters of salvation in abundant streams through the human channels. If men in humble life were encouraged to do all the good they could do, if restraining hands were not laid upon them to repress their zeal, there would be a hundred workers for Christ where now there is one.

God takes men as they are, and educates them for His service, if they will yield themselves to Him. The Spirit of God, received into the soul, will quicken all its faculties. Under the guidance of the Holy Spirit, the mind that is devoted unreservedly to God develops harmoniously, and is strengthened to comprehend and fulfill the requirements of God. The weak, vacillating character becomes changed to one of strength and steadfastness. Continual devotion establishes so close a relation between Jesus and His disciple that the Christian becomes like Him in mind and character. Through a connection with Christ he will have clearer and broader views. His discernment will be more penetrative, his judgment better balanced. He who longs to be of service to Christ is so quickened by the life-giving power of the Sun of Righteousness that he is enabled to bear much fruit to the glory of God.

Men of the highest education in the arts and sciences have learned precious lessons from Christians in humble life who were designated by the world as unlearned. But these obscure disciples had obtained an education in the highest of all schools. They had sat at the feet of Him who spoke as 'never man spake.'"

Also, read what Sister White says in her book, *Last Day Events,* on p. 154, "Afflictions, crosses, temptations, adversity, and our varied trials are God's workmen to refine us, sanctify us, and fit us for the heavenly garner."

Just recently, God wrote me this four-line poem I saw in my dream. Here it is as follows:

"Through all the dangers ahead of me,

The pain and trials and sorrows—

I'll press on in faith and courage knowing that,

Jesus is in all my tomorrows!"

Acknowledgements & Introductory

I want to dedicate this book to Jesus and to acknowledge Him for helping me to write this book. I want to especially thank Jesus, who gave me the dream to write this book and even gave me the title for the book in the dream, ***Don't Be Trapped in the Cities!! Get Out* <u>Now!</u>** Also, Jesus showed me in the dream how He wanted me to sign my name on the book, Linda Clore. Jesus inspired me to write this book and impressed me, through the Holy Spirit and through much prayer, how to write it. Jesus is really the author of this book. I want to give Jesus all the praise and honor and glory and thanks for what He has done to make this book possible. I'm not a writer, but He is. Ps. 45:1, "My heart is inditing a good matter: I speak of the things which I have made touching the king: my tongue is the pen of a ready writer."

God gave me a dream that said, "These dreams are for real. Tell others what I've told you." May this book inspire each reader to have more faith and trust in God and develop a personal relationship with Jesus and step out in faith and allow the Lord to have complete control of your life and plans and surrender all to Him. God bless you, dear reader, as you see the importance and urgency to leave the big wicked cities for the country, for time is truly running out Fast! Like another dream I had, saying, "You haven't much time left!" Another dream said, "NOW is the time to work!" Also, these words were spoken in a dream to me, "Work while you can, the day cometh when no man can work!" John 9:4, 5: "I must work the works of him that sent me, while it is day: the night cometh, when no man can work. As long as I am in the world, I am the light of the world."

Sister White, in her book, *Last Day Events,* on page 42 says, "May the Lord give no rest, day nor night, to those who are now careless and indolent in the cause and work of God. The end is near. This is that which Jesus would have us keep ever before us — the shortness of time."

In another dream I had, I saw the people of God moving out of the cities into retired country places. This is just like the dream Sister White had, and is recorded on p. 21 in her book, *Country Living*, where she said, "The Protestant world have set up an idol sabbath in the place where God's Sabbath should be, and they are treading in the footsteps of the Papacy. For this reason I see the necessity of the people of God moving out of the cities into retired country [places,] where they may cultivate the land and raise their own produce. Thus they may bring their children up with simple, healthful habits. I see the necessity of making haste to get all things ready for the crisis."

We haven't much time to prepare a Christ-like character and warn the world of these coming events. Sister White writes in *Testimonies for the Church,* vol. 9, the chapter entitled, "Called to be Witnesses," on pp. 19, 20 she says, "In a special sense Seventh-day Adventists have been set in the world as watchmen and light bearers. To them has been entrusted the last warning for a perishing world. On them is shining wonderful light from the Word of God. They have been given a work of the most solemn import — the proclamation of the first, second, and third angels' messages. There is no other work of so great importance. They are to allow nothing else to absorb their attention... Christ says of His people: "Ye are the light of the world." Matt. 5:14. It is not a small matter that the counsels and plans of God have been so clearly opened to us. It is a wonderful privilege to be able to understand the will of God as revealed in the sure word of prophecy. This places on us a heavy responsibility. God expects us to impart to others the knowledge that He has given us. It is His purpose that divine and human instrumentalities shall unite in the proclamation of the warning message."

I also, wanted a Spirit of Prophecy quote to put on the cover of my book and asked the Lord to let me know what quote He wanted. That night, in a dream, God showed me the E. G. White quote in *Testimonies for the Church,* vol. 3, p. 281, "If God abhors one sin above another, of which His people are guilty, it is doing nothing in case of an emergency. Indifference and neutrality in a religious crisis is regarded of God as a grievous crime and equal to the very worst type of hostility against God."

The Lord has been helping me to write this book for the last two years. God has been impressing me, through the Holy Spirit and dreams, that NOW is the time to get this information out to His people!

One day I felt like not writing any more on my book and just put it all away. Then, that night, in a dream, God spoke to me and said, "Finish your book!" So I kept writing and working on it with the Lord's help. Thank you, Jesus! Ps. 9:1, 2.

Sister White says in *Last Day Events,* p. 89, "Publications should be issued, written in the plainest, simplest language, explaining the subjects of vital interest, and making known the things that are to come upon the world."

In a recent dream, the Lord showed me the people of God moving out of the cities. Sister White writes in *Country Living,* pp. 28, 29, 30, 31, "The instruction is still being given, move out of the cities... Many now will plead to remain in the cities, but the time will come ere long when all who wish to avoid the sights and sounds of evil will move into the country; for the wickedness and corruption will increase to such a degree that the very atmosphere of the cities will seem to be polluted...

God means that we shall not locate in the cities, for there are very stormy times before us...

Men will arise speaking perverse things, to counterwork the very movements that the Lord is leading His servants to make. But it is time that men and women reasoned from cause to effect... Conditions are arising in the cities that will make it very hard for those of our faith to remain in them...

The Lord desires His people to move into the country, where they can settle on the land, and raise their own fruit and vegetables, and where their children can be brought in direct contact with the works of God in nature. Take your families away from the cities is my message...

The cities are to be worked from outposts. Said the messenger of God, "Shall not the cities be warned? Yes; not by God's people living in them, but by their visiting them, to warn them of what is coming upon the earth." ...

As God's commandment-keeping people, we must leave the cities. As did Enoch, we must work in the cities but not dwell in them...

When iniquity abounds in a nation, there is always to be heard some voice giving warning and instruction, as the voice of Lot was heard in Sodom. Yet Lot could have preserved his family from many evils had he not made his home in this wicked, polluted city. All that Lot and his family did in Sodom could have been done by them, even if they had lived in a place some distance away from the city. Enoch walked with God, and yet he did not live in the midst of any city, polluted with every kind of violence and wickedness, as did Lot in Sodom...

Repeatedly the Lord has instructed us that we are to work the cities from outpost centers. In these cities we are to have houses of worship, as memorials for God, but institutions for the publication of our literature, for the healing of the sick, and for the training of workers, are to be established outside the cities. Especially is it important that our youth be shielded from the temptations of city life...

"Out of the cities; out of the cities!" — This is the message that the Lord has been giving me. The earthquakes will come; the floods will come; and we are not to establish ourselves in the wicked cities, where the enemy is served in every way, and where God is so often forgotten. The Lord desires that we shall have clear spiritual eyesight. We must be quick to discern the peril that would attend the establishment of institutions in these wicked cities. We must make wise plans to warn the cities, and at the same time live where we can shield our children and ourselves from the contaminating and demoralizing influences so prevalent in these places."

I believe in the promises God gave us in Joel 2:28, 29 and Acts 2:17, 18, so please don't think I'm trying to be a prophet, I'm not. I don't consider myself a prophet. I'm only trying to fulfill a work God has given me to do for Him, and He is helping me to do it by writing this book in answer to my prayers for help. I'm only repeating what God's prophet, Sister White, has already said in her warnings given to God's people in the Spirit of Prophecy books.

On pp. 12, 13 of *Country Living,* by Sister White, she gives this warning, "Get out of the large cities as fast as possible…

I am instructed by the Lord to warn our people not to flock to the cities to find homes for their families…

The Lord has sent us warning and counsel to get out of the cities… Fathers and mothers, how do you regard the souls of your children…? 'What shall it profit a man, if he shall gain the whole world and lose his own soul?' How will ease, comfort, convenience, compare with the value of the souls of your children?"

Years ago the Lord impressed me and my husband to build an "Ark" of safety for God's people to come to when the Sunday Laws would be passed and God's people would have nowhere prepared to flee to and survive during the early time of trouble, when we won't be able to buy or sell, because we won't go along with the Sunday Laws passed, but would be true to God and His 7th day Sabbath and all His 10 Commandments. As we read in Sister White's writings, about leaving the large cities preparatory to leaving the smaller ones and during the great time of trouble, after probation closes and there'll be a death sentence on those who hadn't received the mark of the beast by keeping Sunday, as man's made sabbath and won't give up God's true 7th day Sabbath, then we saw in Is. 33:15–17, that our bread and water will be sure during these terrible seven last plagues and that God will take care of us and protect us.

But we saw in reading in the Spirit of Prophecy writings of E. G. White that there's an early time of trouble we'll need to endure and go through before the Great Time of Trouble, when we're fleeing for our lives to desolate and solitary places. During this little time of trouble, when the Sunday Laws have been passed, and we can't buy or sell and our utilities cut off and every earthly support cut off, then we'll have to survive that early time of trouble living out of our own gardens, out of cities and out in the country and having set up and prepared ahead of time for this time in history with our little "Ark" of safety all prepared out in the country with our own well, hand pump, our own woods to be able to cut our own firewood for our woodstoves, and our own little dwelling places out of the cities. Remember, there'll be no buying and selling for those who stay faithful to God's 7th day Sabbath and not going along with the man-made Sunday Law, and you can't go to the grocery store for your food and no job with a paycheck coming in, and no utilities, and like no refrigerator, washing machine, no telephone, or computers or Internet or air-conditioners or gas or electric heaters, no way to buy gas for your car or machinery, no electricity for lights or anything like microwaves, blenders, juicers, no water to your home, it's been cut off, too, no checking accounting, no buying your medicines, or seeing a doctor, or going to the hospital, etc. You are totally dependent on God to get you through this small time of trouble, when you can't buy or sell, and you'll have to rely on Jesus and your little "Ark" of safety you've prepared ahead of this time of trouble you'll be going through when the Sunday Laws are passed and you won't go along with man's Sunday sabbath laws and you won't receive the mark of the beast. These are things we need to be thinking about and praying about and preparing for now, before the Sunday Laws are passed! It takes time to get set up and ready to live during this no buy, no sell crisis we'll have to face, if we're planning on staying true to our God and receive the seal of God by keeping His 7th day Sabbath and all His 10 Commandments and not receiving the Mark of the Beast and his number and his name. (Rev. 13:1–18).

There is going to be only two sides when the Sunday Law is passed — those who go along with it by keeping the man-made sabbath, Sunday and being able to buy and sell and still function in the system, OR those who refuse to go along with the Sunday Law passed and remain true to God and His 7th day Sabbath and all His 10 Commandments and being refused to buy or sell and being put out of the system, but God will care for you and provide for you during this time, while you're living off the land in the country, free from the dangers living in the city. These are the two choices we'll all have to face and the decision we'll all have to make at this time. Will we choose God or man to worship? The decisions we're making each day is deciding the decision we'll be making then. Are we now putting Jesus 1st in our lives and obeying His warnings to leave the cities and prepare to live in the country where you can exist out of your garden and in the little "Ark" you've prepared for this time?

We don't only need to be preparing physically for this small time of trouble, but we need to be preparing our hearts and minds for this time when we'll need to have our own personal relationship with Jesus and learn to love Him and obey Him and have faith and trust in Him with our very lives and know He'll keep His promises to care for us like, Phil 4:19 says, "But my God shall supply all your need according to His riches in glory by Christ Jesus." Also, Ps. 56:3, "What time I am afraid, I will trust in thee." Also, 1 Peter 5:7, "Casting all your care upon him; for he careth for you." Claim, also, the promise in Ps. 55:22, "Cast thy burden upon the Lord, and he shall never suffer the righteous to be moved." Our only safety is in Jesus and staying close and faithful to Him, like Ps. 32:7 & 8 promises, "Thou art my hiding place; thou shalt preserve me from trouble; thou shalt compass me about with songs of deliverance. Selah. I will instruct thee and teach thee in the way which thou shalt go: I will guide thee with mine eye." Also, Ps. 46; and Ps. 91; Ps. 34; Ps. 37; Prov. 3; Is. 41:10, 13 says, "Fear thou not; for I am with thee; be not dismayed for I am thy God. I will strengthen thee; yea, I will help thee; yea, I will uphold thee with the right hand of my righteousness. For I the Lord thy God will hold thy right hand, saying until thee, Fear not; I will help thee." Praise God!

I, also, want to acknowledge and thank the staff at my publishing company for all they've done to help me make my book a reality! Thank you and God bless each one of you for letting God use you!

Table of Contents

My Own Personal Testimony 12
The Founding of the "ARK" 16
Are You Ready and Prepared For What's Coming? 19
Getting Ready For the Crisis Ahead! 33
    Making the Decision 33
Things to Consider
    Get Out of Debt 40
    What to Look For In a Place 41
    What to Put On Your Property 42
Closing Events Charts 46
Pictures 49
Poems 54
    TRUST HIS NAME 55
    THE ARK 56
    GOD LOVES US STILL! 60
    JESUS SUFFERED FOR ME 61
    NOW IS THE TIME! 62
    PREPARE YOUR HEART FOR THE SECOND COMING OF CHRIST! 64
    STAY TRUE TO JESUS! 65
Letters 66
    Step Fast! 71
    God's People, Wake Up! 73
    Why Didn't Someone Warn Us?! 74
    Urgent! 76
    Satan is Wroth! 79
Following the Blueprint in Medical Missionary Work
    Quotes from The Ministry of Healing 82
    Learning Natural Remedies 85
    Experiences 85
    The Great Controversy Above Silver or Gold! 89
Stories
    A CRISIS IS JUST UPON US! 94
    IT MUST HAVE BEEN AN ANGEL! 97
    VISITED BY AN ANGEL IN DISGUISE! 99
    GOD OVERSAW IT ALL! 101
    PAPA, MAMA, BABY BEAR'S CHAIR, AND THE MYSTERY CHAIR! 103
    GOD PARTS THE RED SEA! 105
    I SAW DAVID'S GUARDIAN ANGEL! 106
    LED BY GOD'S PROVIDENTIAL GUIDANCE! 109
    LOST IN THE WOODS 113
    THE MYSTERIOUS CLOUDS! 116

A TEST OF FAITH!	118
THE LOST BILLFOLD	122
A CHRISTMAS STORY	126
FOR HE SHALL GIVE HIS ANGELS CHARGE OVER THEE!	128
GOD WILL PROVIDE!	131
GOD IS ALWAYS RIGHT ON TIME	133
THROUGH THE MAIL WITH AN ANGEL!	135
GOD BROUGHT US THROUGH!	136
TRAPPED!	137
CAMP MEETING DREAM	140

More Stories 142

CHRISTMAS SURPRISES!	142
ANGEL TO THE RESCUE!	145
GOD SENT AN ANGEL!	146
THE POWER OF PRAYER	148
THE PARCEL	149
MATTHEW 21:22	151
WHO WAS IT?	152
THE ANGELS DID IT!	153
THE DREAM	156
GOD SHOWED HIS POWER!	158
GOD KEEPS HIS PROMISES!	161
GOD PUTS A DOUBLE RAINBOW OVER THE 'ARK' TWICE!	162
THE TWO PRAYERS	163
ANGELS HELP!	165
A TIRE, A SCREW, AND A PRAYER	166
ALL THINGS WORK TOGETHER FOR GOOD	167
AN EXCITING AND THRILLING EXPERIENCE!	169
FIGHT THE ENEMY!	170
GOD WROTE US A PERSONAL MESSAGE!	172
THE LOST WAS FOUND!	175
WHY, LORD?	176
STRANDED!	178

Growing Faith for the Time of Trouble

Part 1	179
Part 2	185
Part 3	186
Part 4	188
READY TO COMMIT SUICIDE!	192
THE MYSTERIOUS DATE: 1-22-16	194
PANIC ATTACK!	195
OUR SON, JONATHAN	197

My Own Personal Testimony

My life began on February 28, 1943, being born in Kansas City, KS. My mom, Gladys, was raised a second generation S.D.A. Christian but stopped attending church after she married my dad, Harry, a non-S.D.A., although my dad was a good Baptist Christian. Before my dad died at age 68 years he became a S.D.A. and said at his baptism that it was because he saw Jesus living in me, as I was growing up, that he wanted to join the S.D.A. church. It was at the time my mom was raising her three children: me and my two older brothers, that she became convicted to return back to attending the S.D.A. church. I was nine years old then and began going to church with my mom and was put in our S.D.A. church school, and at age ten years I was baptized. I'm a third generation S.D.A. I have always been a S.D.A. and have enjoyed my walk with Jesus as He has led me through church school, academy, and college. I was married to my S.D.A. husband, David Clore, from Hartford City, Indiana on August 28, 1968.

David is a second generation S.D.A. God blessed us with a son in 1970, who we name Jonathan Paul, which means, "Little Gift of God." That really began my journey learning to rely more and more upon the Lord to train the child God had given to me. Jonathan is a fourth generation S.D.A. We raised him in the country like Sister White admonishes us to do. David and I decided I would not work outside the home but remain home so I could train and teach our son for the Lord. By the time Jonathan was three years old he had memorized over 500 Bible texts and where they were found in the KJV Bible. At age three years old he said he wanted to be a preacher. At eight years of age we placed him in a S.D.A. church school. Then I homeschooled him for a while. Then he attended one of our S.D.A. academies but dropped out in grade 10. He was getting more and more in with the wrong crowd, which was taking away his Christian experience. He passed his GED test and passed his college entrance exams and entered a S.D.A. college. Jonathan is legally blind, and after two-and-a-half months of college he could see his eyes weren't strong enough to take the heavy load, and he dropped out. He had gotten more and more into the wrong crowd and into harmful drugs and drinking and smoking. Through a lot of trials and heartaches, as a mother, I had to witness seeing my son drift from the Lord because of his choices of friends and peer pressure and go out into the world of sin.

There was six-and-a-half years of my life I took care of my son in our home when he became completely paralyzed from his head to his feet. He was reaping the results of his sinful pleasures that caught up with him and he almost died as the paralysis began entering his throat and lungs and other organs. Then God miraculously worked a miracle to stop the paralysis as we earnestly prayed and pleaded with God that He would please spare our son's life and give him more time to live and come back to Jesus again! God in His love and mercy heard our prayers, and the paralysis started reversing, and God has restored all Jonathan's paralysis, except in his ankles, he can't walk. He's in a wheelchair. He's still making poor choices and still reaping the results with poor health and depression and no real joy in life. God is still working on him! He loves Jesus but not willing to obey Him.

These experiences that God has allowed me to go through has brought me closer and closer to the Lord as I realize more and more I need to realize my need to rely more and more on Jesus to see me through these times of trial and heartache in my life. And I know God has a plan for me and for each one of us, if we'll just surrender all to Jesus and let Him control our life. I, also, know God has a plan for my son, Jonathan that I've raised for the Lord. I can claim the promise in Prov. 22:6, "Train up a child in the way he should go: and when he is old, he will not depart from it." God has spared my son's life so very many, many times, for which I'm so very grateful! God's still giving him time to return back to Him with all his heart and deny himself these sinful pleasures and take up his cross and follow where the Lord leads, like Luke 9:23 says, "And he said to them all, if any man will come after me, let him deny himself, and take up his cross daily, and follow me." Even now, as I share my testimony, my son is being cared for in a care center and he's still in a wheelchair unable to walk. He's still experiencing addictions to drugs and depression. We're trying to get him dismissed to bring home and off all these addictions and with the Lord's help restore him to good health again and be able to walk again and hopefully find the Lord again this time around. Please pray for us and our son, Jonathan. Thanks.

Without the Lord's help and courage, I could never go through these experiences in my life. I'm being brought closer to the Lord and He's teaching me faith in His promises and patience in waiting on the Lord to be able to witness the conversion and healing of my son, Jonathan. I'm a firm believer in prayer and God's help and power to heal and to save. And with the coming of the Lord so very near I want to be ready and to help my son and others to be ready to find the joy I have found in living for Jesus! I try to encourage others and young people to stay close and faithful to Jesus as they're making their choices in life because the choices they're making now will determine their destiny then, and I try to encourage other parents who are going through the same broken-hearted experience of seeing their loved ones going down the wrong road and let them know Jesus loves them and is strong to save and is always working behind the scenes to bring our wayward children back to Him. We need to trust Jesus and His Word more and don't lose faith! Hold onto God's promises, He won't lie. Isaiah 49:25, "But thus saith the Lord, Even the captives of the mighty shall be taken away, and the prey of the terrible shall be delivered; for I will contend with him that contendeth with thee, and I will save thy children." In the *Adventist Home* by E. G. White, pp. 264–267 she writes, "By your fervent prayers of faith you can move the arm that moves the world." *Adventist Home,* p. 264. Jeremiah 31:16, 17, "Thus saith the Lord; Refrain thy voice from weeping, and thine eyes from tears: for thy work shall be rewarded, saith the Lord; and they shall come again from the land of the enemy. And there is hope in thine end, saith the Lord that thy children shall come again to their own border." Isaiah 44:3, "For I will pour water upon him that is thirsty, and floods upon the dry ground: I will pour my spirit upon thy seed, and my blessing upon thine offspring."

It's now 2015 and my husband and I are kept busy building the "ARK" God impressed us to build years ago and to prepare a place of refuge for our family and friends and people God will send here at the right time who's needing a place to go through the early time of trouble, when you can't buy or sell, and you'll need to survive the Sunday Laws that will be passed, and we won't go along with them and will be persecuted and fined and imprisonment and some martyrs before the close of probation. (GC 603–612; 5T pp. 449–454) Also, read through E. G. White's book, *Maranatha*.

In Heb. 11:7, God warned Noah to build an "ARK" for the flood coming, and Noah obeyed. In Gen. 6 God told Noah how it was to be made, and Noah obeyed. Today, God is ready to allow the Sunday Laws to be passed, and He's letting His people know to prepare "Little ARKS" of safety to be able to go through the early time of trouble when you can't buy or sell and you'll need to be set up out of the cities, out in the country, so you can have a garden and fruit trees and berries, etc. to eat from and water from your own well hand pump, and woods for firewood to burn in your woodstove. God has instructed His people in the Spirit of Prophecy the importance of being ready for this crisis ahead of us and what they need to do to survive through the Sunday Laws. Some good books to read are: *Coming Events & the Crisis at the Close* and *Another Ark to Build*, both by W. D. Frazee.. Also, *Last Day Events* and *Country Living*, by E.G. White, plus so many more! Like, Jere Franklin's book, *You Can Survive!, and Maranatha by E.G. White.*

As I was writing this article, God gave me a dream: I was in a public store and I noticed a lady making a copy of a log cabin off her Internet, and I said to her, "More and more people are becoming interested in things like that and moving out."

Also, in a recent magazine on rural living, I read how the trend is that more and more people are getting more and more back to gardening and growing their own food, and it showed pictures of back when everyone had their own gardens and fruit trees and lived off the land. Also, just recently, my husband was talking to one of the nurses at the care center where our son is living, until we can get him dismissed and brought home to get him well and off all his drugs he's on, and this nurse was wanting to grow her own garden, and David was encouraging her to do that, and she wanted to get off meat, and we sent her a copy of *Ministry of Healing* and a few standard seeds to get her started, and she was so interested in all he was saying to her. People are open to these truths we're sharing.

People all over are sensing something great and decisive is about to take place, that the world is on the verge of a stupendous crisis. This is what Sister White says in her book, *Education,* pp. 178–184. The question is, are we listening to the Holy Spirit and obeying God's command to leave the large cities as soon as possible and be prepared for what is soon to take the world by surprise? It reminds me of the dream I had. It was quoting Sister White in *Selected Messages*, book 2, p. 142, where she says, "The work of the people of God is to prepare for the events of the future, which will soon come upon them with blinding force." Also, *Testimonies for the Church,* vol. 8, p. 28, "Transgression has almost reached its limit. Confusion fills the world, and a great terror is soon to come upon human beings. The end is very near. We who know the truth should be preparing for what is soon to break upon the world as an overwhelming surprise."

Like Sister White says in *Testimonies for the Church*, vol. 9, pp. 19–29, the chapter, "Called to be Witnesses," on pp. 19, 20 she says, "In a special sense S.D.A. have been set in the world as watchmen and light bearers. To them has been entrusted the last warning for a perishing world. On them is shining wonderful light from the Word of God. They have been given a work of the most solemn import — the proclamation of the 1st, 2nd, and 3rd angels' messages. There is no other work of so great importance. They are to allow nothing else to absorb their attention…

It is not a small matter that the counsels and plans of God have been so clearly opened to us. It is a wonderful privilege to be able to understand the will of God as revealed in the sure word of prophecy. This places on us a heavy responsibility. God expects us to impart to others the knowledge He has given us. It is His purpose that divine and human instrumentalities shall unite in the proclamation of the warning message.

So far as his opportunities extend, everyone who has received the light of truth is under the same responsibility as was the prophet of Israel to whom came the word: "Son of man, I have set thee a watchman unto the house of Israel; therefore thou shalt hear the word at my mouth, and warn them from me." (Read Ezekiel 33:7–9)

Are we to wait until the fulfillment of the prophecies of the end before we say anything concerning them? Of what value will our words be then? Shall we wait until God's judgments fall upon the transgressor before we tell him how to void them? Where is our faith in the Word of God? Must we see things foretold come to pass before we will believe what He has said? In clear, distinct rays light has come to us, showing us that the great day of the Lord is near at hand, 'even at the door.' Let us read and understand before it is too late.

"We are to be consecrated channels, through which the heavenly life is to flow to others… Upon us is laid a sacred charge. The commission has been given us." Matt. 28: 19, 20.

I have been having dreams for many years, probably beginning back in 1996 when I began taking care of our son, Jonathan, who had become completely paralyzed from his bad lifestyle he was living. I never told anyone of my dreams I was having, for fear they'd think I was trying to be a prophet or something. I never did feel I was a prophet and I still don't consider myself a prophet. But through the years I kept receiving these dreams, so I began to write them down but not sharing them with anyone except my husband, David, and our son, Jonathan, and my mom. They enjoyed hearing them and were blessed and helped by them and so was I. My husband kept trying to encourage me to share these dreams with others so they, too, could be helped and blessed by them, but I was too shy and embarrassed to let people know I was having dreams, for fear what they would say or think of me. Finally, after many years, I had a dream that said, "These dreams are for real. Tell others what I've told you."

Then, another night, I heard a voice in my dream call my name, "Linda." I didn't want the people's blood on my hands like Ez. 33 and Ez. 3 and Joel 2 says. So, I felt I should maybe begin sharing these dreams with a few of my friends and close family members. They seemed interested in hearing them and helped and blessed by them, they said.

Then, God laid it on my heart to write a book about the "ARK" we were building for the early time of trouble, when you wouldn't be able to buy or sell. He wanted me to encourage our people to move out of the wicked cities, as soon as possible, and prepare for the Sunday Law crisis ahead of us and to prepare spiritually, too.

I asked the Lord to please help me write the book. I, then, asked the Lord what I should call the book He would help me to write. In a dream I saw the words, ***Don't Be Trapped in the Cities!! Get Out Now!*** I, then, asked the Lord how I was to sign my name on the book. Then in another dream He showed my name written, "Linda Clore." I told the Lord I would like to have a Spirit of Prophecy quote on the cover of the book, but I didn't know what quote to use and for Him to please let me know what He wanted. Then in a dream I saw the quote written by Sister White taken from *Testimonies for the Church,* vol. 3, p. 281, "If God abhors one sin above another, of which His people are guilty, it is doing nothing in case of an emergency. Indifference and neutrality in a religious crisis is regarded of God as a grievous crime and equal to the very worse type of hostility against God." I asked the Lord to please help me design the cover of the book that I was writing for Him, and I feel He did. Praise God He answered all my requests, as I've been literally writing this book on my knees, praying and asking God for His help and guidance and for His Holy Spirit power to write these urgent and solemn words for Him, and to encourage His people to have faith in God and trust in His Word and His promises, as they face the coming Sunday Law crisis, soon to come upon us!

Then, God put it in the heart of Bill and Mary to become interested in my dreams and letters and articles I sent them, and they put them on DVDs for me. So this began the way my book became put on DVDs and shared with others. It has been two years that I have been writing and compiling all this information for my book that God has given me to write. I just pray it will be used of God to be a source of help and a blessing to those who hear my book read on DVDs. To God be the glory! Or read in my book, ***Don't Be Trapped in the Cities!! Get Out Now!*** It's being published in book form now. Thank you Bill and Mary for your love and kindness to help me get this information out on DVDs as soon as possible, and may God richly bless you!

The Founding of the "ARK"

What's the story behind the founding of the "ARK" as it is called by David and Linda Clore, the founders and builders of the "Ark" in Quenemo, Kansas?

Let's go back in time to the year 1941. David Clore was being born in Hartford City, Indiana. Two years later in 1943 Linda Clore was being born in Kansas City, Kansas.

Now how is God going to bring these two individuals together in marriage, being raised so far apart?

Let's fast forward to the year 1968. David was praying for directions in his life and was being impressed by God to leave his home in Hartford City, Indiana, and go to Hinsdale Sanitarium & Hospital to get a job and find him a good S.D.A. woman to marry. So off to Hinsdale, Illinois, he went. Linda, at this same time, was praying what God's plans were for her life and felt impressed by God to leave Union College in Lincoln, Nebraska, and go to Hinsdale Sanitarium & Hospital to get a job. She, too, went. Both were raised S.D.A. Christians wanting to do God's will in their lives and letting the Lord direct as they claimed the promise in Prov. 3:5, 6, "Trust in the Lord with all thine heart; and lean not unto thine own understanding. In all thy ways acknowledge Him, and He shall direct thy paths."

Seven months later after meeting at Hinsdale Sanitarium & Hospital they were married, August 28, 1968. It was now 1973, and in time they moved to five acres in the country in Wellsville, Kansas, with their two-year-old son, Jonathan Clore, born April 21, 1970.

For many years while raising their son, Jonathan, at Wellsville, Kansas, in the country, as Sister E. G. White says to do in her book, *Country Living*, they also kept reading other of her books where Sister E. G. White says to prepare for the time of trouble when you won't be able to buy and sell, because you won't go along with the Sunday Laws passed, and have a garden to raise your own food. Also, they read the book, *Another Ark to Build*, by W. D. Frazee from Wildwood Sanitarium & Hospital in Wildwood, Georgia, where he talked about God's people building little "Arks" of safety to have to go through the early time of trouble ahead of us, before probation closes and the Great time of trouble begins. It was during this time their son, Jonathan, had grown up and had gone out of the S.D.A. church and began bad habits that caused him to go completely paralyzed and have to be cared for.

They chose to care for their son themselves in their small little home they had built on their five acres in Wellsville, Kansas. They felt they could win him back to the Lord as they cared for him at home and not in a nursing home facility.

But then in 2001 Linda's mother became seriously ill, at age eight-four, and was dying of cancer and needed to be cared for, and she didn't want to die in a nursing home, so Linda decided to care for her mom along with her paralyzed son in their home in Wellsville, Kansas. But their small little home wasn't big enough to care for two invalids, so what were they to do?

They prayed, and God directed them to rent a big house in the small town of Ottawa, Kansas.

While caring for their son and Linda's mother and paying rent for this bigger home, they kept thinking that all this rent money could be put on a place to buy so Linda could still have room to care for her mom and son and save all this rent money. They kept praying and David watched the papers and checked with realtors. And then one day in May 2001, David came home from work and said, "I've found just the right place to buy! It's a beautiful 14 acres with woods and a live creek and it's out in the country in Quenemo, Kansas, just a few miles from here. We could buy a big mobile home to put on it and have a place big enough to take care of Jonathan and your mom. It's got really good garden soil for a garden and lots of producing walnut trees and other producing berry bushes. It's real reasonably priced, too. We could use the rent money to make payments on this place in the country!" So they prayed about it and everything worked out with the bank to get the place. They had put $100 down on the contract with the realtor to secure the place while the loan approval went through.

Then the unexpected happened! Linda's mother died and so they wouldn't need to go in debt to purchase a bigger place to care for both Linda's mother and son. They could return back to their little home in Wellsville, Kansas, and care for their son there and not have to rent this big house anymore.

When they explained this to the realtor, that Linda's mother had passed away and they wouldn't need to purchase the 14 acres now, the realtor said, "You put $100 down on the contract and you signed it, you can't back out now, or they could take you to court!"

So they prayed and God worked it out for them to have to go through with the purchase of the 14 acres. So was the beginning of the building of the "Ark." They prayed and asked God what to call their place. Read Heb. 11:7. God impressed them to call it the "Ark," like Noah's Ark. Through the years God has worked miracle after miracle to make the "Ark" a place of safety for people to come to during the time of trouble when the Sunday Laws are passed and people who are just accepting the truth on the 7th day Sabbath and leaving the cities, with nowhere to go, will find shelter and safety on the "Ark." These eleventh-hour people haven't known to prepare a place in the country like S.D.A.'s have known to do from reading Sister White's counsel to leave the cities and prepare a place in the country where you can grow your own provisions when you can't buy or sell. (Read the quotes from E.G. White's book, *Country Living* pp. 9, 10, 17.) They moved forward with a lot of faith and a lot of hard work and a lot of hard times and a lot of prayer and claiming a lot of promises like: James 1:5, "If any of you lack wisdom, let him ask of God, that giveth to all men liberally, and upbraideth not; and it shall be given him."

Luke 1:37, "For with God nothing shall be impossible."

Mark 10:27, "And Jesus looking upon them saith, with men it is impossible, but not with God; for with God all things are possible."

Philippians 4:13, "I can do all things through Christ which strengtheneth me."

Psalm 32:8, "I will instruct thee and teach thee in the way which thou shalt go: I will guide thee with mine eye."

They continue to depend on God to supply all their needs as Philippians 4:19 promises, "But my God shall supply all your need according to his riches in glory by Christ Jesus."

The "Ark," in 2014 is finally a reality, thanks to the good Lord! God has helped them every step of the way as they have had to fight the devil every step of the way, who has tried to stop the building of the "Ark" for God's people to find a shelter in the time of storm. David and Linda still continue to build on the "Ark" and trust God to bring the right people to the "Ark" at the right time. They still continue to claim God's promises and pray and like Noah, before the flood, prepared an ark to save God's people, so they continue to move forward in faith as God directed them to do in a dream, to save God's people through the small time of trouble, as God is directing others to do this, too, by making other "little Arks." Hebrews 11:7, "By faith Noah, being warned of God of things not seen as yet, moved with fear, prepared an Ark to the saving of his house; by which he condemned the world, and became heir of the righteousness which is by faith." Praise God from whom all blessings flow! They give God all the praise and glory for what He has done!

In 2011, during many terribly dangerous tornadoes hitting all around the "Ark," God placed a beautiful double rainbow of promise over the "Ark" assuring them that God's protective hand was over the "Ark" of safety to protect them from the storms ahead during the terrible time of trouble soon to break upon us and protect those, too, who find shelter on the "Ark."

God impressed Linda Clore to write a book, ***Don't Be Trapped in the Cities!! Get Out Now!*** encouraging people to develop faith and trust in God and His promises to be able to hold up under the pressures coming with the Sunday Laws passed and encourage people to leave the large cities, as soon as possible, preparatory to leaving the smaller ones for retired homes in secluded places among the mountains. Read about it in *Testimonies for the Church,* vol. 5, pp. 451, 464–465; *The Great Controversy,* pp. 626–628, 614–615; *Early Writings,* pp. 283–285, 36, 37; *Country Living* by E.G. White pp. 5–32.

As I studied the Spirit of Prophecy quotes and my Bible, I realized God's judgments were soon to fall on these wicked cities and God was warning His people to get out, as soon as possible, so they wouldn't be trapped in the cities with all these calamities coming and people will be unable to leave and martial laws passed saying, "no one can leave the city and no one can be allowed to come into the city." I knew God wanted me to write a book, so I asked the Lord what He wanted me to name the book. He showed me in a dream that night the words, ***Don't Be Trapped in the Cities!! Get Out Now!*** I thanked the Lord for answering me, and then I prayed and asked the Lord how He wanted me to sign my name on the book He would help me write? Then in a dream that night, He showed my name written: Linda Clore. Again, I thanked the Lord for answering my prayers. In my studies and earnestly praying that the Lord would please send the Holy Spirit to guide and direct me as I wrote and claiming James 1:5 promise, I ran across a quote by Sister White in *Testimonies for the Church*, vol. 2, p. 579, "All who are pursuing the onward Christian course should have, and will have, an experience that is living, that is new and interesting. A living experience is made up of daily trials, conflicts, and temptations, strong efforts and victories, and great peace and joy gained through Jesus. A simple relation of such experiences gives light, strength, and knowledge that will aid others in their advancement in the divine life." This quote helped me to realize some of what God wanted me to write about to be an encouragement to others how God will be with us to help us in our time of trials and needs and to have faith in Him and His promises to them. So I began to write experiences my husband and I and our son, Jonathan, have gone through and how God saw us through it all as we relied on Him and how He'll do the same for all His beloved children during the early time of trouble and through the Great time of trouble. We need to let our faith and love for Jesus and His Word grow day by day as we trust in Him to show His power to watch over us and supply all our needs through all our trials and troubles and conflicts and temptations.

As I related some of my experiences to others and my dreams I was having, the word reached Mary and Bill, and Mary became interested in my dreams and wanted me to send them to her and she put them on a DVD and sent them out to help encourage others. I asked her if I sent these dreams and experiences to her if she would put them on a DVD so I wouldn't have to spend a lot of time and money compiling it all in a book form. She said she wanted to put it on a DVD. So I thanked her and felt God had chosen her to be my mouthpiece and avenue to get this information out to encourage and help God's people to let God develop their faith and trust in Him and His promises. Luke 18:8; Heb. 11:5, 6.

Thank you my dear sweet friend, Mary, for doing this for me! I really do appreciate your assistance in doing this kind deed! God bless you and Bill in your DVD ministry! Keep on keepin' on for Jesus! Gal. 6:9. Jesus loves you and I love you, too. Thanks, Lord, for bringing me in touch with Mary!

Mary, I don't mind you giving my name out in these articles I'm sending you. We're just not ready yet to have people come here on the "Ark" yet, as a refuge, until the Sunday Laws. We're still in the process of building the "Ark," 2015.

I finished my book, ***Don't Be Trapped in the Cities!! Get Out Now!*** in 2015, and it's in the process of being published in a book. Praise God!

Are You Ready and Prepared For What's Coming?

We are living in a very critical time in earth's history. The pope in September 2015 is appealing the Sunday Law before congress. Sister White says in *Testimonies for the Church*, vol. 9, p. 11, "Great changes are soon to take place in our world, and the final movements will be rapid ones." Jesus is very soon to come! Are we seriously thinking and planning for the days ahead of us when the Sunday Law will finally be passed? In these last days God is developing a people who will stand through the crisis ahead and will follow Him wherever He leads the way. Read Rev. 14:1–5 about the 144,000. I think of some of the encouraging songs we need to be memorizing, as well as encouraging Bible promises to cheer us on our way during the Sunday Law crisis, when we could be without our song books and Bibles. Songs like: "A Shelter in the Time of Storm" and "Follow, I will Follow Thee, My Lord" and the song, "He Leadeth Me," and the song, "O Let Me Walk with Thee My God," and "All the Way My Savior Leads Me," and "A Mighty Fortress is our God."

It's so important to memorize God's promises and what we believe and be able to prove our beliefs from God's Word. It's so important to get to know Jesus as our own personal Savior and learn to trust and obey Him and rely on Him in our everyday walk with Him, like Enoch did. There's a storm and a crisis coming, are you ready and prepared for what's coming?! Do you love Jesus and His truth, and are you willing to die for Him and His cause? Do you have faith to trust Him when all earthly support is cut off? When the time finally comes to make your decision as to whose side you'll choose to be on, will you be willing to go through persecution and pain and deprivation and oppression and imprisonment and maybe being treated as a slave or be exiled and still stay true to Jesus and all His Ten Commandments, especially the 7th day Sabbath? These are serious and solemn questions we need to be asking ourselves. Joshua 24:15, "…but as for me and my house, we will serve the Lord." We need to be deciding now how we will stand, so we'll be ready and prepared then when the choice will have to be made. We're in the "testing time" right now to be getting prepared and ready for what's coming with the Sunday Law crisis. Satan is tempting more and more people to move into the cities, which is a trap of Satan. That's why God impressed me to write the book, ***Don't Be Trapped in the Cities!! Get Out <u>Now</u>!***

Are you putting your priorities in order, by putting God first in all you do? Read Matt. 6:33. We need to know our Bible and the author of the Bible—God. We need to be seriously thinking about what preparation we need to be making physically and spiritually for the time when we won't be allowed to buy or sell because we choose to follow and obey Jesus and not man and continue to keep God's true 7th day Sabbath and not Sunday, the man-made sabbath. Are you ready and prepared for the hardships ahead of you when all your utilities will be cut off—no electricity, no running water, no gas or propane to heat your home or cook with, no microwave, gas for your car or chainsaw or generator, lawnmower, no telephones, no computers or Internet, no bank, no buying medicine or healthcare or doctor or food or clothes, cars or houses, there'll be no TVs, no washer and dryers or refrigerators or fans and air-conditioners, no paychecks coming in because there'll be no jobs, no video games and DVDs, etc. ...

Before you despair and think how can anyone make it and be able to survive a life like that, let me tell you that it is possible and God will be with you and take care of you because He loves you and will supply all your needs as you learn to trust Him and rely on Him and not man. Please read Phil. 4:19. Some people think the early time of trouble may be for several years, and others think it could be for several months. But nowhere do I find that Sister White says for sure how long this early time of trouble will be. We just need to have faith in God and His promises to see us through the days ahead of us when the Sunday Law is passed and the time comes when we can't buy or sell. Learn promises like: Ps. 91; Ps. 46; 1 Peter 5:7; Matt. 6:33; Phil. 4:13, 19; Ps. 27; Is. 41:10; Is. 41 and 43; Is. 33:15, 16, 17; Ps. 20:1, 6, 7; Ps. 121:1–8; Matt. 11:28–30; Is. 40:21–31; Ps 32:8; Joshua 1:9.

Let me share with you an experience me and my husband, David, and son, Jonathan, went through years ago. We lived in Tennessee for several years out in the back woods in the forest in a little 16' x 16' cabin with no utilities. We had no running water. We had to haul our water, and use an outhouse and bathe in a wash tub and do all my washing by hand, yes, even the sheets. We had a woodstove and cut firewood with a hand bow saw. We had our own garden and no telephone or refrigerator. We used candles and kerosene lamps. My husband colporteured on his own, selling paperback books by E.G. White like: *The Great Controversy, Desire of Ages, Ministry of Healing, Steps to Christ, Patriarchs and Prophets,* etc. We asked for donations only for the books, which we didn't receive very much money for the books.

I remember one time we were short of money and needed food and gas money, so David went to a temporary job place where they line you up with a job for a day or two and they'd pay you the same day what you earned from your temporary job for that day you worked. Well, this particular job they gave David was putting tarred roofs on buildings and shingles on home roofs. He worked ten hours that day pushing a wheelbarrow uphill full of gravel and carrying big heavy stacks of shingles on his shoulder up a tall ladder to the roof. Not being used to this type of work (slave labor) using those muscles he wasn't used to using, he ended up the next day flat on his back and couldn't move! We had no health insurance for any medical help, so we prayed and asked God to please help us in our time of need and please heal daddy. I gave him hot and cold water treatments and massages. With prayer and the Lord's help God healed daddy! Praise God! It was painful for him to walk much for a while.

But we were in need of money, so we prayed and asked God to please bless our canvassing to meet our needs for food and gas money. We drove to a small town close by because we didn't have much gas in the car. I carried the canvassing case of books, and we went together door to door. God was blessing us with sales to pastors and interested people who were giving us large donations for our books! Praise God! He was meeting our needs and helping daddy to be able to walk and meeting the spiritual needs of the people receiving the truth-filled books. It wasn't long before daddy was completely well and able to go canvassing alone. Our faith and trust in Jesus to meet all our needs and care for us through our hard times was tested, but God brought us through it all! Praise God! And God will do the same for each of His children who will be faithful to Him through the Sunday Law crisis ahead of us all. We need to be pressing together and encouraging each other in the Lord.

David's colporteur instructor, when he saw how we were living said, "Well, all I can say is, when the time of trouble comes upon us, you'll certainly be ready and prepared for it, when others who aren't used to hardships will be in a state of shock!" Sister White says in *Country Living,* p. 19, "Hard work, simple fare, close economy often hardship and privation, would be their lot. But what a blessing would be theirs in leaving the city, with its enticements to evil, its turmoil and crime, misery and foulness, for the country's quiet and peace and purity."

Also, Sister White says in *Testimonies for the Church,* vol. 5, p. 711, "A great crisis awaits the people of God. A crisis awaits the world. The most momentous struggle of all the ages is just before us… Have we faithfully discharged the duty which God has committed to us of giving the people warning of the danger before them?" On p. 712 she continues saying, "There is a prospect before us of a continued struggle, at the risk of imprisonment, loss of property, and even of life itself, to defend the law of God, which is made void by the laws of men."

Soon our faith will be severely tested. Sister White says in *Great Controversy*, p. 618, "Their confidence in God, their faith and firmness, will be severely tested." She goes on to say on p. 621 of *The Great Controversy*, "The season of distress and anguish before us will require a faith that can endure weariness, delay, and hunger—a faith that will not faint though severely tried. The period of probation is granted to all to prepare for that time."

She continues writing on p. 622 of *The Great Controversy*, "Those who exercise but little faith now are in the greatest danger of falling under the power of satanic delusions and decree to compel the conscience. And even if they endure the test they will be plunged into deeper distress and anguish in the time of trouble, because they have never made it a habit to trust in God. The lessons of faith which they have neglected they will be forced to learn under a terrible pressure of discouragement.

We should now acquaint ourselves with God by proving His promises. Angels record every prayer that is earnest and sincere. We should rather dispense with selfish gratifications than neglect communion with God. The deepest poverty, the greatest self-denial, with His approval is better than riches, honors, ease, and friendship without it. We must take time to pray. If we allow our minds to be absorbed by worldly interests, the Lord may give us time by removing from us our idols of gold, of houses, or of fertile land… The 'time of trouble, such as never was,' is soon to open upon us; and we shall need an experience which we do not now possess and which many are too indolent to obtain."

We hope and pray our faith experiences we've shared with you will encourage you to have faith in God and will help you know that with God's help and blessing and care that you, too, will be able to weather the storms ahead of you and help you to be ready and prepared for what's coming! God bless you and yours.

Sister White says in *Country Living*, p. 21, "…I see the necessity of making haste to get all things ready for the crisis." Read the Chapter 39, "The Time of Trouble" in *The Great Controversy* by E. G. White. Read Chapters 9, "Sunday Laws," and Chapter 10, "The Little Time of Trouble" in *Last Day Events*, by E. G. White, pp. 123–154. For further study read: *Selected Messages*, book 3, pp. 380–402; and *Testimonies for the Church*, vol. 5, pp. 711–718, by E. G. White.

In the book *Country Living*, by E. G. White she says on pp. 7, 8, "The same voice that warned Lot to leave Sodom bids us, 'Come out from among them, and be ye separate… and touch not the unclean.' Those who obey this warning will find a refuge for himself, and try to save his family. Let him gird himself for the work. God will reveal from point to point what to do next. …

The time is near when the large cities will be visited by the judgments of God. In a little while, these cities will be terribly shaken…

The ungodly cities of our world are to be swept away by the besom of destruction…

Oh that God's people had a sense of the impending destruction of thousands of cities, now almost given to idolatry."

Again in *Country Living*, by E. G. White she says on pp. 10 and 11, "The work of the people of God is to prepare for the events of the future, which will soon come upon them with blinding force…

But erelong there will be such strife and confusion in the cities that those who wish to leave them will not be able. We must be preparing for these issues. This is the light that is given me…"

On pp. 12, 14, 16, 17, 19, 20, and 21 of *Country Living*, Sister White has these words of counsel and warning, "Get out of the large cities as fast as possible…

Who will be warned? We say again, Out of the cities. Do not consider it a great deprivation, that you must go into the hills and mountains, but seek for that retirement where you can be alone with God, to learn His will and way…

I urge our people to make it their lifework to seek for spirituality. Christ is at the door. This is why I say to our people, Do not consider it a privation when you are called to leave the cities and move out into the country places. Here there await rich blessings for those who will grasp them. By beholding the scenes of nature, the works of the Creator, by studying God's handiwork, imperceptibly you will be changed into the same image…

Instead of dwelling where only the works of men can be seen, where the sights and sounds frequently suggest thoughts of evil, where turmoil and confusion bring weariness and disquietude, go where you can look upon the works of God. Find rest of spirit in the beauty and quietude and peace of nature. Let the eye rest on the green fields, the groves, and the hills. Look up to the blue sky, unobscured by the city's dust and smoke, and breathe the invigorating air of heaven. Go where, apart from the distractions and dissipations of city life, you can give your children your companionship, where you can teach them to learn of God through His works, and train them for lives of integrity and usefulness…

It would be well for you to lay by your perplexing cares, and find a retreat in the country, where there is not so strong an influence to corrupt the morals of the young…

To live in the country would be very beneficial to them, an active, outdoor life would develop health of both mind and body. They should have a garden to cultivate, where they might find both amusement and useful employment…

He [God] wants us to live where we can have elbow room. His people are not to crowd into the cities. He wants them to take their families out of the cities, that they may better prepare for eternal life. In a little while they will have to leave the cities.

These cities are filled with wickedness of every kind—with strikes and murders and suicides. Satan is in them, controlling men in their work of destruction…

If we place ourselves under objectionable influences, can we expect God to work a miracle to undo the results of our wrong course? No, indeed. Get out of the cities as soon as possible, and purchase a little piece of land, where you can have a garden, where your children can watch the flowers growing, and learn from them lessons of simplicity and purity…

Much depends upon laying our plans according to the Word of the Lord, and with persevering energy carrying them out…

If the poor now crowded into the cities could find homes upon the land, they might not only earn a livelihood, but find health and happiness now unknown to them. Hard work, simple fare, close economy, often hardship and privation, would be their lot. But what a blessing would be theirs in leaving the city, with its enticements to evil, its turmoil and crime, misery and foulness, for the country's quiet and peace and purity.

To many of those living in the cities who have not a spot of green grass to set their feet upon, who year after year have looked out upon filthy courts and narrow alleys, brick walls and pavements, and skies clouded with dust and smoke, —if these could be taken to some farming district, surrounded with the green fields, the woods and hills and brooks, the clear skies and the fresh, pure air of the country, it would seem almost like heaven.

Cut off to a great degree from contact with and dependence upon men, and separated from the world's corrupting maxims and customs and excitements, they would come nearer to the heart of nature. God's presence would be more real to them. Through nature they would hear His voice speaking to their hearts of His peace and love, and mind and soul and body would respond to the healing, life-giving power…

We are not to locate ourselves where we will be forced into close relations with those who do not honor God… A crisis is soon to come in regard to the observance of Sunday…

The Sunday party is strengthening itself in its false claims, and this will mean oppression to those who determine to keep the Sabbath of the Lord. We are to place ourselves where we can carry out the Sabbath commandment in its fullness. 'Six days shalt thou labor,' the Lord declares, and do all thy work, but the seventh day is the Sabbath of the Lord thy God: in it thou shalt not do any work.' And we are to be careful not to place ourselves where it will be hard for ourselves and our children to keep the Sabbath.

If in the providence of God we can secure places away from the cities, the Lord would have us do this. There are troublous times before us…

The Protestant world have set up an idol Sabbath in the place where God's Sabbath should be, and they are treading in the footsteps of the Papacy. For this reason I see the necessity of the people of God moving out of the cities into retired country [places,] where they may cultivate the land and raise their own produce. Thus they may bring their children up with simple, healthful habits."

Also, on pp. 24, 28, 29–32 of *Country Living,* by E. G. White, she gives this advice on what God wants His people to do: "The time has come, when as God opens the way, families should move out of the cities. The children should be taken into the country. The parents should get as suitable a place as their means will allow. Though the dwelling may be small, yet there should be land in connection with it, that may be cultivated…

Parents can secure small homes in the country, with land for cultivation, where they can have orchards and where they can raise vegetables and small fruits to take the place of flesh meat, which is so corrupting to the life blood coursing through the veins. On such places children will not be surrounded with the corrupting influences of city life. God will help His people to find such homes outside the cities…

More and more as time advances, our people will have to leave the cities…

We cannot have a weak faith now, we cannot be safe in a listless, indolent, slothful attitude. Every jot of ability is to be used, and sharp, calm, deep thinking is to be done. The wisdom of any human agent is not sufficient for the planning and devising in this time. Spread every plan before God with fasting, [and] with the humbling of the soul before the Lord Jesus, and commit thy ways unto the Lord. The sure promise is, He will direct thy paths. [Prov. 3:6] He is infinite in resources. The holy One of Israel, who calls the host of heaven by name, and holds the stars of heaven in position, has you individually in His keeping…

The instruction is still being given, move out of the cities. Establish your sanitariums, your schools, and offices away from the centers of population. Many now will plead to remain in the cities, but the time will come erelong when all who wish to avoid the sights and sounds of evil will move into the country; for wickedness and corruption will increase to such a degree that the very atmosphere of the cities will seem to be polluted…

God means that we shall not locate in the cities; for there are very stormy times before us…

Conditions are arising in the cities that will make it very hard for those of our faith to remain in them. It would therefore be a great mistake to invest money in the establishment of business interests in the cities….

But it is not God's will that His people shall settle in the cities where there is constant turmoil and confusion. Their children should be spared this; for the whole system is demoralized by the hurry and rush and noise…

The cities are to be worked from outposts. Said the messenger of God, 'Shall not the cities be warned? Yes; but not by God's people living in them, but by their visiting them, to warn them of what is coming upon the earth.'…

As God's commandment-keeping people, we must leave the cities. As did Enoch, we must work in the cities but not dwell in them…

Enoch walked with God, and yet he did not live in the midst of any city, polluted with every kind of violence and wickedness, as did Lot in Sodom…

'Out of the cities; out of the cities!'—this is the message the Lord has been giving me. The earthquakes will come; the floods will come, and we are not to establish ourselves in the wicked cities, where the enemy is served in every way, and where God is so often forgotten. The Lord desires that we shall have clear spiritual eyesight… We must make wise plans to warn the cities, at the same time live where we can shield our children and ourselves from the contaminating and demoralizing influences so prevalent in these places…

It is no time now for God's people to be fixing their affections or laying up their treasure in the world. The time is not far distant when, like the early disciples, we shall be forced to seek a refuge in desolate and solitary places. As the siege of Jerusalem by the Roman armies was the signal for flight to the Judean Christians, so the assumption of power on the part of our nation, in the decree enforcing the papal Sabbath will be a warning to us. It will then be time to leave the large cities, preparatory to leaving the smaller ones for retired homes in secluded places among the mountains. And now, instead of seeking expensive dwellings here, we should be preparing to move to a better country, even a heavenly. Instead of spending our means in self-gratification, we should be studying to economize."

The following are quotes from the book, *Last Day Events,* written by Ellen G. White, taken from pp. 123, 125, 126, 127–139, 141 and 142: (The Lord impressed me to add these quotes to this article.) "God made the world in six days and rested on the seventh, sanctifying this day, and setting it apart from all others as holy to Himself, to be observed by His people throughout their generations. But the man of sin, exalting himself above God, sitting in the temple of God, and showing himself to be God, thought to change times and laws. This power, thinking to prove that it was not only equal to God, but above God, changed the rest day, placing the first day of the week where the seventh should be. And the Protestant world has taken this child of the papacy to be regarded as sacred. In the Word of God this is called her fornication… [Rev. 14:8]

The Sunday movement is now making its way in darkness. The leaders are concealing the true issue, and many who unite in the movement do not themselves see whither the undercurrent is tending… They are working in blindness. They do not see that if a Protestant government sacrifices the principles that have made them a free, independent nation, and through legislation brings into the Constitution principles that will propagate papal falsehood and papal delusion, they are plunging into the Roman horrors of the Dark Ages…

Those who are making an effort to change the Constitution and secure a law enforcing Sunday observance little realize what will be the result…

As faithful watchmen, you should see the sword coming and give the warning, that men and women may not pursue a course through ignorance that they would avoid if they knew the truth…

I do hope that the trumpet will give a certain sound in regard to this Sunday-law movement…

We should now be doing our very best to defeat this Sunday law…

When our nation shall so abjure the principles of its government as to enact a Sunday law, Protestantism will in this act join hands with popery…

Sooner or later Sunday laws will be passed…

Soon Sunday laws will be enforced and men in positions of trust will be embittered against the little handful of God's commandment-keeping people…

The prophecy of Rev. 13 declares that the power represented by the beast with the lamblike horns shall cause 'the earth and them which dwell therein' to worship the papacy—there symbolized by the beast 'like unto a leopard'… This prophecy will be fulfilled when the United States shall enforce Sunday observance, which Rome claims as the special acknowledgement of her supremacy…

Political corruption is destroying love of justice and regard for truth, and even in free America rulers and legislators, in order to secure public favor, will yield to the popular demand for a law enforcing Sunday observance…

Satan puts his interpretation upon events, and they think, as he would have them, that the calamities which fill the land are a result of Sunday breaking. Thinking to appease the wrath of God these influential men make laws enforcing Sunday observance…

This very class put forth the claim that the fast-spreading corruption is largely attributable to the desecration of the so-called 'Christian sabbath' and that the enforcement of Sunday observance would greatly improve the morals of society. This claim is especially urged in America, where the doctrine of the true Sabbath has been most widely preached…

How the Roman Church can clear herself from the charge of idolatry we cannot see…. And this is the religion which Protestants are beginning to look upon with so much favor, and which will eventually be united with Protestantism. This union will not, however, be effected by a change in Catholicism, for Rome never changes. She claims infallibility. It is Protestantism that will change. The adoption of liberal ideas on its part will bring it where it can clasp the hand of Catholicism…

The professed Protestant world will form a confederacy with the man of sin, and the church and the world will be in corrupt harmony…

When the leading churches of the United States, uniting upon such points of doctrine as are held by them in common, shall influence the state to enforce their decrees and to sustain their institutions, then Protestant America will have formed an image of the Roman hierarchy, and the infliction of civil penalties upon dissenters will inevitably result…

The enforcement of Sunday keeping on the part of Protestant churches is an enforcement of the worship of the papacy…

In the very act of enforcing a religious duty by secular power, the churches would themselves form an image to the beast; hence the enforcement of Sunday keeping in the United States would be an enforcement of the worship of the beast and his image…

When Protestantism shall stretch her hand across the gulf to grasp the hand of the Roman power, when she shall reach over the abyss to clasp hands with spiritualism, when under the influence of this three-fold union, our country shall repudiate every principle of its Constitution as a Protestant and republican government and shall make provision for the propagation of papal falsehoods and delusions, then we may know that the time has come for the marvelous working of Satan and that the end is near…

As we approach the last crisis it is of vital moment that harmony and unity exist among the Lord's instrumentalities. The world is filled with storm and war and variance. Yet under one head—the papal power—the people will unite to oppose God in the person of His witnesses. This union is cemented by the great apostate…

The religion of the papacy will be accepted by the rulers, and the law of God will be made void…

In the movements now in progress in the United States to secure for the institutions and usages of the church the support of the state, Protestants are following in the steps of papists. Nay, more, they are opening the door for the papacy to regain in Protestant America the supremacy which she has lost in the old world…

We must take a firm stand that we will not reverence the first day of the week as the Sabbath, for it is not the day that was blessed and sanctified by Jehovah, and in reverencing Sunday we should place ourselves on the side of the great deceiver…

Roman Catholic principles will be taken under the care and protection of the state. This national apostasy will speedily be followed by national ruin…

History will be repeated. False religion will be exalted…

Foreign nations will follow the example of the United States. Though she leads out, yet the same crisis will come upon our people in all parts of the world…

The substitution of the false for the true is the last act in the drama…

The whole world is to be stirred with enmity against S.D.A.s because they will not yield homage to the papacy by honoring Sunday, the institution of the antichristian power…

All Christendom will be divided into two great classes—those who keep the commandments of God and the faith of Jesus, and those who worship the beast and his image and receive his mark…

As the decree issued by the various rulers of Christendom against commandment keepers shall withdraw the protection of government, and abandon them to those who desire their destruction, the people of God will flee from the cities and villages and associate together in companies, dwelling in the most desolate and solitary places…

Take the students out to hold meetings in different places, and do medical missionary work. They will find the people at home and will have a splendid opportunity to present the truth. This way of spending Sunday is always acceptable to the Lord… The adherents of the truth are now called upon to choose between disregarding a plain requirement of God's Word or forfeiting their liberty. If we yield the Word of God and accept human customs and traditions, we may still be permitted to live among men, to buy and sell and have our rights respected. But if we maintain our loyalty to God it must be at the sacrifice of our rights among men, for the enemies of God's law have leagued together to crush out independent judgment in matters of religious faith and control the consciences of men…

The Word of God must be recognized and obeyed as an authority above that of all human legislation. 'Thus saith the Lord' is not to be set aside for a 'Thus saith the church or the state.' The crown of Christ is to be uplifted above all the diadems of earthly potentates."

I had wanted to hurry and get this article written and copies made and mailed out on Friday, April 17, but David got so busy hurrying to plant things in our garden, before a lot of rain came in, so it didn't get done. But it was God's will that they not be sent out yet, until I had added these following thoughts at the end of the article to arouse God's people to think seriously about their life and the choices and decisions they're making right now. These are life and death decisions being made!

God woke me up Sabbath morning with these thoughts in my mind to add to the end of this article that God had impressed me to write. The following are the words God gave me: "Friends, the decisions we're making day by day now, will determine whose side we'll be on when the Sunday Law is passed, God's side OR man's side. The decision we make then will decide our destiny. Friends, can't you see how very important it is for you and me to decide now to follow Jesus with all our heart and love and obey Him and learn to trust in Him and His Word now, so when the final decision comes to every one of us, ' Will we obey God or man?' We'll be ready and prepared to say, 'I will serve the Lord and keep his seventh day Sabbath holy and obey all His Ten Commandments, no matter what!' God is putting us all through tests and trials right now to show us our character and where we need to improve to be like Jesus. This is what Jesus is waiting for, to develop a Christ-like character in each one of us, so we'll be ready and prepared to pass our test when the Sunday Law is passed. We need, now to be examining ourselves and see how we stand. May God help us! 2 Cor. 13:5, "Examine yourselves whether ye be in the faith, prove your own selves, know ye not your own selves, how that Jesus Christ is in you, except ye be reprobates?" Also, in the same dream God gave me when He woke me up Sabbath morning with this picture of the stamp that says: "Casting all your care upon him; for he careth for you." 1 Peter 5:7. Jesus cares for you, my friend, and wants you to come to Him and be saved. We need not fear the future if we're on God's side. Jesus will supply all our needs as Phil. 4:19 promises: "But my God shall supply all your need according to his riches in glory by Christ Jesus." Sister White in the book, *Last Day Events,* p. 205 says, "The laborers will be qualified rather by the unction of His Spirit than by the training of literary institutions. Men of faith and prayer will be constrained to go forth with holy zeal, declaring the words which God gives them… Those who receive Christ as a personal Savior will stand the test and trial of these last days."

Over on p. 204 of *Last Day Events,* Sister White pens these words: "He [God] will raise up from among the common people men and women to do His work, even as of old He called fishermen to be His disciples."

Another quote of Sister White found in *Last Day Events,* p. 221 is: "Those who receive the seal of the living God and are protected in the time of trouble must reflect the image of Jesus fully."

Again we read the words of God's prophet, Sister White, in *Last Day Events,* p. 215: "There can be only two classes. Each party is distinctly stamped, either with the seal of the living God, or with the mark of the beast or his image."

On p. 55 of *Last Day Events,* by Sister White she tells us: "We cannot now step off the foundation that God has established. We cannot now enter into any new organization, for this would mean apostasy from the truth."

Read on pp. 224 and 225 these words of Sister White in *Last Day Events,* "The mark of the beast is the papal Sabbath...

When the test comes, it will be clearly shown what the mark of the beast is. It is the keeping of Sunday...

The sign, or seal, of God is revealed in the observance of the seventh-day Sabbath, the Lord's memorial of creation... The mark of the beast is the opposite of this—the observance of the first day of the week...

The Sabbath will be the great test of loyalty, for it is the point of truth especially controverted. When the final test shall be brought to bear upon men, then the line of distinction will be drawn between those who serve God and those who serve Him not."

In *Last Day Events,* on pp. 186–196 Sister White shares this light with us: "Before the final visitation of God's judgments upon the earth there will be among the people of the Lord such a revival of primitive godliness as has not been witnessed since apostolic times. The Spirit and power of God will be poured out upon His children...

At that time the refreshing from the presence of the Lord, will come, to give power to the loud voice of the third angel, and prepare the saints to stand in the period when the seven last plagues shall be poured out...

We may have had a measure of the Spirit of God, but by prayer and faith we are continually to seek more of the Spirit. It will never do to cease our efforts. If we do not progress, if we do not place ourselves in an attitude to receive both the former and the latter rain, we shall lose our souls, and the responsibility will lie at our own door...

The convocations of the church, as in camp meetings, the assemblies of the home church, and all occasions where there is personal labor for souls, are God's appointed opportunities for giving the early and latter rain...

A revival of true godliness among us is the greatest and most urgent of all our needs. To seek this should be our first work... But it is our work, by confession, humiliation, repentance, and earnest prayer, to fulfill the conditions upon which God has promised to grant us His blessing. A revival need be expected only in answer to prayer...

I tell you that there must be a thorough revival among us. There must be a converted ministry. There must be confessions, repentance, and conversions. Many who are preaching the Word need the transforming grace of Christ in their hearts. They should let nothing stand in the way of their making thorough work before it shall be forever too late...

A revival and a reformation must take place, under the ministration of the Holy Spirit...

If we stand in the great day of the Lord with Christ as our refuge, our high tower, we must put away all envy, all strife for the supremacy... We must place ourselves wholly on the side of the Lord...

True conversion is a change from selfishness to sanctified affection for God and for one another...

The strongest argument in favor of the gospel is a loving and lovable Christian...

God will accept nothing less than unreserved surrender. Half-hearted, sinful Christians can never enter heaven... The true Christian keeps the windows of the soul open heaven-ward. He lives in fellowship with Christ. His will is conformed to the will of Christ. His highest desire is to become more and more Christlike...

We cannot use the Holy Spirit. The Spirit is to use us. Through the Spirit God works in His people 'to will and to do of His good pleasure.' (Phil. 2:13) But many will not submit to this. They want to manage themselves. This is why they do not receive the heavenly gift. Only to those who wait humbly upon God, who watch for His guidance and grace, is the Spirit given...

I saw that none could share the 'refreshing' unless they obtain the victory over every besetment, over pride, selfishness, love of the world, and over every wrong word and action. We should therefore be drawing nearer and nearer to the Lord and be earnestly seeking that preparation necessary to enable us to stand in the battle in the day of the Lord...

It is left with us to remedy the defects in our character, to cleanse the soul temple of every defilement. Then the latter rain will fall upon us as the early rain fell upon the disciples on the Day of Pentecost...

There is nothing that Satan fears so much as that the people of God shall clear the way by removing every hindrance, so that the Lord can pour out His Spirit upon a languishing church... Every temptation, every opposing influence, whether open or secret, may be successfully resisted 'not by might, nor by power, but by my Spirit, saith the Lord of Hosts.' (Zech. 4:6)

The latter rain will come, and the blessing of God will fill every soul that is purified from every defilement. It is our work today to yield our souls to Christ, that we may be fitted for the time of refreshing from the presence of the Lord—fitted for the baptism of the Holy Spirit…

The great outpouring of the Spirit of God, which lightens the whole earth with His glory, will not come until we have an enlightened people, that know by experience what it means to be laborers together with God. When we have entire, wholehearted consecration to the service of Christ, God will recognize the fact by an outpouring of His Spirit without measure; but this will not be while the largest portion of the church are not laborers together with God…

The answer may come with sudden velocity and overpowering might, or it may be delayed for days and weeks, and our faith receive a trial. But God knows how and when to answer our prayer. It is our part of the work to put ourselves in connection with the divine channel. God is responsible for His part of the work. He is faithful who hath promised. The great and important matter with us is to be of one heart and mind, putting aside all envy and malice and, as humble supplicants, to watch and wait. Jesus, our Representative and Head, is ready to do for us what He did for the praying, watching ones on the Day of Pentecost…

I have no specific time of which to speak when the outpouring of the Holy Spirit will take place—when the mighty angel will come down from heaven and unite with the third angel in closing up the work for this world. My message is that our only safety is in being ready for the heavenly refreshing, having our lamps trimmed and burning…

Only those who are living up to the light they have will receive greater light. Unless we are daily advancing in the exemplification of the active Christian virtues, we shall not recognize the manifestations of the Holy Spirit in the latter rain. It may be falling on hearts all around us, but we shall not discern or receive it."

Are you and me ready and prepared for what's coming? This is the question we need to be asking ourselves. *Last Day Events,* by Sister White says on p. 12–14, "The time of trouble—trouble such as was not since there was a nation [Dan. 12:1]—is right upon us, and we are like the sleeping virgins. We are to awake and ask the Lord Jesus to place underneath us His everlasting arms, and carry us through the time of trial before us.

So now we are given warning of Christ's second coming and of the destruction to fall upon the world. Those who heed the warning will be saved…

We should study the great waymarks that point out the times in which we are living."

Sister White tell us on p. 23 of *Last Day Events,* "We know that the Lord is coming very soon. The world is fast becoming as it was in the days of Noah. It is given over to selfish indulgence. Eating and drinking are carried to excess. Men are drinking the poisonous liquor that makes them mad…

The labor unions are quickly stirred to violence if their demands are not complied with…

The terrible reports we hear of murders and robberies, of railway accidents and deeds of violence, tell the story that the end of all things is at hand. Now, just now, we need to be preparing for the Lord's second coming."

Also, in *Last Day Events,* by Sister White on pp. 26–29 she reveals this information to us: "Satan is working in the atmosphere; he is poisoning the atmosphere, and here we are dependent upon God for our lives—our present and eternal lives. And being in the position that we are, we need to be wide awake, wholly devoted, wholly converted, wholly consecrated to God. But we seem to sit as though we were paralyzed. God of heaven, wake us up!

The Lord will not interfere to protect the property of those who transgress His law, break His covenant, and trample upon His Sabbath, accepting in its place a spurious rest day…

As the wheel-like complications were under the guidance of the hand beneath the wings of the cherubim, so the complicated play of human events is under divine control. Amidst the strife and tumult of nations, He that sitteth above the cherubim, still guides the affairs of the earth."

Talking about Satan poisoning the atmosphere, that reminds me of the "chemtrails aluminum" with aluminum sulfides spraying out of spraying devices installed on planes and as they fly over the earth this terribly dangerous poison is sprayed into the air contaminating our air and food, and water and crops and human beings, causing Alzheimer's Disease, that's becoming so prevalent. Also, Satan is using man to G.M.O. our food, causing all kinds of problems in animals and man. Sister White says in *The Great Controversy,* pp. 589, 590, "Satan works through the elements also to garner his harvest of unprepared souls. He has studied the secrets of the laboratories of nature, and he uses all his power to control the elements as far as God allows… It is God that shields His creatures and hedges them in from the power of the destroyer… Satan has control of all whom God does not especially guard…

While appearing to the children of men as a great physician who can heal all their maladies, he [Satan] will bring disease and disaster, until populous cities are reduced to ruin and desolation. Even now he is at work. In accidents and calamities by sea and by land, in great conflagrations, in fierce tornadoes and terrific hailstorms, in tempests, floods, cyclones, tidal waves, and earthquakes, in every place and in a thousand forms, Satan is exercising his power. He sweeps away the ripening harvest, and famine and distress follow. He imparts to the air a deadly taint, and thousands perish by the pestilence. These visitations are to become more and more frequent and disastrous. Destruction will be upon both man and beast." Read Is. 24:4–5. Also, in *Ministry of Healing,* by E. G. White on p. 262 she says, "The noise and excitement and confusion of the cities, their constrained and artificial life, are most wearisome and exhausting to the sick. The air, laden with smoke and dust, with poisonous gases, and with germs of disease, is a peril to life." Read in *The Great Controversy,* Chapter 36, "The Impending Conflict," by E. G. White.

In *Last Day Events,* by Sister White, pp. 37–52, are quotes from the pen of Sister White, "The time of test is just upon us, for the loud cry of the third angel has already begun in the revelation of the righteousness of Christ, the sin pardoning Redeemer…

The long night of gloom is trying, but the morning is deferred in mercy, because if the Master should come so many would be found unready… It is the unbelief, the worldliness, unconsecration, and strife among the Lord's professed people that have kept us in this world of sin and sorrow so many years…

The angels of God in their messages to men represent time as very short…

Christ is waiting with longing desire for the manifestation of Himself in His church. When the character of Christ shall be perfectly reproduced in His people, then He will come to claim them as His own…

There is a limit beyond which the judgments of Jehovah can no longer be delayed…

Transgression has almost reached its limit. Confusion fills the world, and a great terror is soon to come upon human beings. The end is very near. We who know the truth should be preparing for what is soon to break upon the world as an overwhelming surprise…

May the Lord give no rest, day nor night, to those who are now careless and indolent in the cause and work of God. The end is near. This is that which Jesus would have us keep ever before us – the shortness of time. There is no need to doubt, to be fearful that the work will not succeed. God is at the head of the work, and He will set everything in order. If matters need adjusting at the head of the work, God will attend to that and work to right every wrong. Let us have faith that God is going to carry the noble ship which bears the people of God safely into port…

The church, enfeebled and defective, needing to be reproved, warned, and counseled, is the only object upon earth upon which Christ bestows His supreme regard."

Sister White says in *Last Day Events*, pp. 172–182: "It is a solemn statement that I make to the church, that not one in twenty whose names are registered upon the church books are prepared to close their earthly history, and would be as verily without God and without hope in the world as the common sinner…

Divisions will come in the church. Two parties will be developed. The wheat and tares grow up together for the harvest…

The history of the rebellion of Dathan and Abiram is being repeated, and will be repeated till the close of time. Who will be on the Lord's side? Who will be deceived, and in their turn become deceivers…

The Lord is soon to come. There must be a refining winnowing process in every church, for there are among us wicked men who do not love the truth or honor God…

We are in the shaking time, the time when everything that can be shaken will be shaken. The Lord will not excuse those who know the truth if they do not in word and deed obey His commands…

Prosperity multiplies a mass of professors. Adversity purges them out of the church…

The time is not far distant when the test will come to every soul. The mark of the beast will be urged upon us. Those who have step by step yielded to worldly demands and conformed to worldly customs will not find it a hard matter to yield to the powers that be, rather than subject themselves to derision, insult, threatened imprisonment, and death. The contest is between the commandments of God and the commandments of men. In this time the gold will be separated from the dross in the church…

In the absence of the persecution there have drifted into our ranks men who appear sound and their

Christianity unquestionable, but who, if persecution should arise, would go out from us…

When the law of God is made void the church will be sifted by fiery trials, and a larger proportion than we now anticipate will give heed to seducing spirits and doctrines of devils…

The work which the church has failed to do in a time of peace and prosperity she will have to do in a terrible crisis under most discouraging, forbidding circumstances. The warning that worldly conformity has silenced or withheld must be given under the fiercest opposition from enemies of the faith. And at that time the superficial, conservative class, whose influence has steadily retarded the progress of the work, will renounce the faith…

Those who have had privileges and opportunities to become intelligent in regard to the truth and yet who continue to counterwork the work God would have accomplished will be purged out, for God accepts the service of no man whose interest is divided…

As trials thicken around us, both separation and unity will be seen in our ranks. Some who are now ready to take up weapons of warfare will in times of real peril make it manifest that they have not built upon the solid rock, they will yield to temptation. Those who have had great light and precious privileges but have not improved them will, under one pretext or another, go out from us…

I asked the meaning of the shaking I had seen, and was shown that it would be caused by the straight testimony called forth by the counsel of the True Witness to the Laodiceans. This will have its effect upon the heart of the receiver, and will lead him to exalt the standard and pour forth the straight truth. Some will not bear this straight testimony. They will rise up against it, and this will cause a shaking among God's people…

The Lord calls for a renewal of the straight testimony borne in years past. He calls for a renewal of spiritual life. The spiritual energies of His people have long been torpid, but there is to be a resurrection from apparent death. By prayer and confession of sin we must clear the King's highway…

When the shaking comes, by the introduction of false theories, these surface readers, anchored nowhere, are like shifting sand. They slide into any position to suit the tenor of their feelings of bitterness…

One thing is certain: Those S.D.A.s who take their stand under Satan's banner will first give up their faith in the warnings and reproofs contained in the Testimonies of God's Spirit…

The very last deception of Satan will be to make of none effect the testimony of the Spirit of God. 'Where there is no vision, the people perish.' (Prov. 29:18) Satan will work ingeniously, in different ways and through agencies, to unsettle the confidence of God's remnant people in the true testimony…

It is Satan's plan to weaken the faith of God's people in the Testimonies. Next follow skepticism in regard to the vital points of our faith, the pillars of our position, then doubt as to the Holy Scriptures, and then the downward march to perdition. When the Testimonies, which were once believed, are doubted and given up, Satan knows the deceived ones will not stop at this; and he redoubles his efforts till he launches them into open rebellion, which becomes incurable and ends in destruction…

The great issue so near at hand [enforcement of Sunday Laws] will weed out those whom God has not appointed and He will have a pure, true sanctified ministry prepared for the latter rain…

The church may appear as about to fall, but it does not fall. It remains, while the sinners in Zion will be sifted out—the chaff separated from the precious wheat. This is a terrible ordeal, but nevertheless it must take place…

As the storm approaches, a large class who have professed faith in the third angel's message, but have not been sanctified through obedience to the truth, abandon their position and join the ranks of the opposition…

Let opposition arise, let bigotry and intolerance again bear sway, let persecution be kindled, and the half-hearted and hypocritical will waver and yield the faith; but the true Christian will stand firm as a rock, his faith stronger, his hope brighter than in days of prosperity…

Some had been shaken out and left by the way. The careless and indifferent, who did not join with those who prized victory and salvation enough to perseveringly plead and agonized for it, did not obtain it, and they were left behind in darkness, and their places were immediately filled by others taking hold of the truth and coming into the ranks…

The broken ranks will be filled up by those represented by Christ as coming in at the eleventh hour. There are many with whom the Spirit of God is striving… Large numbers will be admitted who in the last days hear the truth for the first time."

Sister White writes on p. 212–214 of *Last Day Events*, "There will be thousands converted to the truth in a day who at the eleventh hour see and acknowledge the truth and the movements of the Spirit of God…

A good many do not see it now, to take their position, but these things are influencing their lives, and when the message goes with a loud voice they will be ready for it. They will not hesitate long; they will come out and take their position…

Soon the last test is to come to all inhabitants of the earth. At that time prompt decisions will be made. Those who have been convicted under the presentation of the Word will range themselves under the blood-stained banner of Prince Emmanuel…

In a large degree through our publishing houses is to be accomplished the work of that other angel who comes down from heaven with great power and who lightens the earth with his glory."

On pp. 256–260 in *Last Day Events,* by Sister White we read, "The remnant church will be brought into great trial and distress. Those who keep the commandments of God and the faith of Jesus will feel the ire of the dragon and his host. Satan numbers the world as his subjects. He has gained control of the apostate churches; but here is a little company that are resisting his supremacy. If he could blot them from the earth, his triumph would be complete. As he influenced the heathen nations to destroy Israel, so in the near future he will stir up the wicked powers of earth to destroy the people of God…

Let all read carefully the 13th chapter of Revelation, for it concerns every human agent, great and small…

The time of trouble is about to come upon the people of God. Then it is that the decree will go forth forbidding those who keep the Sabbath of the Lord to buy or sell, and threatening them with punishment, and even death, if they do not observe the first day of the week as the Sabbath…

All who refuse compliance will be visited with civil penalties, and it will finally be declared that they are deserving of death…

If the people of God will put their trust in Him and by faith rely upon His power, the devices of Satan will be defeated in our time as signally as in the days of Mordecai…

This small remnant, unable to defend themselves in the deadly conflict with the powers of earth that are marshaled by the dragon host, make God their defense. The decree has been passed by the highest earthly authority that they shall worship the beast and receive his mark under pain of persecution and death. May God help His people now, for what can they then do in such a fearful conflict without His assistance…

As the decree issued by the various rules of Christendom against commandment keepers shall withdraw the protection of government and abandon them to those who desire their destruction, the people of God will flee from the cities and villages and associate together in companies, dwelling in the most desolate and solitary places. Many will find refuge in the strongholds of the mountains… But many of all nations and of all classes, high and low, rich and poor, black and white, will be cast into the most unjust and cruel bondage. The beloved of God pass weary days bound in chains, shut in by prison bars, sentenced to be slain, some apparently left to die of starvation in dark and loathsome dungeons…

The people of God are not at this time all in one place. They are in different companies and in all parts of the earth, and they will be tried singly, not in groups. Everyone must stand the test for himself…

The faith of individual members of the church will be tested as though there were not another person in the world."

While writing on this article God gave me these dreams: "I saw a group of God's people heading into the mountains. I was saying to them, "Don't go empty handed." Each person was carrying something in their hands. Read *Testimonies for the Church, vol. 5,* pp. 464–466. The other dream said, "Seize the moment." Read *Testimonies for the Church,* vol. 5, pp. 612, 613. (Take advantage of the moment you now have.) The dictionary says "seize" means, "to pursue diligently or persistently."

Also, I dreamed I heard these words: "Stay on the straight and narrow path and take time to pray." Read, Matt. 7:13, 14 and Luke 13:24; and also, 1 Thess. 5:17, "Pray without ceasing." Read also, Phil. 4:1-23. Now is the time when we need to hang onto Jesus' hand tight and never let it go, no matter what! Does Jesus have all your heart, soul, mind, and spirit? Have you surrendered all to Jesus? Are you letting Jesus control your life and your decisions you're making day by day? Are you and your family ready and prepared for what's coming?!

Friends, things are shaping up FAST and the last movements will be rapid ones! None of us know how long we have left in this world. Those dear people who went to work on 9-11 to the twin towers never dreamed that would be their last day on earth. Are we ready and prepared to close our life's record? Are we ready and prepared to meet the crisis ahead of us and to meet Jesus face to face? Now is the time to decide how we will stand in the days ahead of us. Tomorrow may not be given to you or me. What are we doing with our life today? We need to put Jesus first in our life, and as Matt. 6:33 says, "But seek ye first the kingdom of God, and his righteousness; and all these things shall be added unto you."

Sister White says in *Country Living,* pp. 5–13, "Few realize the importance of shunning, so far as possible, all associations unfriendly to religious life. In choosing their surroundings, few make their spiritual prosperity the first consideration…

Instead of the crowded city, seek some retired situation where your children will be, so far as possible, shielded from the temptation, and there train and educate them for usefulness…

Through the working of trusts and the results of labor unions and strikes the conditions of life in the city are constantly becoming more and more difficult. Serious troubles are before us, and for many families removal from the cities will become a necessity.

The physical surroundings in the cities are often a peril to health. The constant liability to contact with disease, the prevalence of foul air, impure water, impure food, the crowded, dark, unhealthful dwellings, are some of the many evils to be met.

It was not God's purpose that people should be crowded into cities, huddled together in terraces and tenements. In the beginning He placed our first parents amidst the beautiful sights and sounds He desires us to rejoice in today. The more nearly we come into harmony with God's original plan, the more favorable will be our position to secure health of body, and mind, and soul…

Had Lot hastened as the Lord desired him to, his wife would not have become a pillar of salt. Lot had too much of a lingering spirit. Let us not be like him. The same voice that warned Lot to leave Sodom bids us, 'Come out from among them, and be ye separate,… and touch not the unclean.' Those who obey this warning will find a refuge. Let every man be wide awake for himself, and try to save his family. Let him gird himself for the work. God will reveal from point to point what to do next.

Hear the voice of God through the apostle Paul: 'Work out your own salvation with fear and trembling. For it is God which worketh in you both to will and to do of His good pleasure.' Lot trod the plain with unwilling and tardy steps…

In harmony with the light given me, I am urging people to come out from the great centers of population. Our cities are increasing in wickedness, and it is becoming more and more evident that those who remain in them unnecessarily do so at the peril of their soul's salvation…

The time is fast coming when the controlling power of the labor unions will be very oppressive. Again and again the Lord has instructed that our people are to take their families away from the cities into the country, where they can raise their own provisions, for in the future the problem of buying and selling will be a very serious one. We should now begin to heed the instruction given us over and over again: Get out of the cities into rural districts, where the houses are not crowded closely together, and where you will be free from the interference of enemies…

The trades unions will bring upon this earth a time of trouble such has not been since the world began…

The work of the people of God is to prepare for the events of the future, which will soon come upon them with blinding force. In the world gigantic monopolies will be formed. Men will bind themselves together in unions that will wrap them in the folds of the enemy. A few men will combine to grasp all the means to be obtained in certain lines of business. Trade unions will be formed, and those who refuse to join these unions will be marked men…

The trade unions and confederacies of the world are a snare. Keep out of them, and away from them, brethren. Have nothing to do with them. Because of these unions and confederacies, it will soon be very difficult for our institutions to carry on their work in the cities. My warning is: Keep out of the cities. Build no sanitariums in the cities. Educate our people to get out of the cities into the country, where they can obtain a small piece of land, and make a home for themselves and their children…

These unions are one of the signs of the last days. Men are binding up in bundles ready to be burned. They may be church members, but while they belong to these unions, they cannot possibly keep the commandments of God; for to belong to these unions means to disregard the entire Decalogue.

'Thou shalt love the Lord thy God with all thy heart, and with all thy soul, and with all thy strength, and with all thy mind; and thy neighbor as thyself.' These words sum up the whole duty of man. They mean the consecration of the whole being, body, soul, and spirit to God's service. And how can men obey these words, and at the same time pledge themselves to support that which deprives their neighbors of freedom of action? And how can men obey these words, and form combinations that rob the poorer classes of the advantages which justly belong to them, preventing them from buying and selling, except under certain conditions?...

Those who claim to be children of God are in no case to bind up with the labor unions that are formed or that shall be formed. This the Lord forbids. Cannot those who study the prophecies see and understand what is before us...

Before the overflowing scourge [this is referring to the Sunday Laws] shall come upon the dwellers of the earth, the Lord calls upon all who are Israelites indeed to prepare for that event. To parents He sends the warning cry, Gather your children into your own houses, gather them away from those who are disregarding the commandments of God, who are teaching and practicing evil. Get out of the large cities as fast as possible. Establish church schools. Give your children the Word of God as the foundation of all their education.

I am instructed by the Lord to warn our people not to flock to the cities to find homes for their families. To fathers and to mothers I am instructed to say, Fail not to keep your children within your own premises...

Let children no longer be exposed to the temptations of the cities that are ripe for destruction. The Lord has sent us warning and counsel to get out of the cities. Then let us make no more investments in the cities. Fathers and mothers, how do you regard the souls of your children? Are you preparing the members of your families for translation into the heavenly courts? Are you preparing them to become members of the royal family? Children of the heavenly King? 'What shall it profit a man, if he shall gain the whole world and lose his own soul?' How will ease, comfort, convenience, compare with the value of the souls of your children?

In *Testimonies for the Church*, vol. 5, p. 612, Sister White writes: "They are a solemn warning to churches and individuals that the watcher who never slumbers is measuring their course of action. It is only by reason of his marvelous patience that they are not cut down as cumberers of the ground. But His Spirit will not always strive. His patience will wait but little longer.

Your faith must be something more than it has been, or you will be weighed in the balances and found wanting...

It is not yet too late to redeem the neglects of the past. Let there be a revival of the first love, the first ardor."

Read *Testimonies for the Church* vol. 4, p. 312 by Sister White. Continuing to read in *Testimonies for the Church*, vol. 5, p. 612, 613, Sister White says, "Let the tenderness and mercy that Jesus has revealed in His own precious life be an example to us of the manner in which we should treat our fellow beings, especially those who are our brethren in Christ. Many have fainted and become discouraged in the great struggle of life, whom one word of kindly cheer and courage would have strengthened to overcome. Never, never become heartless, cold, unsympathetic, and censorious. Never lose an opportunity to say a word to encourage and inspire hope. We cannot tell how far reaching may be our tender words of kindness, our Christlike efforts to lighten some burden. The erring can be restored in no other way than in the spirit of meekness, gentleness, and tender love."

Read the chapter entitled: "Practical Godliness," in *Testimonies for the Church*, vol. 5, by Sister White, pp. 532–541.

Getting Ready For the Crisis Ahead!

Making the Decision

We all should ask ourselves the question: What is God's will for me? One of the best ways to make a decision about something is to go to God in prayer and pray for divine guidance and fast over the matter and seek counsel in God's Word and Spirit of Prophecy. James 1:5–8, "If any of you lack wisdom, let him ask of God, that giveth to all men liberally, and upbraideth not; and it shall be given him. But let him ask in faith, nothing wavering. For he that wavereth is like a wave of the sea driven with the wind and tossed. For let not that man think that he shall receive anything of the Lord. A double minded man is unstable in all his ways."

Desire of Ages, p. 348, "It is for our own benefit to keep every gift of God fresh in our memory. Thus faith is strengthened to claim and to receive more and more. There is greater encouragement for us in the least blessing we ourselves receive from God than in all the accounts we can read of the faith and experiences of others. The soul that responds to the grace of God shall be like a watered garden. His health shall spring forth speedily; his light shall rise in obscurity and the glory of the Lord shall be seen upon him. Let us then remember the loving kindness of the Lord, and the multitude of His tender mercies. Like the people of Israel, let us set up our stones of witness, and inscribe upon them the precious story of what God has wrought for us. And as we review His dealings with us in our pilgrimage, let us, out of hearts melted with gratitude, declare, "What shall I render unto the Lord for all His benefits toward me? I will take the cup of salvation, and call upon the name of the Lord. I will pay my vows unto the Lord now in the presence of all His people." Ps. 116:12–14.

Please read page 668 in *Desire of Ages*, my favorite page. Here's a quote from there: "The Lord will teach us our duty just as willingly as He will teach somebody else. If we come to Him in faith, He will speak His mysteries to us personally. Our hearts will often burn within us as One draws nigh to commune with us as He did with Enoch. Those who decide to do nothing in any line that will displease God, will know, after presenting their case before Him, just what course to pursue. And they will receive not only wisdom, but strength. Power for obedience, for service, will be imparted to them, as Christ has promised… And 'whatsoever we ask, we receive of Him, because we keep His commandments, and do those things that are pleasing His sight.'" 1 John 3:22.

Testimonies for the Church, vol. 6, p. 393, "The word of the living God is not merely written, but spoken. The Bible is God's voice speaking to us, just as surely as though we could hear it with our ears. If we realized this, with what awe would we search its precepts! The reading and contemplation of the Scriptures would be regarded as an audience with the Infinite One… Many fail of imitating our holy Pattern because they study so little the definite features of that character. So many are full of busy plans, always active; and there is no time or place for the precious Jesus to be a close, dear companion. They do not refer every thought and action to Him, inquiring: 'Is this the way of the Lord?' If they did they would walk with God, as did Enoch."

Some good books to read to help you in making your decision as to what to do at this time is: Robert W. Olson, Compiler of—Ellen White comments on *"The Crisis Ahead."* This is a book on Answers to Questions about the end-time. (What if you could sit down with Ellen White and ask her any question you wished about the end of the world? Now you can, in a way.) In this book Sister White explains not only WHAT will happen, but HOW to get ready for it. The compiler of this book, Robert W. Olson is the former director of the Ellen G. White Estates.

Another good reference book is Ellen G. White's, *Last Day Events,* and her valuable book for our day, *The Great Controversy,* and her *Country Living* book. Also, read W.D. Frazee's books, *Another Ark to Build,* and *Coming Events & Crisis at the Close.* A book that you must have is Jere Franklin's book, *You Can Survive.* A good reference book to have on hand is: *Natural Remedies Encyclopedia,* by Vance Ferrell. Also, *Today's Herbal Health,* by Louise Tenney, M.H. Another good herb book is *From the Shepherd's Purse,* by Max G. Burlow. *Back to Eden,* by Jethro Kloss; *From City to Country Living,* by Arthur L. White and E.A. Sutherland. *The Country Way,* by Lloyd E. Eighme.

These are a few good books to help you in making your decision to leave the city for country living and for learning Medical Missionary Joel 3:14, "Multitudes, multitudes in the valley of decision: for the day of the Lord is near in the valley of decision."

Some reasons people give for why they live in the cities are:

1. More and better jobs to pick from.

2. Everything is so convenient and easy access to the malls, schools, hospitals, doctors' offices, grocery stores, and other stores, restaurants, fast foods, entertainment.

3. You can save gas and time by not having to commute long distances to the city from out in the country and save wear and tear on the car and tires.

BUT --Some of the reasons why we shouldn't locate in the cities, but be out in the country is First of all, it's a command from God through His prophet Sister White, "Out of the cities, out of the cities! This is the message the Lord has been giving me." *Country Living*, p. 31. The cities are a TRAP of Satan to get the people to flock to the cities with their families.

Sister White says in *Country Living,* pp. 5, 6, "Few realize the importance of shunning, so far as possible, all associations unfriendly to religious life. In choosing their surroundings, few make their spiritual prosperity the first consideration. Parents flock with their families to the cities, because they fancy it easier to obtain a livelihood there than in the country. The children, having nothing to do when not in school obtain a street education. From evil associates, they acquire habits of vice and dissipation. The parents see all this, but it will require a sacrifice to correct their error, and they stay where they are, until Satan gains full control of their children. Better sacrifice any and every worldly consideration than to imperil the precious souls committed to your care… Instead of the crowded city, seek some retired situation where your children will be, so far as possible, shielded from temptation, and there train and educate them for usefulness…

The world over cities are becoming hotbeds of vice. On every hand are the sights and sounds of evil. Everywhere are enticements to sensuality and dissipation… Every day brings the record of violence, robberies, murders, suicides, and crimes unnamable…

One of the most subtle and dangerous temptations that assails the children and youth in the cities is the love of pleasure…

Through the working of trusts and the results of labor unions and strikes the conditions of life in the city are constantly becoming more and more difficult. Serious troubles are before us; and for many families removal from the cities will become a necessity."

Sister White goes on to say in *Country Living,* p. 7, "I am bidden to declare the message that cities full of transgression, and sinful in extreme will be destroyed by earthquakes, by fires, by flood.

On p. 9 of *Country Living*, we read, "The time is fast coming when the controlling power of the labor unions will be very oppressive. Again and again the Lord has instructed that our people are to take their families away from the cities, into the country, where they can raise their own provisions, for in the future the problem of buying and selling will be a very serious one. We should now begin to heed the instruction given us over and over again: Get out of the cities into rural districts, where the houses are not crowded closely together, and where you will be free from the interference of enemies."

I looked up in the dictionary the meaning of provisions and it said: A supply or stock of food; the state of being prepared beforehand; a stock of needed material or supplies; a measure taken beforehand to deal with a need.

In *Country Living*, p. 10–12 Sister White says, "The trade unions will be one of the agencies that will bring upon this earth a time of trouble such as has not been since the world began… Trade unions will be formed, and those who refuse to join these unions will be marked men. The trade unions and confederacies of the world are a snare. Keep out of them, and away from them, brethren. Have nothing to do with them. Because of these unions and confederacies, it will soon be very difficult for our institutions to carry on their work in the cities. My warning is: Keep out of the cities. Build no sanitariums in the cities. Educate our people to get out of the cities into the country, where they can obtain a small piece of land, and make a home for themselves and their children… But erelong there will be such strife and confusion in the cities, that those who wish to leave them will not be able. We must be preparing for these issues. This is the light that is given to me. We are not to unite with secret societies or with trades unions… These unions are one of the signs of the last days. Men are binding up in bundles ready to be burned. They may be church members, but while they belong to these unions, they cannot possibly keep the commandments of God; for to belong to these unions means to disregard the entire Decalogue.

(Read Mark 12:30, 31.) These words sum up the whole duty of man. They mean consecration of the whole being, body, soul, and spirit, to God's service. How can men obey these words, and at the same time pledge themselves to support that which deprives their neighbors of freedom of action? And how can men obey these words, and form combinations that rob the poorer classes of the advantages which justly belong to them, preventing them from buying and selling, except under certain conditions? Those who claim to be children of God are in no case to bind up with the labor unions that are formed or that shall be formed. This the Lord forbids. Cannot those who study the prophecies see and understand what is before us?"

Read in *Country Living*, by Sister White, pp. 12–17, "An Appeal to Parents." In this section she says, "Before the overflowing scourge (she's referring to the Sunday Laws) shall come upon the dwellers of the earth, the Lord calls upon all who are Israelites indeed to prepare for that event… Get out of the large cities as fast as possible… Give your children the Word of God as the foundation of all their education… Fathers and mothers, how do you regard the souls of your children? Are you preparing the members of your family for translation into the heavenly courts?… How will ease, comfort, convenience, compare with the value of the souls of your children?… God gave to our first parents the means of true education, when He instructed them to till the soil and care for their garden home…

As it was in the days of Noah, every kind of evil is on the increase. Divorce and marriage is the order of the time. At such a time as this, the people who are seeking to keep the commandments of God should look for retired places away from the cities… Do not consider it a great deprivation, that you must go into the hills and mountains, but seek for that retirement where you can be alone with God, to learn His will and way. I urge our people to make it their lifework to seek for spirituality. Christ is at the door."

I looked up in the dictionary the meaning of deprivation and it said: Deprived of the necessities of life; to take away from by force; the lack of things needed to live or be comfortable.

Sister White continues to say on pp. 12–17 in *Country Living*, "What were the conditions chosen by the infinite Father for His son? A secluded home in the Galilean hills… Better than any other inheritance of wealth you can give to your children will be the gift of a healthy body, a sound mind, and a noble character. Those who understand what constitutes life's true success will be wise betimes. They will keep in view life's best things in their choice of a home. Instead of dwelling where only the works of men can be seen, where the sights and sounds frequently suggest thoughts of evil, where turmoil and confusion bring weariness and disquietude, go where you can look upon the works of God. Find rest of spirit in the beauty and quietude and peace of nature. Let the eye rest on the green fields, the groves, and the hills. Look up to the blue sky, unobscured by the city's dust and smoke, and breathe the invigorating air of heaven. Go where, apart from distractions and dissipations of city life, you can give your children your companionship, where you can teach them to learn of God through His works, and train them for lives of integrity and usefulness."

I looked up in the dictionary the meaning of the word dissipation and it said: to spend or use foolishly, waste; to spend much time in wild or harmful pleasures; wasteful expenditure; intemperate living, especially excessive drinking; amusements; to spread thin to the point of vanishing; to be extravagant or dissolute in the pursuit of pleasure.

Sister White continues saying on pp. 16, 17 of *Country Living*, "It would be well for you to lay by your perplexing cares, and find a retreat in the country, where there is not so strong an influence to corrupt the morals of the young... To live in the country would be very beneficial to them; an active, out-of-door life would develop health of both mind and body. They should have a garden to cultivate, where they might find both amusement and useful employment. The training of plants and of flowers tends to the improvement of taste and judgment, while an acquaintance with God's useful and beautiful creation has a refining and ennobling influence upon the mind, referring it to the Maker and Master of all...

He wants us to live where we can have elbow room. His people are not to crowd into the cities, He wants them to take their families out of the cities, that they may better prepare for eternal life. In a little while they will have to leave the cities. These cities are filled with wickedness of every kind,—with strikes and murders and suicides. Satan is in them, controlling men in their work of destruction. Under his influence they kill for the sake of killing, and this they will do more and more... If we place ourselves under objectionable influences, can we expect God to work a miracle to undo the results of our wrong course? No, indeed. Get out of the cities as soon as possible, and purchase a little piece of land, where you can have a garden, where your children can watch the flowers growing, and learn from them lessons of simplicity and purity."

The decision to go to the country or remain in the cities is a choice everyone is going to have to make, but will have to live with the consequences of their decision they have made.

The Sunday Law crisis is another decision everyone is going to have to make, but will have to live with the consequences of the choice they have made; to obey man and his Sunday Law and still be able to buy and sell and be a part of society, but receive the mark of the beast and the seven last plagues and lose eternal life; or choose to obey God's true seventh-day Sabbath and all his commandments and have the seal of God, and be filled with the Holy Spirit and give the Loud Cry message and be persecuted and fined and imprisoned and can't buy or sell and be shut off from all utilities and food and clothes and medical assistance, etc., but have angels care for you and provide for you and have your garden to eat from and be able to exist on your little Ark of safety out in the country during the early time of trouble and then, finally, cared for when you'll have to leave your little Arks of safety and the death decree will be enforced and we'll have to flee for our lives to desolate and solitary places in the mountains and forests, and caves and go through the Great Time of Trouble when the seven last plagues will be falling but God promises us that our bread and water will be sure in Is. 33:15, 16 and angels will protect and care for us, and we'll have eternal life given to us. Ps. 34:6–9; Ps. 91; Ps. 46; Ps 27. *Great Controversy*, chapter, "The Time of Trouble", pp. 611–634. *Testimonies for the Church*, vol. 5, p. 147, "Choose poverty, reproach, separation from friends, or any suffering rather than to defile the soul with sin. Death before dishonor or the transgression of God's law should be the motto of every Christian."

Yes, again there is a showdown coming for God's people over God's seventh-day Sabbath, Saturday versus Sunday, the first day of the week, a man-made Sabbath and the choice we'll all have to make to obey and worship God or man at that time when the Sunday Law will be enforced upon us. We'll all have to face that decision and make that choice who we will obey, like God's people on Mt. Carmel when they had to decide who they would serve and obey, God or Baal? (1 Kings 18, 19) Also, in Joshua 24:14–25, God's people had to make a decision who they were going to obey back then.

We, too, are going to have to make choices and a decision when the Sunday Law is passed to worship and obey God or man?

Please read *Testimonies for the Church*, vol. 5, pp. 132–137. I quote from pp. 136, 137, "To stand in defense of truth and righteousness when the majority forsake us, to fight the battles of the Lord when champions are few—this will be our test... The test will surely come... Now is the time when we should closely connect with God, that we may be hid when the fierceness of His wrath is poured upon the sons of men. We have wandered away from the old landmarks. Let us return. If the Lord be God, serve Him; if Baal, serve him. Which side will you be on?"

Testimonies for the Church, vol. 5, p. 573, "Time is very short, and all that is to be done must be done quickly. The angels are holding the four winds, and Satan is taking advantage of everyone who is not fully established in the truth. Every soul is to be tested. Every defect in the character, unless it is overcome by the help of God's Spirit, will become a sure means of destruction... The Lord has much work to be done; and if we do what He has appointed for us to do, He will work with our efforts."

The choices and decisions we're making now, day by day is determining the final choice we will make when we face the Sunday Law crises. We need to be obeying God and His law now and getting rid of our sins that separate us from God. Then we'll be able to receive the early rain by reforming our lives to God's will and developing a Christ-like character now, so we can receive the outpouring of the latter rain, and be able to share in the loud cry message. We won't receive the latter rain if we've not received the early rain first, which is the time for making reforms in our lives, like: Dress reform; Health reform; Education reform; Sabbath reform.

Sister White warns us in *Country Living*, p. 20, 21, "The Sunday party is strengthening itself in its false claims, and this will mean oppression to those who determine to keep the Sabbath of the Lord. We are to place ourselves where we can carry out the Sabbath commandment in its fullness... And we are to be careful not to place ourselves where it will be hard for ourselves and our children to keep the Sabbath."

I looked up the word oppression in the dictionary and it said: unjust or cruel exercise of authority or power; a sense of being weighed down in body or mind. depression; to burden spiritually or mentally; harsh rule; a feeling of being weighed down with problems, worries, etc.

Sister White continues her counsel by saying on pp. 20, 21 in *Country Living*, "If in the providence of God we can secure places away from the cities, the Lord would have us do this. There are troublous times before us."

I looked up the word secure in the dictionary and it said: lasting possession or control of; to put beyond hazard of losing or not receiving; free from risk of loss, harm, attack, etc., to get; obtain.

This means to obtain a place, free from debt, in your possession which means: the fact of possessing, holding, or owning; ownership; something that one owns. This means not renting a place, but owning it, making it secure.

Sister White continues her counsel on p. 21 of *Country Living*, "the Protestant world have set up an idol Sabbath in the place where God's Sabbath should be, and they are treading in the footsteps of the Papacy. For this reason I see the necessity of the people of God moving out of the cities, into retired country [places,] where they may cultivate the land and raise their own produce. Thus they may bring their children up with simple, healthful habits. I see the necessity of making haste to get all things ready for the crisis."

I looked up retired in the dictionary and it said: Retreat; to withdraw, especially for privacy; secluded; withdrawn from one's position or occupation; hidden or private. (It's like a retired cabin.)

I, also, looked up produce and it said: agricultural products, especially fresh fruits and vegetables; to bear, make, or yield something, like trees producing apples.

In *Country Living,* Sister White says on p. 19, 20, "If the poor now crowded into the cities could find homes upon the land, they might not only earn a livelihood, but find health and happiness now unknown to them. Hard work, simple fare, close economy, often hardship and privation, would be their lot. But what a blessing would be theirs in leaving the city, with its enticements to evil, its turmoil and crime, misery and foulness, for the country's quiet and peace and purity. To many of those living in the cities who have not a spot of green grass to set their feet upon, who year after year have looked out upon filthy courts and narrow alleys, brick walls and pavements, and skies clouded with dust and smoke; if these could be taken to some farming district, surrounded with the green fields, the woods and hills and brooks, the clear skies and the fresh, pure air of the country, it would seem almost like heaven. Cut off to a great degree from contact with and dependence upon men, and separated from the world's corrupting maxims and customs and excitements, they would come nearer to the heart of nature. God's presence would be more real to them. Many would learn the lesson of dependence upon Him. Through nature they would hear His voice speaking to their hearts of His peace and love, and mind and soul and body would respond to the healing, life giving power...

Believers who are now living in the cities will have to move to the country, that they may save their children from ruin... All that needs to be done cannot be specified till a beginning is made. Pray over the matter, and remember God stands at the helm, that He is guiding in the work of the various enterprises a place in which the work is conducted on right lines is an object lesson to other places."

On p. 17 in *Country Living,* Sister White tells us, "If the land is cultivated, it will, with the blessing of God, supply our necessities."

I looked up the word cultivate and it said: the act or art of cultivating or tilling; to prepare or prepare and use for the raising of crops; to loosen or break up the soil about (growing plants); to improve by labor, care and study; to break up the soil around plants in order to kill weeds and help the plants grow.

In *Selected Messages*, vol. 3, Chapter 44, entitled, "Specific Light on Gardening", pp. 328, 329, Sister White gives instruction in planting fruit trees, "I ordered my hired man to dig a deep cavity in the ground, then put in a layers of earth and dressing until the hole was filled."

In *Country Living,* pp. 21, 22, we read the advice of Sister White, "Many of the members of our large churches are doing comparatively nothing. They might accomplish a good work if, instead of crowding together, they would scatter into places that have not yet been entered by the truth. Trees that are planted too thickly do not flourish. They are transplanted by the gardener that they may have room to grow and not become dwarfed and sickly. The same rule would work well for our large churches. Many of the members are dying spiritually for want of this very work. They are becoming sickly and inefficient. Transplanted, they would have room to grow strong and vigorous."

Read pp. 24–28 in *Country Living,* entitled, "Guided by God's Providences." "More and more as time advances, our people will have to leave the cities. For years we have been instructed that our brethren and sisters, and especially families with children, should plan to leave the cities as the way opens before them to do so. Many will have to labor earnestly to help open the way. But until it is possible for them to leave, so long as they remain, they should be most active in doing missionary work, however limited their sphere of influence may be.

Those who have felt at last to make a move, let it not be in a rush, in an excitement, or in a rash manner, or in a way that hereafter they will deeply regret that they did move out. Do nothing without seeking wisdom of God, who hath promised to give liberally to all who ask and who upbraideth not. All that anyone can do is to advise and counsel, and then leave those who are convicted in regard to duty to move under divine guidance and with their whole hearts open to learn and obey God…

Not a move should be made but that movement and all that it portends are carefully considered—everything weighed… To every man was given his work according to his several ability. Then let him not move hesitatingly, but firmly, and yet humbly trusting in God.

There may be individuals who will make a rush to do something and enter into some business they know nothing about. This God does not require. Think candidly, prayerfully, studying the Word with all carefulness and prayerfulness, with mind and heart awake to hear the voice of God to understand the will of God is a great thing. Do not go in a rush, without knowing what you are about. Let there be much praying done, and even with fasting, that not one shall move in darkness, but move in the light as God is in the light. Let there be wise generalship in this matter, and all move under the guidance of a wise, unseen Counselor, which is God. Submit all your ways and your will to God's ways and to God's will. If everyone will come to Jesus in a teachable spirit, with contrition of heart, then he is in a condition of mind to be instructed and to learn of Jesus and obey His orders. We cannot have a weak faith now, we cannot be safe in a listless, indolent, slothful attitude. Every jot of ability is to be used, and sharp, calm, deep thinking is to be done. The wisdom of any human agent is not sufficient for planning and devising in this time. Spread every plan before God with fasting and with the humbling of the soul before the Lord Jesus, and commit thy ways unto the Lord. The sure promise is, He will direct thy paths. He is infinite in resources. The Holy One of Israel, who calls the host of heaven by name, and holds the stars of heaven in position, has you individually in His keeping. I would that all could realize what possibilities and probabilities there are for all who make Christ their sufficiency and their trust. The life hid with Christ in God ever has a refuge; he can say, "I can do all things through Christ which strengthens me." (Phil. 4:13)

Prov. 11:14, "Where no counsel is, the people fall: but in the multitude of counselors there is safety."

Remember, to vacate the city for the country is not something to do on impulse. It will take a great amount of careful planning and education to avoid financial disaster and unhappiness. Let each one seek the Lord for instruction and guidance and direction. Claim His promises like: James 1:5, "If any of you lack wisdom, let him ask of God, that giveth to all men liberally, and upbraideth not, and it shall be given him."

Prov. 3:5–8, "Trust in the Lord with all thine heart; and lean not unto thine own understanding. In all thy ways acknowledge him, and he shall direct thy paths. Be not wise in thine own eyes; fear the Lord, and depart from evil. It shall be health to thy naval and marrow to thy bones." Also, read Ps. 37:3–5, "Trust in the Lord, and do good; so shalt thou dwell in the land, and verily thou shalt be fed. Delight thyself also in the Lord; and he shall give thee the desires of thine heart. Commit thy way unto the Lord, trust also in him; and he shall bring it to pass."

Read E.G. White's book, "Maranatha" — The Lord is coming!

> "If any of you lack wisdom, let him ask of God, that giveth to all men liberally, and upbraideth not; and it shall be given him. But let him ask in faith, nothing wavering. For he that wavereth is like a wave of the sea driven with the wind and tossed. For let not that man think that he shall receive any thing of the Lord. A double minded man is unstable in all his ways."
>
> James 1:5-8

Things to Consider

Get Out of Debt

A. Deny Yourself

a. *Counsels on Stewardship*, p. 256, 257, E. G. White, "You must see that one should not manage his affairs in a way that will incur debt… When a man sees that he is not successful, why does he not betake himself to prayer, or change his work? There are stormy times before us, and the Lord will accept all who can cooperate with Him. Practice self-denial and self-sacrifice. Consider every movement carefully and prayerfully. Walk softly before the Lord. We must preserve a devotedness to God, and make straight paths for our feet, lest the lame be turned out of the way." "Be determined never to incur another debt. Deny yourself of a thousand things rather than run into debt. Avoid it as you would the smallpox. Make a solemn covenant with God that by His blessing you will pay your debts and then owe no man anything if you live on porridge and bread… Take care of the pennies, and the dollars will take care of themselves. It is the mites here and the mites there that are spent for this, that, and the other, that soon run up into dollars. Deny self at least while you are walled in with debts… Do not falter, be discouraged, or turn back. Deny your taste, deny the indulgence of appetite, save your pence and pay your debts. Work them off as fast as possible. When you can stand forth a free man again, owing no man anything, you will have achieved a great victory."

B. Pray and Fast for Wisdom and Knowledge

a. James 1:5
b. *Country Living,* by E. G. White, pp. 24–28, "Guided by God's Providences."
c. Prov. 3:5, 6
d. Ps. 37:3–5
e. *Desire of Ages*, pp. 121 & 122. "Every earthly support cut off."
f. Ps. 32:8

g. *Evangelism* by E. G. White, pp. 61–65, "Moving Forward by Faith." "Money will soon depreciate in value very suddenly…"
h. *Testimonies for the Church*, vol. 5, p. 152 by E. G. White.
i. Sell your city home, to buy a country home
j. God gives you power to get wealth. Deut. 8:18
k. *Review and Herald,* 3-21-1878, p. 91—"Hoarded wealth will soon be worthless when the decree shall go forth that none shall buy or sell except they have the mark of beast, very much means will be of no avail."
l. Can you afford a place and pay it off quickly?
m. Is this place out of the city limits?

What to Look For In a Place

A. Garden Site

a. *Country Living,* by E. G. White, p. 9, "Again and again the Lord has instructed that our people are to take their families away from the cities, into the country, where they can raise their own provisions…"
b. *Country Living,* by E. G. White, pp. 17, 18. "Get out of the cities as soon as possible, and purchase a little piece of land, where you can have a garden where your children can watch the flowers growing, and learn from them lessons of simplicity and purity.
c. *Country Living*, p. 18, "Work in the garden and field will be an agreeable change from wearisome routine of abstract lessons, to which their young minds should never be confined."
d. Is your garden site:
   1. Good soil? To improve soil sow cover crop of clover, rye, vetch, peas, soybeans, other beans.
   2. Cleared for full sunshine—at least 6–8 hours of open sun.
   3. Is the site too high or too dry?
   4. Is it too low or too wet?
   5. Are there berries and fruit trees already growing on the site?
   6. Is there a southern slope to your garden?
e. Have a compost pile and fertilizer, like grass clippings, leaves, and garbage.

B. Climate

a. Is the place too hot or too cold?
b. Will it be a tolerable place when you can't buy or sell utilities to it?

C. Water

a. Is there sweet well water, not too deep?
b. Is there a surface stream or spring or pond or creek?
c. Do you have water rights?
d. Hand well pump and a rain barrel
e. Need a lot of water for drinking, bathing, dishes, washing clothes, gardening, cooking, and cleaning jobs.

D. House

a. Privacy
b. Livable with minimal repairs
c. Is the soil the kind you can have a septic?
d. By a few S.D.A. friends?
e. A few non-hostile neighbors in area?
   1. Check out what's in the area.
   2. What are neighbors like? Druggies? Drunks? Friendly?
f. Check out easements
   1. Are there public roads or driveways crossing your property; will you have to maintain the road to your place?
   2. Are there large power lines or pipe lines?
g. Have several acres away from neighbors. The more the better.

E. Wood

a. Different uses for wood.
   1. Keeping warm
   2. Cooking with
   3. For shade
   4. For health: *Ministry of Healing*, p. 264,

by E. G. White, "There are life-giving properties in the balsam of the pine, in the fragrance of the cedar and the fir, and other trees also have properties that are health restoring."

b. Different Types of Wood:
 1. Cedar
 2. Pine
 3. Fir
 4. Red bud
 5. Oak.
 6. Maple
 7. Hickory
 8. Ash
 9. Sycamore

c. Have a good supply of woods to cut (several acres) for firewood

What to Put On Your Property

A. Fruit Trees (These take years to grow and produce)

a. A variety of fruits grown in your area
 1. Peach
 2. Pear
 3. Plum
 4. Cherry
 5. Apricot
 6. Mulberry
 7. Apple
 8. Persimmon
 9. Pawpaw
 10. Prune
 11. Lemon
 12. Orange
 13. Grapefruit

B. Berry Bushes (These grow faster, so plant first)

a. A variety of berries
 1. Boysenberry
 2. Gooseberry
 3. Strawberry
 4. Blackberries
 5. Raspberries
 6. Elderberry
 7. Blueberry
 8. Autumn olives

C. Variety of Things for Your Area

a. Nut trees
 1. Walnut
 2. Pecan
 3. Almond
 4. Coconut
 5. Chestnuts
b. Peanuts
c. Grape vines
d. Asparagus

D. Herb Garden

a. Parsley
b. Basil
c. Sage
d. Hops
e. Catnip
f. Rosemary
g. Alfalfa
h. Thyme
i. Comfrey
j. Dill
k. Stevia
l. Red clover
m. Aloe Vera

E. Flowers

a. Roses
b. Daffodils
c. Lilacs
d. Tulips

e. Iris
   f. Hydrangea
   g. Morning Glories
   h. Jonquils
   i. Forsythia
   j. Echinacea

F. Clothes Line and Clothes Pins

   a. Scrub board
   b. Wash tubs
   c. Buckets
   d. Soap/Clorox

G. Woodshed

   a. Keep firewood dry
   b. Use a tarp over wood
   c. Stack wood to let air flow through it

H. Outhouse

   a. At least 25 feet from the house
   b. Lime in outhouse and for garden (Can use ashes from woodstove)

I. Woodstove

   a. Stove pipe
   b. Elbows
   c. Cap over stove pipe outside
   d. Tools for wood stove fire
      1. Poker
      2. Shovel
      3. Bucket for ashes
      4. Cast iron kettle to heat water for bathing, dishes, and washing clothes

J. Cast Iron Pans

   a. Skillets and lids
   b. Pans and lids
   c. Cookie sheet
   d. Big cast iron pot (You can use on open fire outside — like a Dutch oven)
   e. Utensils

K. Root Cellar

   a. To store garden things
   b. To store fruit
   c. To put your canning jars in so they won't freeze

L. Greenhouse

   a. To grow things during winter months
   b. To start your seeds in for gardening and transfer to garden
   c. Small containers to start seeds in
   d. Trays on shelves made
   e. Hand sprinkler, bucket with spout
   f. Near to a water source

M. Candles or Kerosene Oil Lamps

   a. Wicks
   b. Matches or disposable cigarette lighters
   c. Kerosene
   d. Flashlights and batteries, extra ones

N. Canning Jars and Extra Lids and Rings for Jars

   a. Salt (for canning)
   b. Big kettle with lid (to can in)

O. Hand-Powered Mill for Grinding Flour or Meal

P. Seeds

   a. For sprouting (like lentils, Alfalfa, red clover, corn, mung
      1. one-quart canning jar, a cheesecloth or

screen, rubber band, and water to be able to sprout seeds. Use quart jar to soak seeds overnight covered with water. Then keep rinsed and moist every day until they sprout — usually one week, more or less.
b. For growing (standard seeds that reproduce themselves and grow good in your area)
c. Store in a cool, dry, dark place (Use bay leaves to keep the bugs out and also out of beans.)
d. Have at least a two-year supply

Q. Drying Foods Rack

a. Like apples, banana, tomatoes, etc. (Use two screens, one on top of the other and place food to dry between the two screens and place out in the sun or hang over your woodstove in winter to dry it out.)

R. Tools

a. Hand bow saw/crosscut saw to cut firewood
b. Rakes
c. Hoe
d. Shovels
e. Spade
f. Pick or mattock
g. Turning fork
h. Wheelbarrow
i. Wheel hoe and wheel push plow
j. Pipe for irrigation and water hose
k. Little hand rake and claw and scoop shovel
l. Mauls—To split firewood
m. Sledge hammer—to split firewood
n. Hatchet
o. Axe
p. Hammer/ Level/Tape measure/Screwdriver/ Pliers/ Square
q. Carpenter hand saw
r. Assorted sizes—nails, nuts, bolts, screws
s. Flashlight
t. Sevin® Dust, 5% (safest insecticide)
u. Ant spray, Decon®, wasp spray

S. Clothes

a. Winter clothes
b. Coats warm and rain coat and neck scarves
c. Sweaters
d. Sweatshirts
e. Gloves for work and warmth
f. Stocking hats and bill hats
g. Warm socks
h. Jeans/practical coveralls
i. Long underwear
j. Warm boots, waterproof
k. Warm blankets/sleeping bags/pillows
l. Have extra clothes to share with others
m. Extra bedding, towels, wash cloths, and toiletries
n. Durable, practical shoes and boots
o. Needle and thread and safety pins

T. Books

a. Bible (King James Version) (Learn your Bible and what you believe and the promises)
b. Spirit of Prophecy Books
c. Pens and paper
d. How to Garden books
e. Herb books:
Back to Eden by Jethro Kloss;
Natural Remedies Encyclopedia by Vance Ferrell;
From the Shepherd's Purse by Max C. Barlow;
Today's Herbal Health by Louise Tenny, M. H.
f. *You Can Survive* by Jere Franklin
g. *From City to Country Living* by Arthur White and E. A. Sutherland
h. *The Country Way* by Lloyd E. Eighme
i. Visit county agent in your area and get free gardening material to read and soil test done

U. Things to Have on Hand

a. Toiletries:
   1. Toilet paper
   2. Hand soap/dish soap, detergent, Clorox
   3. Toothbrushes
   4. Toothpaste

5. Razor blades
   6. Shaving cream
   7. Sanitary napkins
   8. Shampoo
b. Have dried foods like beans, raisins, prunes, dates, apricots, dried herbs, sunflower seeds, and pumpkins seeds, flax seeds, sesame seeds, etc., and nuts.
c. Home canned foods
d. First aid kit:
   1. Band-Aids®/sterile dressings, roll of gauze, cloth tape, scissors, knife, and tweezers
   2. Alcohol
   3. Peroxide
   4. Mentholatum® Ointment
   5. PRID® salve (to draw splinters out of fingers)
   6. Ace® bandages—different sizes and safety pins
   7. Activated charcoal powder
   8. Variety of herbs
   9. Cleansing wipes
   10. First aid manual

V. Survival Kit

a. Compass
b. Bandana
c. First aid kit
d. Rope
e. Whistle
f. Flashlight
g. Concentrated food
h. Knife
i. Space blanket
j. Large trash bag—one for each person
k. Water bottle full of water
l. Matches and lighter and flint, magnifying glass
m. Candle
n. Backpack

o. Know how to build a fire
p. Know how to build a shelter outside
q. Bible (King James Version)
r. Mirror
s. Soap and towel and wash cloth
t. Extra socks to keep feet dry
u. Paper and pencil
v. Sleeping bag
w. Utensils/ice chest
x. Toilet paper
y. Map and survival book and identification of edible plants book (Know how to identify things you can eat off the land.)
z. Remember this if you get lost:

S — Stay

T — Think

O — Observe

P — Plan

Survival Priorities

1. Pray and Trust God
2. Shelter
3. Fire
4. Water
5. Rest
6. Food

W. Witnessing

a. Have books and materials to witness with
b. Give Bible studies in your area you move to
c. Have books and literature to pass out in your area
d. Know medical missionary work, how to help people
e. Learn to colporteur

Closing Events Charts

"The follower of Christ has a chart pointing out every waymark on the heavenward journey, and he ought not to guess at anything." G.C. 598

CLOSING EVENTS CHART
6T 128, 129. 7T 157, 158

1844

Investigative judgement began
Dan 8:14; GC 479-491

Three angels
Rev 14:6-12; EW 42-45, 85-86, 66-78, 111-114

The Heavenly sanctuary cleansed (1844-close of probation)
EW 36, 48, 58, 224 279-281; GC 352, 390, 417-425, 485, 490, 600-628; 5T 475, 575, 692, 343, 358; 1T58; Dan 8:14; Heb 8-9; Rev 14:6-12; Acts 3:19; 1Tim 5:24; 1Pet 4:17, Ez 9:4-6; 7; BC 605-607 ; PP 343-358; Evangelism 224

"The Protestant world have set up an idol Sabbath in place where God's Sabbath should be, and they are treading in the footsteps of the Papacy. For this reason I see the necessity of the people of God moving out of the cities into retired country places, where they may cultivate the land and raise their own produce. Thus they may bring their children up with simple, healthful habits. I see the necessity of making haste to get all things ready for the crisis." Country Living p. 21.

Now

Time to prepare! Troubles increasing!
GC 625, 626; 5T 449-454, 206-216; EW 42-45, 66-73, 85-86, 111-114, WM 134-139, MYP 89-90

Three angels messages
EW 269-273, 50-51 1T 429

National Sunday Law

Final call to leave LARGE CITIES preparatory to leaving the smaller ones, for retired homes in secluded places among the mountains.
5T 464-465; GC 626; EW 232-285; Country Living 3-32

Three angels/sounding & swelling into loud cry
8T 19-23, 6T 401; Rev 18:1-4; 7 BC 983-985; LDE 197-214; EW 277-282

Early time of trouble
GC 593-612; EW, 33-39, 48-71 & 85-86, 7 BC 976; Rev 13; Matt 24; Mark 13; Luke 21; Maranatha 198-199

Persecution
GC 48, 507, 610; 2Tim 3:12; EW 33-34, 85-86

Charts by Linda Clore 2013

CLOSING EVENTS CHART

6T 128, 129. 7T 157, 158

"I saw the powers of earth are now being shaken, and that events come in order."

E.W. 41

Close of Probation

Four Angels loose the 4 winds
Rev 7:1-4; 5T 152; EW 36, 38; Dan 12:1; 7 BC 968

Great time of trouble
GC 613-634; EW, 56-58 & 282-285; Dan 12:1; IS 33:15-16

Seven last plagues
Rev 16; GC 624-629; EW 52

Remnant remain true
Rev 12:17, 19:10, 14:12

Jacob's trouble
GC 616-622; E.W, 37-38, 282-285

Death decree
GC 631; EW 282-285

Saints delivered
GC 635-678; EW 285-288

"The Lord has shown me repeatedly that it is contrary to the Bible to make any provision for our temporal wants in the time of trouble… Then will be the time for us to trust wholly in god, and He will sustain us."
Early Writings p. 56; Is 33:15-16

2nd Coming/Millennium

Second Coming of Christ
GC 635-661; EW 13-24, 74-81, 285-288; Matt 24; Mark 13; Luke 21; Acts 1:9-11, Rev 1:7; 1Thess 4:15-18; 1Cor 15:50-58; Titus 2:11-15; Rev 22:10-21

Millennium begins
Rev 20; EW 51, 288

Saints in heaven 1,000 years and Satan bound on earth 1,000 years.
EW 289-295

The New Jerusalem comes down to earth.
Rev 21-22

Satan and his followers destroyed with fire.
Mal 4:1-3; 2Peter 3:10-13; GC 655-678

Charts by Linda Clore 2013

Pictures

David and Linda Clore

Jonathan Clore in the front room of our 14' x 80' mobile home.

David Clore, digging in the garden, with one of our cabins in the background.

Linda Clore, pumping water from our hand-pump well.

Inside the classroom and treatment room on the "Ark."

52 — *Don't Be Trapped in the Cities!! Get Out Now!*

Two of our cabins.

Jonathan Clore in 1996, 2½ months before he became totally paralyzed at the age of 27.

The 12' x 20' cabin that we built.

Linda Clore, on the front porch of the 12' x 20' cabin we built on the hill, back in the forest.

David Clore, on a snowy day, near the storage building and the classroom building.

Linda Clore, bringing firewood into our 14' x 80' mobile home, to burn in the wood stove.

A storage building, cabin and the classroom building

The 12' x 20' cabin that we built over the basement.

On the left, is our enclosed back porch, connected to our 14' x 80' mobile home. In the center, is the 12' x 24' dining hall, and behind it, the chapel.

Poems

This "ARK" poem written by Linda Clore was encouraged to be written by David's sister, Hilma, from Chicago, a S.D.A. Christian. Back in November 2009, Hilma came down from Chicago, Illinois, to visit us and see how things were going on the "ARK" we were building for our family and for people to come to in the early time of trouble, when they'll have nowhere to go when they are forced to leave the big wicked cities and can't buy or sell, cause of the Sunday Law passed.

She saw the buildings we were putting up on our 14 acres of woods with a live creek, outside a little town, out in the country. She saw the few cabins we had for people to stay in and a small 12 x 20 building for a classroom and treatment room. She knew, too, we were preparing the "ARK" for not only a place of refuge in the small time of trouble, but also for a small medical missionary training center, on a very small scale, for when people leave the large cities they can learn the eight natural remedies Sister White mentions in The Ministry of Healing, p. 127, "Pure air, sunshine, abstemiousness, rest, exercise, proper diet, the use of water, trust in Divine power—these are the true remedies. Every person should have a knowledge of nature's remedial agencies and how to apply them. It is essential both to understand the principles involved in the treatment of the sick and to have a practical training that will enable one rightly to use this knowledge."

Some of the other things people also will be learning is how to survive the early time of trouble, gardening, herbs, and healthful living, and learning their Bibles and the Spirit of Prophecy, and the Last Day Events and how God will get us througwxh the seven last plagues and the Great Time of Trouble ahead of us, when we'll have to flee for our lives when the death decree will be passed.

During Hilma's visit in our home, she went into our bathroom where she saw a poem hanging on the wall that I had written back in 2006, entitled: "Trust His Name." Hilma liked this poem so much and she said to me, "Why don't you write a poem about the "ARK" you're building?"

So as time went by, I kept praying about it and asked God to please help me write it, and I feel He did.

TRUST HIS NAME

God has a plan,
We may not understand.
He'll make it plain,
If we'll just trust His name.
Don't run ahead, Just walk with Him instead.
He'll make it plain, If we'll just trust His name.
We don't always see, What God has for you and me.
He'll make it plain, If we'll just trust His name.
God knows what's best, And helps us through our tests.
He'll make it plain, If we'll just trust His name.
We walk by faith, And believe in His grace.
He'll make it plain, If we'll just trust His name.
Hold His strong hand, He will help us to stand.
He'll make it plain, If we'll just trust His name.
Soon He's to come, When our race here is done.
He'll make it plain, If we'll just trust His name.
Heartaches no more, Just joys forever more.
He'll make it plain, If we'll just trust His name.
The end of sin, So keep your eyes on Him.
He'll make it plain, If we'll just trust His name.
There's hope, my friend, Our broken hearts He'll mend.
He'll make it plain, If we'll just trust His name.
What of the pain, God's power's still the same.
He'll make it plain, If we'll just trust His name.
So don't be so sad, Jesus will make you glad.
He'll make it plain, If we'll just trust His name.
Be faithful then, And true until the end.
He'll make it plain, If we'll just trust His name.

Written by Linda Clore
Ps. 33:21; Ps. 20:7; Ps. 9:9, 10; Isa. 50:10

THE ARK

There is a place of safety, It's found only in the Lord!
He's our City of Refuge, He's our Anchor in the storm!
He's "THE ARK" of our salvation, It is in Him we can trust.
He's the Rock of our foundation, He'll never leave nor fail us!
Cause He'll never leave nor fail us, We can abide in His love.
We can go to Him in Prayer, Knowing He watches from above!
When He warns us of His coming, When He tells us we're to prepare,
Then we'll do what the Lord tells us, Having faith and trust without fear!
By daily studying God's Word, We're to follow His directions,
Then we know what we are to do, We're to build "THE ARK" for protection!
Angels are promised to watch, While we prepare for the storm.
Before the Sunday laws are passed, Like Noah, the people we will warn!
Like the Schools of the prophets, Way back there in Bible times,
We'll teach the people God's Word, And how to live through hard times!
In "THE ARK", we will teach them how to Grow gardens and depend on God,
Also, to learn God's promises, And to have faith and trust in God!
We'll teach Medical Missionaries How to heal the sick and help the poor,
How to share God's Final message, And then help them learn so much more!
Like having a Christ-like character, And keeping all God's commandments,
Being filled with His Holy Spirit, And reaching higher attainments!
Being in the ark of safety, Just like back in Noah's day,
We'll be able to ride the storms, Until comes God's delivery day!
So even though the time will come For the 'death sentence' on our life,
We'll be ready and trusting in God, Waiting for our eternal life!
So, now while probation lingers, And we're sheltered in His arms of love,
Let us not put off deeds of kindness, Nor fail to enter our home above!
There awaits our Master's words Of admonition and words, "WELL DONE,"
Because we've followed our Savior, And the victory we've finally won!
Isaiah 33:15 and 16, God's promise is given
To care for those who'll do His will, And a Christ-like life they'll be livin'!
So get in "THE ARK" of safety, While there is still a little time,
Since there's still a lot of storms ahead, We'll need Jesus till the end of time!
So, heed His call and heed His warnings, Take that final step and get aboard!
Be a part of God's closing work, By giving your all to the Lord!

Written by: Linda Clore and the help of the Lord!

We still have a lot to learn so we can help others learn. This is why David and I have gotten training from different places and people so we can be of help to others who want to learn to be medical missionaries like Sister White says to do.

Healthful Living, p. 271, "As religious aggression subverts the liberties of our nation, those who would stand for freedom of conscience will be placed in unfavorable positions. For their own sakes they should, while they have opportunity, become intelligent in regard to disease, its causes, prevention, and cure. Those who do this will find a field of labor anywhere. (Read pp. 271–273, "The Medical Missionary Work" chapter XL.)

Testimonies for the Church, vol. 7, pp. 62, 63, "We have come to a time when every member of the church should take hold of the medical missionary work. The world is a lazar house filled with victims of both physical and spiritual disease… The message to God's people today is, 'Arise, Shine: for thy light is come, and the glory of the Lord is risen upon thee…' Let our people show that they have a living interest in medical missionary work. Let them prepare themselves for usefulness by studying the books that have been written for our instruction in these lines."

Read: *The Ministry of Healing*, pp. 17–28. Jesus is our Great Example as the True Medical Missionary as Matthew 4:23 says, "And Jesus went about all Galilee, teaching in their synagogues, and preaching the gospel of the kingdom, and healing all manner of sickness and all manner of disease among the people." Also, read Is. 58, the great medical missionary chapter for us to follow.

Counsels on Health, p. 533, "I wish to tell you that soon there will be no work done in ministerial lines but medical missionary work… You will never be ministers after the gospel order till you show a decided interest in medical missionary work, the gospel of healing and blessing and strengthening… I wish to say that the medical missionary work is God's work. The Lord wants every one of His ministers to come into line. Take hold of the medical missionary work, and it will give you access to the people. Their hearts will be touched as you minister to their necessities. As you relieve their suffering, you will find opportunity to speak to them of the love of Jesus…" Also, p. 531, "We were to have an institution where the sick could be relieved of suffering and that without drug medication. God declared that He Himself would go before His people in this work." Also, p. 534, "Medical missionary work, ministering to the sick and suffering, cannot be separated from the gospel." The *Ministry of Healing*, chapter, "The Physician an Educator" pp. 125–136.

God even gave us the name for our place, the "ARK." Heb. 11:7

What's in the name, "ARK"?

A = Agriculture

R = Religion

K = Knowledge

What does it stand for?

A = Agriculture

This is so important to know that Sister White said in *Testimonies for the Church*, vol. 6, p. 179, "Working the soil is one of the best kinds of employment, calling muscles into action and resting the mind. Study in agricultural lines should be the A, B, and C of the education given in our school…"

R = Religion

2 Timothy 2:15, "Study to show thyself approved unto God, a workman that needeth not to be ashamed, rightly dividing the word of truth." Read *Last Day Events*, p. 209, Sister White says that we should know our Bibles and what we believe and be able to prove it from the Scriptures. We should be memorizing our Bible. Sister White says in *Last Day Events*, p. 67, "The time will come when many will be deprived of the written Word. But if this Word is printed in the memory, no one can take it from us." Also, pp. 67 & 68, "Study the Word of God. Commit its precious promises to memory so that when we shall be deprived of our Bibles, we may still be in possession of the Word of God… In these last days it is our duty to ascertain the full meaning of the first, second, and third angels' messages." Also, p. 69, "God will flash the knowledge obtained by diligent searching of the scriptures into their memory at the very time when it is needed."

One night I had a dream and it was quoting *The Great Controversy*, pp. 593, 594, the chapter on "The

Scriptures a Safeguard." "None but those who have fortified the mind with the truths of the Bible will stand through the last great conflict. To every soul will come the searching test: Shall I obey God rather than men? The decisive hour is even now at hand. Are our feet planted on the rock of God's immutable word? Are we prepared to stand firm in defense of the commandments of God and the faith of Jesus?"

Again on another night God gave me this dream: A quote from *Selected Messages*, book 2, p. 142, "The work of the people of God is to prepare for the events of the future, which will soon come upon them with blinding force." Another quote that goes along with that is: *Testimonies for the Church*, vol. 8, p. 28, "Transgression has almost reached its limit. Confusion fills the world, and a great terror is soon to come upon human beings. The end is very near. We who know the truth should be preparing for what is soon to break upon the world as an overwhelming surprise."

While writing on my book, I had asked God for a title, and in a dream He showed me this title, **Don't Be Trapped in the Cities!! Get Out Now!** God gave me this dream, too, during the same night I had asked God for a Spirit of Prophecy quote to put on the cover of my book. It was the quote from God taken from *Testimonies for the Church*, vol. 3, p. 281, "If God abhors one sin above another, of which His people are guilty, it is doing nothing in case of an emergency. Indifference and neutrality in a religious crisis is regarded of God as a grievous crime and equal to the very worst type of hostility against God."

K = Knowledge

2 Pet. 1:4–8, "Whereby are given unto us exceeding great and precious promises: that by these ye might be partakers of the divine nature, having escaped the corruption that is in the world through lust. And beside this, giving all diligence, add to your faith virtue; and to virtue knowledge; and to knowledge temperance; and to temperance patience; and to patience godliness; and to godliness brotherly kindness; and to brotherly kindness charity. For if these things be in you, and abound, they make you that ye shall neither be barren nor unfruitful in the knowledge of our Lord Jesus Christ."

Col. 1:9, 10: "For this cause we also, since the day we heard it, do not cease to pray for you, and to desire that ye might be filled with the knowledge of his will in all wisdom and spiritual understanding, that ye might walk worthy of the Lord unto all pleasing, being fruitful in every good work, and increasing in the knowledge of God."

There is so much knowledge to be learned in so many areas of a person's practical and educational training. Like: Living and learning the eight natural remedies and how to apply them, found in the book, *Ministry of Healing* and other natural remedies books. Also, being able to gain a knowledge of God and His will and His word, and Present truth and how to prepare for the future events so soon to break upon us, and how to survive the days ahead and remain faithful to God and all his ten commandments and to develop a Christ-like character. Also, how to prepare to live in the country and ("get out of the large cities as fast as possible," *Country Living*, p. 12.)

"Before the overflowing scourge shall come upon the dwellers of the earth, the Lord calls upon all who are Israelites indeed to prepare for that event. To parents He sends the warning cry, Gather your children into your own houses; gather them away from those who are disregarding the commandments of God, who are teaching and practicing evil. Get out of the large cities as fast as possible. Establish church schools. Give your children the Word of God as the foundation of all their education." *Testimonies for the Church*, vol. 6, p. 195

"…Out of the cities is my message for the education of our children. God gave to our first parents the means of true education when He instructed them to till the soil and care for their garden home. *Country Living*, p. 13

And how did Enoch walk with God? He educated his mind and heart to ever feel that he was in the presence of God, and when in perplexity his prayers would ascend to God to keep him… Now Enoch was a representative of those who will be upon the earth when Christ shall come, who will be translated to heaven without seeing death." *Last Day Events*, p. 73.

"We have nothing to fear for the future, except as we shall forget the way the Lord has led us, and His teaching in our past history." *Last Day Events*, p. 72.

"We should ask ourselves, 'For what are we living and working?' And what will be the outcome of it all?" *Last Day Events*, p. 73

"We should watch and work and pray as though this were the last day that would be granted us." *Testimonies for the Church*, vol. 5, p. 200.

"The time is fast coming when the controlling power of the labor unions will be very oppressive." *Selected Messages*, book 2, p. 141.

"The time is soon coming when God's people, because of persecution, will be scattered in many countries. Those who have received an all-round education will have the advantage where they are," Last *Day Events*, p. 152.

This is what we're trying to do on the "ARK", is to give an all-round education to God's people He brings here. God is impressing others around the world to prepare little ARKS of safety for God's people to flee to when the time comes. May God help us to be about our Father's business and prepare for the events of the future, which will soon come upon us with blinding force and is soon to break upon the world as an overwhelming surprise, as Sister White warns us in her writings: (*Selected Messages*, book 2, p. 142 and *Testimonies for the Church*, vol. 8, p. 28)

God gave me a dream showing me this article, "The Story Behind the "ARK" poem I had started writing this article, maybe a year ago, and had laid it aside and hadn't written on it. But God must want it completed, because He brought it to my attention in a recent dream. So this is why I'm getting it written and finished and may it be a help and blessing and encouragement to those who read it.

My thanks to my dear sweet sister-in-law, Hilma Sue, who encouraged me to write the poem about the "ARK" and what it's all about. God bless her.

A very valuable book to read is, *Another ARK to Build*, by W. D. Frazee. This explains what we are doing on the "ARK" and how others around the world should be preparing for the crisis ahead, too, by preparing places of refuge for God's people to come to when the right time comes. And we need to be preparing spiritually, too.

Thank you, Jesus, for helping me write this book and this article and for helping me and my husband to build the "ARK" for the time of trouble ahead when we can't buy or sell because we'll keep God's seventh day Sabbath holy and not man's Sunday sabbath. Praise God!

GOD LOVES US STILL!

Even though God we have all disobeyed,
Even though we like sheep have gone astray,
God loves us still!
Even though we have turned our back on Him,
Even though we have followed after sin,
God loves us still!
Even though parents love their wayward child,
Even though they have rebelled for a while,
We love them still!
Even though from God we have run away,
Even though promises we break each day,
God loves us still!
Even though God is love, for sin we'll pay,
Even though there's for us payday someday,
God loves us still!
Even though there'll come a time we repent,
Even though the Holy Spirit we resent,
God loves us still!
Even though God waits for us to come back,
Even though His promises do not lack,
God loves us still!
Even though on the cross God proved His love,
Even though Jesus left heaven above,
God loves us still!
Even though we be like little black sheep,
Even though the angels in heaven weep,
God loves us still!
Even though we'll always be God's little child,
Even though we are saved or lost and wild,
God loves us still!
Even though the choice is up to us to make,
Even though His free gift of love we forsake,
God loves us still!
Even though we're finally saved at last,
Even though His scars He'll wear for our past,
God loves us still!

John 3:16; Isa. 53

By Linda Clore

JESUS SUFFERED FOR ME

We were out working on the "Ark" one day in winter.
While handling the lumber I got a bad splinter.
The splinter was deep and the pain was unbearable.
I tried real hard to remove it and was so careful.
As I dug at the splinter, the blood came from my sore.
It made me think of Christ on the cross, and the pain He bore.
How He must have hurt with those nails hammered in His hands.
I was in pain with only a splinter in my hand.
Then they thrust Christ onto the cross and into the hole with a bang!
And He suffered in anguish as they left Him there to hang!
While digging on my splinter I prayed, "Please help me, Lord!"
This was so very painful as my flesh bled and tore.
I thought of all the pain Christ must have endured for me!
Because of His great love for me, He went to Calvary!
"Lord, I'm so very sorry for the times I have sinned,
And put you through the pain of Calvary once again!"
"Forgive me, Lord, for the times I didn't resist Satan,
But went ahead and yielded to the power of Satan."
May this experience of this splinter in my hand,
Help me realize more the pain you bore and understand,
That God is love and wants me saved and go to heaven.
To be with Him where there'll be no more pain in heaven.
Help me to be willing to endure the trials of life.
And keep my eyes on Jesus and my goal—eternal life.
May I value more the pain you bore in saving me!
That only in Christ will I gain over sin, victory!
And may I never forget what my salvation cost.
And how your heart will break, like on the cross, if I am lost.
May I be willing to die to self and take up my cross,
Like you were willing to die for me on the cruel cross.
"Thank you, Lord, for your great love and sacrifice for me!
I love you, Lord, and of your love I'm so unworthy!"

By Linda Clore
John 3:16; Rev. 21:4; The Desire of Ages, "Calvary"

NOW IS THE TIME!

God's merciful and kind, To give us all more time,
To be ready for Him, And overcome our sins.
Now is our time to work, And our duty not shirk.
We will certainly win, If we're relying on Him.
We should do all we can, To save our fellow man.
Time here is running out, God's work we are about.
Pray for the Spirit's Power, God's blessings He'll shower.
Never give up your faith. Soon we'll see Jesus' face.
It will be worth it all, When Jesus gives His call,
To leave this world and fly, With angels through the sky.
All sorrow and pain past, Home with Jesus at last.
Oh! There'll be no crying there. Just heaven's joys to share.
Don't you want to be there? Friends, Jesus wants you there.
He gave His life for you, What more then could He do?
Now's the time to be saved, Don't wait another day.
These are serious times With violence and bad crimes.
Don't put salvation off, Jesus died on the cross,
To ransom you from sin, Then, forever with Him.
The choice is up to you. Friends, what then will you do?
Jesus is soon to come. Friends, don't from Jesus run.
Friends, Satan wants you lost, Because he knows he's lost.
Don't keep following him, Cut loose from all your sins.
Now's the time to decide. Don't run from Christ and hide.
Jesus loves you my friends. Let Him cleanse you from sin.
You can decide your fate. Tomorrow is too late.
Jesus is calling now. Friends, surrender all now.
Soon judgment hour will pass. Soon we'll be Home at last,
Seeing Jesus and loved ones, The race of life all done.
That will be a grand time. The climax of all time!
We just have to be there! "Together" we'll be there!
We'll be safe in the fold, To walk the streets of gold,
With angels and with God, To walk on Heaven's sod.
Make your decision now. Jesus will help you now.
Have faith and trust in God. Walk hand in hand with God.
He'll see you through your trials, And all of Satan's wiles,
Follow God's plan for you. Just see what God can do!
Friends, Jesus is pleading, He's now interceding,
Don't say no to His call, Just surrender your all.
Things just won't be the same, If no one calls your name.
When Jesus looks for you, Won't you please be there, too?!
You don't want to be lost, And become useless dross.
Jesus wants you with Him. Won't you now accept Him?!
You haven't much time left, To pass your final test.
(cont.)

So won't you do it now? Walk the narrow road now?
The things of earth will pass, Get on the narrow path.
Follow Christ every day. He'll see you through each day.
He'll make you a new man, Following in His plans.
There's a future for you. In Christ you'll be made new.
So don't delay longer, God will make you stronger.
Real joy is found in Christ, And doing what is right.
Friends, take that step today, Now, no longer delay!
Give up your life of sin, And give it all to Him!
He'll take you by the hand, Make you strong so you'll stand.
Never fear, just hold on! Christ's in control from now on!
What peace and joy you'll find, Serving Christ all the time!
Now living to please Him, Not pleasing self and sin.
Victories, day by day! Staying close to Christ each day.
Gaining strength, through God's Word.
Through prayer, the Spirit's heard.

2 Cor 6:2; Rom 13:11-14; Jude 24

by Linda Clore

PREPARE YOUR HEART FOR THE SECOND COMING OF CHRIST!

No one knows what tomorrow holds! Only Jesus knows our future!
We must obey what we are told, In God's Word He shows our future!
Life is very solemn indeed, With decisions we make each day!
That's why God's counsel we should heed, Get rid of sin without delay!
Christ's coming is right upon us! We have no time to play in sin!
So, in God's Word we put our trust, And ask God's Spirit to come in.
God's power helps us overcome, When we surrender all our heart
Then, we will hear God's words, "Well done"! In Jesus a new life we'll start!
It's NOW that we are to prepare, Every day, time is running out!
God's truth with others we are to share, 'Cause soon God will come with a SHOUT!
What are we doing with our life? Our life's record is written down.
Are our days filled with cares and strife? Be ready when the trumpet sounds!
Satan is out to steal our crown! We must be faithful to Jesus!
And our names in heaven be found, Ready and prepared for Jesus!
No one knows what tomorrow brings, Nor how soon our life here may end!
Prepare NOW in heaven to sing, And be ready when the earth ends!
Things on earth are shaping up FAST! Jesus is calling you, TODAY!
Answer His call! Forget the past! Come to Jesus without delay!
Tomorrow it may be too late! All anyone has is right **_Now!_**
Right now you're deciding your fate! Open your heart to Jesus **_Now!_**
Jesus is stronger than Satan! Jesus will give you, "victory"!
Cling to Jesus and not Satan. Then, when Christ comes you'll shout, "Glory"!
So, prepare now to take your stand! Be true and loyal to Jesus!
And be in the Lord's will and plan. Be ready now to meet Jesus!
Oh! Get ready for Judgment Day! Friends, we now have no time to lose!
Now's the time to put sins away! It's time to decide whom we'll choose!

Written by Linda Clore

*David's dream on 5-28-15, "Prepare your heart for the second coming of Christ!" This dream inspired me to write this poem! I prayed God would help me write it fast, and in half an hour, God helped me write this poem! Praise God!

Read: *The Desire of Ages*, chapter 13, "The Victory," by E. G. White; 2 Cor. 6:2; Acts 24:25; Eccles. 12:13, 14; Matt. 24:36-51; *Early Writings*, p. 119, by E. G. White; *Testimonies for the Church*, vol. 6, p. 404-410, by E.G. White.

STAY TRUE TO JESUS!

Whatever it takes to be true, That's what I'm going to do!
And when the Sunday Laws are here, Trusting Jesus, I'll have no fears.
No matter what the test may be, I'll remain loyal to Thee!
Now's the time to show faith in God, Trust in His Word, and be like God.
Soon, troubles and trials will all be gone. Soon, we'll be singing a new song
So, keep your eyes fixed on Jesus, 'Cause soon we'll be home with Jesus.
There, there'll be no heartaches or cares, Only joys of heaven to share.
Decide now whose side you'll be on, Because soon, time will all be gone.
Where will you spend eternity? We have to face reality!
There's a showdown we must all face, Everyone in this human race.
Will you choose Christ or follow man? Will you keep God's Sabbath or man's?
Friends, there's no more time for delay! Choose to follow Jesus TODAY!
He'll help you through the days ahead. Trust His Word, and do what He says!
So, just be true and do His will. Through the storms you'll be calm and still.
Come what may, remain in His love, 'Cause soon Christ will come from above.
I want to be ready, don't you? And to be found faithful and true.
Christ says we can do it through Him, And live on this earth without sin.
Won't you put Christ first in your life? Then, you will have eternal life.
It will be worth it all my friends. Stay true to Christ until the end.
Don't be one of those shaken out. Right now, friends, you can turn about.
And put away your sinful life. Be true to Jesus without strife.
Just live for Jesus in all you do. Have Christ's character and be true.
So when the Sunday Laws are passed, Friends, the choice you make then will last.
There'll be no turning around then. Decide NOW what you will do then.
Friends, there's serious times ahead! It's time to put Christ at the head!
And let Him have control of all. Then you'll be ready when He calls.
No matter what the future holds, In Christ you can be true and bold.
Be true to Christ and don't give in, Because with Christ we will soon win!
Whether we live or whether die, We can make it, if we'll just try!
Friends, we can do all things through Christ! We can have hope and trust in Christ!
Friends, Christ will never let you down. Let's decide we won't let Him down!
Christ is stronger than any man! And He is out to help us stand!
The war's between Christ and Satan, Then, choose Christ and don't be shaken!

Written by Linda Clore

***Maranatha**, p. 270, by E. G. White; Ps. 121; Phil. 4:13, 19; Ps. 32:8; Josh. 24:15; Prov. 3:1–8; Ps. 46:1; Ps. 37:1–7; Isa. 33:15–17; Ps. 56; Ps. 91; 1 Kings 18; **Testimonies for the Church**, vol. 6, "The Work for this Time", pp. 14-22 by E. G. White*

Letters

The following are letters we've received through the years from friends and loved ones about the "ARK" and the time of trouble, etc., and letters we've written back to them, by me, to try and encourage them and give them help in seeing what God's will is for His people in leaving the large cities and moving to the country, as God opens the way for them.

Sister White tells us in *Country Living*, pp. 24–28, "The time has come, when, as God opens the way, families should move out of the cities. The children should be taken into the country. The parents should get as suitable a place as their means will allow. Though the dwelling may be small, yet there should be land in connection with it that may be cultivated. Parents can secure small homes in the country, with land for cultivation, where they can have orchards and where they can raise vegetables and small fruits to take the place of flesh meat, which is so corrupting to the life blood coursing through the veins. On such places the children will not be surrounded with the corrupting influences of city life. God will help His people to find such homes outside the cities… More and more, as time advances, our people will have to leave the cities. For years we have been instructed that our brethren and sisters, and especially families with children, should plan to leave the cities as the way opens before them to do so. Many will have to labor earnestly to help open the way. But until it is possible for them to leave, so long as they remain, they should be most active in doing missionary work, however, limited their sphere of influence may be…

Those who have felt at last to make a move, let it not be in a rush, in an excitement, or in a rash manner, or in a way that hereafter they will deeply regret that they did move out… Do nothing without seeking wisdom of God, who hath promised to give liberally to all who ask and who upbraideth not. All that anyone can do is to advise and counsel, and then leave those who are convicted in regard to duty to move under divine guidance and with their whole hearts open to learn and obey God…

The messengers who bear the message of mercy to our world, who have the confidence of the people, will be appealed to for advice. Great caution must be exercised by these men who have not genuine experiences in practical life, and who will be in danger of giving advice, ignorant of what that advice may lead others to do… Some men have insight into matters, having ability to counsel. It is a gift of God… Let everyone take time to consider carefully; and not be like the man in the parable who began to build, and was not able to finish. Not a move should be made but that movement and all that it portends are carefully considered—everything weighed… To every man was given his work according to his several ability. Then let him not move hesitatingly, but firmly, and yet humbly trusting in God. There may be individuals who will make a rush to do something, and enter into some business they know nothing about. This God does not require. Think candidly, prayerfully, studying the Word with all carefulness and prayerfulness, with mind and heart awake to hear the voice of God... To understand the will of God is a great thing...

They (teachers) do not discern the perplexing situation that must necessarily come to every family who shall make a change... and let the individual rely wholly upon God. Let there be much praying done, and even with fasting, that not one shall move in darkness, but move in the light as God is in the light... Let there be wise generalship in this matter, and all move under the guidance of a wise, unseen Counselor, which is God... Now I plead with every soul to look not too strongly and confidently to human counselors, but look most earnestly to God, the one wise in counsel. Submit all your ways and your will to God's ways and to God's will...

If everyone will come to Jesus in a teachable spirit, with contrition of heart, then he is in a condition of mind to be instructed and to learn of Jesus and obey His orders...

We cannot have a weak faith now, we cannot be safe in a listless, indolent, slothful attitude. Every jot of ability is to be used, and sharp, calm, deep thinking is to be done. The wisdom of any human agent is not sufficient for planning and devising in this time. Spread every plan before God with fasting [and] with the humbling of the soul before the Lord Jesus, and commit thy ways unto the Lord. The sure promise is, He will direct thy paths. He is infinite in resources. The Holy One of Israel, who calls the host of heaven by name, and holds the stars of heaven in position, has you individually in His keeping...

I would that all could realize what possibilities and probabilities there are for all who make Christ their sufficiency and their trust. The life hid with Christ in God ever has a refuge; he can say, 'I can do all things through Christ which strengthens me...' for if we walk humbly with God, we shall walk safely."

I'll start with a question from David's S.D.A. sister, Hilma, in Chicago. She said to us that a S.D.A. friend of hers said that she felt people should be living up in the mountains right now, and not in just the hill country.

I'll try and answer her question, as David and I see it, according to how Sister White writes. Everyone will have to go to the Lord for themselves and pray and fast over their own situation and what God wants them to do, individually. Not everyone's case is the same.

Where we're living now, in the Chippewah Hills, with forest all around us and far out away from the big cities, at least 55–75 miles away from two big cities and three and a half miles out on a gravel country road from a small town. This is the place God prepared for us in answer to our fasting and praying for God's guidance, as we prayed over Sister White's *Country Living* book and other of her many quotes referring to being out in the country; especially with children and leaving the large cities now and be getting set up and prepared for the crisis ahead of us. According to what we read in Sister White's counsel, not everyone is going to be in the mountains during this early time of trouble, we're beginning to get into right now, as God's angels are holding the four winds back a little longer, before the Great Time of Trouble comes, when probation has closed, and the seven last plagues are falling and when the death decree is passed on God's faithful ones who are loyal to God's seventh day Sabbath and not going along with the Sunday Law. This is when we'll have to leave our country places and our mountain places we've been living in with our fruit trees and berries and gardens for food, since we can't buy or sell, because we've been cut off from the system and have no electricity, gas, water, food, etc. We will then have to flee to desolate and solitary places. When Jesus comes, God's heirs will be coming from garrets, from hovels, from dungeons, from scaffolds, from mountains, from deserts, from caves of the earth, from the caverns of the sea. (*The Great Controversy*, p. 650) Read the chapter, "God's People Delivered." We read in *Country Living*, p. 32, by E. G. White, "It is no time now for God's people to be fixing their affections in the world. The time is not far distant, when, like the early disciples, we shall be forced to seek a refuge in desolate and solitary places. As the siege of Jerusalem by the Roman armies was the signal for flight to the Judean Christians, so the assumption of power on the part of our nation, in the decree enforcing the papal Sabbath, will be a warning to us. It will then be time to leave the large cities, preparatory to leaving the smaller ones for retired homes in secluded places among the mountains. And now, instead of seeking expensive dwellings here, we should be preparing to move to a better country, even a heavenly. Instead of spending our means in self-gratification, we should be studying to economize." This is the time when God shall supply His faithful children with their food and water, like Isa. 33:15, 16 promises. Read *The Great Controversy*, the chapter, "The Time of Trouble." Read your *Country Living* by E. G. White where she says over and over again to leave the large cities and move out into retired country places where we can have a garden and raise our own produce." (*Country Living*, p. 21)

In the book, *Early Writings*, p. 56, by Sister White, she's referring to the Great Time of Trouble when the seven last plagues are falling and we've had to leave our country or mountain homes and our gardens and are trusting wholly in God to sustain us.

In *Country Living*, p. 10, by E. G. White, she writes, "Get out of the cities into rural districts, where the houses are not crowded closely together, and where you will be free from the interference of enemies." (You can do this in country places and not necessarily have to be up in the mountains.)

"The time is fast coming when the controlling power of the labor unions will be very oppressive. Again and again the Lord has instructed that our people are to take their families away from the cities, into the country, where they can raise their own provisions, for in the future the problem of buying and selling will be a very serious one." Quote by E. G. White in *Country Living*, p. 9, 10.

Sister White entitled her book, *Country Living* and not "Mountain Living." In *Country Living*, p. 14, Sister White warns us, "Who will be warned? We say again, Out of the cities. Do not consider it a great deprivation that you must go into the hills and mountains but seek for that retirement where you can be alone with God, to learn His will and way... I urge our people to make it their lifework to seek for spirituality. Christ is at the door. This is why I say to our people, Do not consider it a privation when you are called to leave the cities and move out into country places. Here there await rich blessings for those who will grasp them. By beholding the scenes of nature, the works of the Creator, by studying God's handiwork, imperceptibly you will be changed into the same image."

In *Country Living*, pp. 14 and 15, Sister White tells us where Jesus lived when on earth growing up: "What were the conditions chosen by the infinite Father for His Son? A secluded home in the Galilean hills..."

Jesus didn't live in the mountains Himself, but in the hills. God's prophet, Sister White, tells us over and over again to be in the country, not telling everyone to go into the mountains to live, yet.

I looked up the word, "country" and the dictionary says, "land with farms and small towns, land outside of cities, rural."

I looked up the word, "mountain" and it said, "a part of the earth's surface that rises high into the air; a very high hill."

In *Country Living*, p. 10, by Ellen White, she writes, "Educate our people to get out of the cities into the country, where they can obtain a small piece of land, and make a home for themselves and their children." Another note from Sister White out of her book, *Country Living*, p. 5, she writes and tells us, "Instead of the crowded city, seek some retired situation where your children will be so far as possible shielded from temptation and there train and educate them for usefulness."

Again this can be done by living in the country and not the city. There are places all over the U.S.A. and the world that have no mountains, but God's people are to be found everywhere as lights shining for Jesus and spreading the truth, but not by living in the cities, but in the country, and not necessarily a mountain dwelling.

Matt. 5:16, "Let your light so shine before men, that they may see your good works, and glorify your Father which is in heaven."

In *Country Living*, p. 30, by E. G. White, she tells us, "As God's commandment-keeping people, we must leave the cities. As did Enoch, we must work in the cities but not dwell in them... Enoch walked with God, and yet he did not live in the midst of any city, polluted with every kind of violence and wickedness... Repeatedly the Lord has instructed us that we are to work the cities from outpost centers."

Mountain places would be the best, but not everyone can move way up in the mountains, especially if they're still working and not retired, and have to commute back and forth to their jobs long distances. But God does tell us to live in the country and not in the cities. This is true of our training schools and places for the sick, etc. Sister White says in *Medical Ministry*, p. 308, 309, "Look for such places just out from the large cities." In the book *Country Living*, p. 11, by Ellen G. White we read, "But erelong there will be such strife and confusion in the cities, that those who wish to leave them will not be able. We must be preparing for these issues. This is the light that is given me."

In *Country Living*, p. 13, by E. G. White, she gives this advice, "There is not one family in a hundred who will be improved physically, mentally, or spiritually by residing in the city. Faith, hope, love, happiness, can far better be gained in retired places, where there are fields and hills and trees. Take your children away from the sights and sounds of the city, away from the rattle and din of streetcars and teams, and their minds will become more healthy. It will be found easier to bring home to their hearts the truth of the Word of God… Send the children to schools in the city, where every phase of temptation is waiting to attract and demoralize them, and the work of character building is tenfold harder for both parents and children. Out of the cities is my message for the education of our children."

In *Selected Messages*, book 2, p. 359, by E. G. White, we are advised, "If in the providence of God we can secure places away from the cities, the Lord would have us do this. There are troublous times before us." Read Ps. 32:8; Prov. 3:5–8; Ps. 37:3–7; Matt. 6:33

Testimonies for the Church, vol. 5, p. 461, Sister White tells us, "The work will be given to those who will take it, those who prize it, who weave its principles into their everyday experience. God will choose humble men who are seeking to glorify His name and advance His cause rather than to honor and advance themselves. He will raise up men who have not so much worldly wisdom, but who are connected with Him, and who will seek strength and counsel from above."

In the book *Maranatha*, p. 270, by Sister White, she says, "During the night a very impressive scene passed before me. There seemed to be great confusion and the conflict of armies. A messenger from the Lord stood before me, and said, 'Call your household. I will lead you; follow me.' He led me down a dark passage, through a forest, then through the clefts of mountains and said, 'Here you will be safe.' There were others who had been led to this retreat. The heavenly messenger said, 'The time of trouble has come as a thief in the night, as the Lord warned you it would come… In the time of trouble just before the coming of Christ, the righteous will be preserved through the ministration of heavenly angels, but there will be no security for the transgressor of God's law. Angels cannot then protect those who are disregarding one of the divine precepts."

In *Maranatha*, p, 278, 279, by E. G. White we read, "The people of God—some in prison cells, some hidden in solitary retreats in the forests and the mountains—still plead for divine protection, while in every quarter companies of armed men, urged on by hosts of evil angels are preparing for the work of death. It is now, in the hour of utmost extremity that the God of Israel will interpose for the deliverance of His chosen… It is at midnight that God manifests His power for the deliverance of His people."

Well, these are just a few quotes from Sister White. You will have to search it out for yourself with fasting and praying over your choice of a home out of the cities and let the Lord lead and guide and direct you. Look to God as your counselor and not man. Don't take what I say or anyone else, but look to Jesus and His Word and the Spirit of Prophecy to advise you and you can't go wrong, as you let the Lord open the way for you. Spread your individual case and situation before the Lord and He won't fail you. We need to be developing faith and trust in God now and His promises, so we will have the faith and courage then to leave our security in our country or mountain home and our gardens for food and be willing to follow the Lord's angels to places of refuge whether in the high mountains or caves or desert or forest where God's angels will cover us over and hide us from our enemies who will want to destroy us.

The next letter comes from a very dear friend, like a sister to me. Her name is, Sandie, from New Jersey. In her letter she writes, "We want to come to Kansas. We talk about it a lot. Only the Lord can take us there. We long for the "ARK" of safety and a true Godly experience with you. God bless you both for what you have done for others. It's amazing all you have done and sacrificed to build the "ARK" to help others needing a refuge, when the Sunday Law will be passed and people have nowhere to go."

Sandie said to me, also, "The Lord is using you in these last days in so many ways to help people in the end time to be saved. Praise God for you and Dave. All that you've done to build the "ARK" and all your dreams God has given you and all the writing you do, God bless you for it all! It's been a journey like no other for you both! Please take care of yourselves. Love to you, David, Linda, and Jonathan. I continue to pray for you and for Jonathan's healing and he'll overcome. Love your sister Sandie." Through the years in other letters she's written to us she has said how she and her daughter are interested in learning to be medical missionaries and live the eight natural remedies and be ready for the soon coming crises ahead with the Sunday Law soon to come upon us. She wants to learn gardening and survival and have Bible studies with us. She sends us encouraging letters and keeps encouraging us to keep up the writing on my book, **Don't Be Trapped in the Cities!! Get Out Now!**

Another letter Sandie wrote me where she said, "I want out of the big wicked cities and to be able to come to the "ARK", but my daughter and I can't read a road map. My husband can't see the importance in leaving our home in the cities and the dangers of staying longer in the big wicked cities. I have obligations of caring for loved ones here, too, who can't see the reasons to leave the large cities. We've had terrible crimes going on right in our very own neighborhood, and robberies happening to our very own family! We've gone through some serious and terrible disaster storms and loss of our electricity and all our food in the freezer and refrigerator. We were affected by the "Sandy hurricane storm," too. Please pray for us, that we'll know what to do!"

To answer her letters and questions, I prayed for God's help and guidance to direct her and her daughter as to what the Lord wanted them to do at this time about their particular situation. Their letters were so touching and I felt so helpless to know how to answer them. I told them to pray and fast over their *Country Living* book by Sister White and other E. G. White references on what to be doing at this time and to get to know Jesus as a personal Saviour and learn to trust Him and have faith in Him and encouraged them to let the Holy Spirit guide them and direct them and claim God's promises to them. I wrote and said I just didn't know what to tell them to do at this time, when to come and how to get here. I encouraged them to pray and fast and draw close to Jesus like never before. My heart ached for them as I read their letters and assured them that there will be a place for them when they feel it's time to come and to keep letting the Lord plan for them. I quoted the promise in Prov. 3:5, 6 "Trust in the Lord with all thine heart, and lean not unto thine own understanding. In all thy ways acknowledge Him, and he shall direct thy paths." I also, quoted Ps. 37:3–5, "Trust in the Lord, and do good; so shalt thou dwell in the land, and verily thou shalt be fed. Delight thyself also in the Lord; and He shall give thee the desires of thine heart. Commit thy way unto the Lord; trust also in him; and He shall bring it to pass. Read Ps. 32:8."

I quoted to her quotes from Sister White to encourage her and others who have written to us feeling trapped in the cities and don't know what to do or where to go! They, too, have to personally decide what God wants them to be doing, at this time, and when and how to do it. There is an urgency people are feeling, knowing they should be getting out of these big wicked cities with all these calamities coming because of the cities' wickedness and crime and violence and to get out while they still can or be trapped and martial law passed and they can't leave and no one can come in. No one can tell each person what they are to do. This is between you and God. I told her and others in letters that God knows their heart and concerns and worries and fears and decisions they have to make and plans for them and their families they'll have to decide what to do and when to do it, when that time finally comes. You hate to wait too long before the next dangerous storm and disaster hits and you may not make it through the next one. I quote *Ministry of Healing* to people in answer to their questions as to what they are to do. On p. 482 Sister White, God's prophet, has this encouraging statement, "Many who profess to be Christ's followers have an anxious troubled heart because they are afraid to trust themselves with God. They do not make a complete surrender to Him, for they shrink from the consequences that such a surrender may involve. Unless they do make this surrender they cannot find peace… Worry is blind and cannot discern the future; but Jesus sees the end from the beginning. In every difficulty He has His way prepared to bring relief. 'No good thing will He withhold from them that walk uprightly.' Ps. 84:11. Our heavenly Father has a thousand ways to provide for us of which we know nothing. Those who accept the one principle of making the service of God supreme, will find perplexities vanish and a plain path before their feet… Let us be hopeful and courageous. Despondency in God's service is sinful and unreasonable. He knows our every necessity… He has means for the removal of every difficulty, that those who serve Him and respect the means He employs may be sustained. His love is as far above all other love as the heavens are above the earth. He watches over His children with a love that is measureless and everlasting. In the darkest days, when appearances seem most forbidding, have faith in God. He is working out His will, doing all things well in behalf of His people. The strength of those who love and serve Him will be renewed day by day. He is able and willing to bestow upon His servants all the help they need. He will give them the wisdom which their varied necessities demand." Read 2 Cor. 12:9, 10.

In my letter to Sandie, and others I've received letters from, and have answered, I tell them how much Jesus loves them and has plans for their life as Jer. 29:11–13, that says, "For I know the thoughts that I think toward you, saith the Lord, thoughts of peace, and not of evil, to give you an expected end. Then shall ye call upon me, and ye shall go and pray unto me, and I will hearken unto you. And ye shall seek me, and find me, when ye shall search for me with all your heart." Also, Jer. 33:3, "Call unto me, and I will answer thee, and show thee great and mighty things, which thou knowest not." Also, Rom. 8:28, "And we know that all things work together for good to them that love God, to them who are the called according to his purpose."

God is testing our faith and trust in Him. He's the only all wise counselor we can depend on. Man will only fail us, but Jesus never fails. He's always there to help and strengthen and guide us as we learn to depend and rely on Him and not weak sinful man. We need to keep our eyes on Jesus and not the problems of life, like Ps. 121 says.

In my letters to people who had children or grandchildren, I tried to encourage them to stay faithful to Jesus and keep Him as their pattern and not follow the crowd or give in to peer pressures. I mentioned how our son, Jonathan, started on the downward road in church school, when he wanted to be liked and accepted and not feel different. But there was so much peer pressure, so he got in with the wrong crowd, which was the popular kids doing the wrong things and he'd follow along instead of standing up for Jesus, and doing what he knew was right. As he got older and out on his own, one step down led to others and others until he was doing and saying things he thought he would never do or say. We now have our son living at home with us, so we can help him get well and come back to Jesus again with all his heart and encourage him to turn his life over to Jesus and find the peace and joy and happiness that comes from living to please Jesus and obey and follow Him with all his heart. We need to spend time with Jesus through prayer and Bible study and pattern our life after Jesus and not the people of the world. We must guard the avenues of our soul, seeing, hearing, smelling, touching, tasting. Sister White admonishes us in *Messages to Young People*, p. 285, "Those who would not fall a pray to Satan's devices must guard well the avenues of the soul; they must avoid reading, seeing, or hearing that which will suggest impure thoughts."

Also, in my letters I've mentioned to people about listening to Hal Mayer's CD on, "The Sunday Movements Gain Momentum." I, also, mentioned to people I've written to about hearing from a good source about our economy situation and they were saying by December 2014 we were supposed to change over to a new currency and the money we now use won't have the value it now has. God in His love and mercy has been holding this off. Praise God! Sister White says in *Evangelism*, p. 63, "Money will soon depreciate in value very suddenly when the reality of eternal scenes opens to the senses of man."

My dear cousins in Florida, Nancy and her sister Diane and her husband, Larry, have written and encouraged us to keep writing on my book, **Don't Be Trapped in the Cities!! Get Out <u>Now</u>!** and keep building on the "ARK." Also, a dear friend, Cynthia, from New York writes and encourages us to keep building on the "ARK." We hear how people are blessed by the DVDs of my book that Bill and Mary are making for me. Now is our time to be praying for the outpouring of the Holy Spirit and receive the latter rain to be able to stand during the time of trouble and give the Loud Cry message. We need to keep our records straight in heaven.

Step Fast!

"Said the angel, 'Deny self; ye must step fast.'" *Early Writings* p. 67

I had been having dreams saying, "HURRY! URGENT! Get Ready! Get Ready! Get Ready! 'What thou doest do Quickly!' "

I had a dream that showed a clock with its hand showing just minutes before midnight. My husband, that same night, had dreamed all night seeing a clock in his dreams! Then my husband and I had both dreamed in the same night the words, "The Midnight Cry." Then I dreamed on another night these words, "The Midnight Cry! Give the trumpet a certain sound!" My husband dreamed the words: "Lift up the Trumpet!" My husband and I on the same night dreamed the same dream: "Come out of her my people!" Rev. 18:4 (Read about it in *The Great Controversy*, the chapter on, "Prophecies Fulfilled—The Midnight Cry.")

One time, David, during the night had had a dream that I had had a dream that very night about the NEARNESS of Christ's SOON coming and that things are almost over. He couldn't remember the dream but he said it was startling! I had been fasting and praying that day and had skipped a meal because there were so many things I had been praying about and I wanted answered. Some of the things I had been praying about was the salvation of our son, Jonathan, and praying for the outpouring of the Holy Spirit in my life and to overcome my sins and I was claiming Bible promises like Matt. 21:22, "And all things whatsoever ye shall ask in prayer, believing, ye shall receive."

After David told me about him dreaming that I had had a frightening dream that night, we prayed that God would please give me the dream He wanted me to have that night. I prayed myself back to sleep that night asking God to please give me a dream about His soon coming and the urgency of getting ready! During that very night God gave me this dream: I saw charts showing the signs of the times of Christ's soon coming!

It said, "STEP FAST!" ("We should study the great way marks that point out the times in which we are living." *Last Day Events*, p. 14, by E. G. White)

The next morning when I told my dream to my husband that God had given me that night he said, "You need to write this in your book you're writing that you've entitled, ***Don't Be Trapped in the Cities!! Get Out Now!*** The people need to be warned to get ready before it's too late! They need to STEP FAST! There's no time to lose in getting ourselves ready and others ready for Christ's soon coming and things are wrapping up FAST! People need to be in earnest in getting out of these big wicked cities as FAST as they can before it will be too late for them to leave and will be TRAPPED! They need to be studying and learning their Bibles and the Spirit of Prophecy books like: *The Great Controversy, Country Living, Last Day Events, Maranatha* by E. G. White and books like: *You Can Survive* by Jere Franklin; and *Another Ark to Build* by W. D. Frazee and also, W. D. Frazee's book, *Coming Events and Crisis at the Close. Everything is so Urgent! Time is* Running Out!"

We both agreed and knelt down and prayed and thanked the Lord for the dream and prayed for us and God's people that their eyes and ours would be opened to the events happening in quick succession and all the signs pointing to the nearness of Christ's soon return! God is trying to wake up His people! "We are standing on the threshold of the crisis of the ages. In quick succession the judgments of God will follow one another—fire, and flood, and earthquake, with war, and bloodshed." *Last Day Events*, p. 12, by E. G. White.

Matt. 24:42 & 44: "Watch therefore: for ye know not what hour your Lord doth come…. Therefore be ye also ready: for in such an hour as ye think not the Son of man cometh." (Read Matt. 24; Mark 13; Luke 21; Matt 25).

Mark 13:29: "So ye in like manner, when ye shall see these things come to pass, know that it is nigh, even at the door."

Just recently I had this quote of E. G. White in my dream: *Selected Messages*, book 2, p. 142: "The work of the people of God is to prepare for the events of the future, which will soon come upon them with blinding force." Also read, *Testimonies for the Church*, vol. 8, p. 28: "Transgression has almost reached its limit. Confusion fills the world, and a great terror is soon to come upon human beings. The end is very near. We who know the truth should be preparing for what is soon to break upon the world as an overwhelming surprise."

Testimonies for the Church, vol. 6, p. 407: "The judgments of God are about to fall upon the world, and we need to be preparing for that great day."

Testimonies for the Church, vol. 5, p. 452: "God has revealed what is to take place in the last days, that His people may be prepared to stand against the tempest of opposition and wrath. Those who have been warned of the events before them are not to sit in calm expectation of the coming storm, comforting themselves that the Lord will shelter His faithful ones in the day of trouble."

Early Writings, p. 119: "I saw that the remnant were not prepared for what is coming upon the earth. Stupidity like lethargy, seemed to hang upon the minds of most of those who profess to believe that we are having the last message. My accompanying angel cried out with awful solemnity, GET READY! GET READY! GET READY! for the fierce anger of the Lord is soon to come. His wrath is to be poured out, unmixed with mercy, and ye are not ready."

Messages to Young People, pp. 99, 100: "Remember, that you will never reach a higher standard than you yourself set. Then set your mark high, and step by step, even though it be by painful effort, by self-denial and sacrifice, ascend the whole length of the ladder of progress. Let nothing hinder you."

Welfare Ministry, p. 136: "I heard someone say, 'We knew that the judgments of God were coming upon the earth, but we did not know that they would come so soon.' Others said, 'You knew? Why then did you not tell us? We did not know.' On every side I heard such words spoken… The prophecies of the eleventh of Daniel have almost reached their final fulfillment."

Early Writings, p. 58: "…Some are looking too far off for the coming of the Lord. Time has continued a few years longer than they expected, therefore they think it may continue a few years more, and in this way their minds are being led from present truth, out after the world… I saw that the time for Jesus to be in the most holy place was nearly finished and that time can last but a very little longer… Live and act wholly in reference to the coming of the Son of man. The sealing time is very short, and will soon be over. Now is the time, while the four angels are holding the four winds, to make our calling and election sure."

Testimonies for the Church, vol. 3, p. 380: "Will you heed the voice of warning which tells you that destruction lies in the path of those who are at ease in the hour of danger? God's patience will not always wait for you, poor, trifling souls. He who holds our destinies in

His hands will not always be trifled with… It shall be more tolerable for Sodom and Gomorrah in the day of judgment than for those who have had the privileges and the great light which shines in our day, but who have neglected to follow the light and to give their hearts fully to God."

Testimonies for the Church, vol. 1, p. 187: "Individuals are tested and proved a length of time to see if they will sacrifice their idols and heed the counsel of the True Witness… Those who come up to every point, and stand every test, and overcome, be the price what it may, have heeded the counsel of the True Witness, and they will receive the latter rain, and thus be fitted for translation."

Country Living, p. 31: "Out of the cities; out of the cities!'—this is the message the Lord has been giving me. The earthquakes will come; the floods will come; and we are not to establish ourselves in the wicked cities, where the enemy is served in every way, and where God is so often forgotten."

Country Living, p. 21: "The Protestant world have set up an idol sabbath in place where God's Sabbath should be, and they are treading in the footsteps of the Papacy. For this reason I see the necessity of the people of God moving out of the cities, into retired country places, where they may cultivate the land and raise their own produce. Thus they may bring their children up with simple, healthful habits. I see the necessity of making haste to get all things ready for the crisis."

Country Living, p. 17: "If we place ourselves under objectionable influences, can we expect God to work a miracle to undo the results of our wrong course? No, indeed. Get out of the cities as soon as possible, and purchase a little piece of land, where you can have a garden…"

Country Living, p. 27: "Let there be much praying done, and even with fasting, that not one shall move in darkness, but move in the light as God is in the light."

I recommend the book, *Country Living* by E. G. White for everyone to read and study and pray and fast over, so the Lord can direct your paths. Claim God's promises in Prov. 3:5, 6; and Ps. 37:3–5; Ps. 32:8; Remember, Jesus loves you and He has plans for you! Jer. 29:11–13; Jer. 33:3; "Remember Lot's wife." Luke 17:32; Great changes are soon to take place in our world, and the final movements will be rapid ones." *Testimonies for the Church*, vol. 9, p. 11

God's People, Wake Up!

At 3:15 AM, 7-29-14, I awoke with this impressive dream on my mind: I was telling someone of the fallout destruction in Kansas City. (There's a big underground nuclear arsenal there.) Continuing on in the dream, some of us were together seeing what it would be like if we were experiencing a disaster and what we needed to do in case of going through one and how one needed to prepare for it. We could see we weren't ready like we should be. I was telling someone of the dream God gave me that we should be using our money to get ready for what's coming and have what things we'll need for such a time ahead of us and be prepared and ready for it. One thing I remember in my dream, "Have your clothes ready." In *Prophets and Kings*, p. 184, Sister White quotes Satan speaking, saying "…Human laws will be made so stringent that men and women will not dare to observe the seventh-day Sabbath. For fear of wanting food and clothing, they will join with the world in transgressing God's law. The earth will be wholly under my dominion." Read the whole chapter 14, pp. 177–189, "In the Spirit and Power of Elias." (I looked up in the dictionary the word, "fallout." It said, "The falling to earth of radioactive particles after a nuclear explosion.")

I, also, looked up in the dictionary the word, "nuclear," it said, "Having to do with a nucleus or nuclei…involving or using the nuclei of atoms… or involving atomic bombs or other nuclear weapons like nuclear warfare."

It won't only be BIG Kansas City involved in terrible disasters, but Sister White says in *Country Living*, p. 8, "O that God's people had a sense of the impending destruction of thousands of cities, now almost given to idolatry."

Also, in *Country Living*, p. 6, Sister White says, "I could not sleep past two o'clock this morning. During the night season I was in council. I was pleading with some families to avail themselves of God's appointed means and get away from the cities to save their children. Some were loitering, making no determined efforts."

On page 8 of *Country Living*, Sister White continues to warn God's people by saying, "There are reasons why we should not build in the cities, on these cities, God's judgments are soon to fall… The time is near when large cities will be swept away, and all should be warned of these coming judgments."

Sister White relates one of her very impressive scenes she had. *Country Living*, p. 8, she relates the dream: "Last Friday morning, just before I awoke, a very impressive scene was presented before me. I seemed to awake from sleep, but was not in my home. From the windows I could behold a terrible conflagration. Great balls of fire were falling upon houses, and from these balls fiery arrows were flying in every direction. It was impossible to check the fires that were kindled, and many places were being destroyed. The terror of the people was indescribable."

Country Living, p. 9, Sister White urges God's people to heed her warning, when she says, "In harmony with the light given me, I am urging people to come out from the great centers of population. Our cities are increasing in wickedness, and it is becoming more and more evident that those who remain in them unnecessarily do so at the peril of their soul's salvation." Sister White, in *Country Living*, pp. 9, 10, 11, and 12, tells of the future problem of buying and selling. "The time is fast coming when the controlling power of the labor unions will be very oppressive. Again and again the Lord has instructed that our people are to take their families away from the cities, into the country, where they can raise their own provisions, for in the future the problem of buying and selling will be a very serious one. We should now begin to heed this instruction given us over and over again: Get out of the cities into rural districts, where the houses are not crowded closely together, and where you will be free from the interference of enemies...

The trades unions will be one of the agencies that will bring upon this earth a time of trouble such as has not been since the world began... The work of the people of God is to prepare for the events of the future, which will soon come upon them with blinding force... But erelong there will be such strife and confusion in the cities, that those who wish to leave them will not be able. We must be preparing for these issues. This is the light that is given me." (This could be like Martial Law passed on cities.) Also, Sister White, referring to the Sunday Law, tells us this, "Before the overflowing scourge shall come upon the dwellers of the earth, the Lord calls upon all who are Israelites indeed to prepare for that event. To the parents He sends the warning cry, gather your children into your own houses, gather them away from those who are disregarding the commandments of God, who are teaching and practicing evil. Get out of the large cities as fast as possible." On pp. 13 and 14, Sister White, in her book, *Country Living* goes on to give this counsel..., "...Fathers and mothers, how do you regard the souls of your children? Are you preparing the members of your families for translation into the heavenly courts?... How will ease, comfort, convenience, compare with the value of the souls of your children?... We cannot fail to see that the end of the world is soon to come. Satan is working upon the minds of men and women, and many seem filled with a desire for amusement and excitement. As it was in the day of Noah, every kind of evil is on the increase. Divorce and marriage is the order of the time. At such a time as this, the people who are seeking to keep the commandments of God should look for retired places away from the cities... Who will be warned? We say again, Out of the Cities. Do not consider it a great deprivation that you must go into the hills and mountains, but seek for that retirement where you can be alone with God, to learn His will and way... I urge our people to make it their life work to seek for spirituality. Christ is at the door."

Why Didn't Someone Warn Us?!

There's a dream my husband, David, had that just makes him shudder to think about it! He said he was up high in the sky. He wasn't in an airplane, he said. But it was at night and he could look down and see fires all over in different places and different size fires. It was cities being burned up and destroyed. Some were little fires on the small cities and some were medium size fires on medium size cities, and there were real BIG fires destroying BIG cities. He remembers hearing the shrieks and screams and cry of the terrified people calling out to one another and arguing with one another and moaning and groaning and wailing and screaming out, "Why didn't someone warn us of these judgments coming?!!" They were turning on each other and blaming each other for not warning them of this terrible destruction they were suffering. Read in *Country Living*, p. 6–8, by E. G. White of the destruction of these cities! David's dream reminded me of the dream God gave me, the words spoken were, "Blow the trumpet! Sound an alarm! Warn my people!" This made me realize I must write my book and warn the people like God says or their blood will be on my hands as Ez. 33 and Joel 2 says and also, Ez. 3.

Read *Testimonies for the Church*, vol. 6, pp. 60–62, the chapter entitled, "The Last Warning" where Sister White says, "The trumpet is to give a certain sound... Lift up the standard—the commandments of God and the faith of Jesus… Our warfare is aggressive. Tremendous issues are before us, yea, and right upon us. Let our prayers ascend to God that the four angels may still hold the four winds, that they may not blow to injure or destroy until the last warning has been given to the world. Then let us work in harmony with our prayers. Let nothing lessen the force of the truth for this time. The present truth is to be our burden. The third angels' message must do its work of separating from the churches a people who will take their stand on the platform of eternal truth. Our message is a life and death message, and we must let it appear as it is, the great power of God. We are to present it in all its telling force. Then the Lord will make it effectual… The perils of the last days are upon us, and in our work we are to warn the people of the danger they are in. Let not the solemn scenes which prophecy has revealed be left untouched. If our people were half awake, if they realized the nearness of the events portrayed in the Revelation, a reformation would be wrought in our churches, and many would believe the message. We have no time to lose; God calls upon us to watch for souls as they must give an account… Let Daniel speak, let the Revelation speak, and tell what is truth. But whatever phase of the subjects presented, uplift Jesus as the center of all hope, the root and offspring of David, and the bright morning star.' "Rev. 22:16.

This is why I'm so earnest to get my book, **Don't Be Trapped in the Cities!! Get Out _Now!_** written. To warn the people of the dangers of remaining unnecessarily in these cities, like Sister White says in her book, *Country Living*, p. 9, "In harmony with the light given me, I am urging people to come out from the great centers of population. Our cities are increasing in wickedness, and it is becoming more and more evident that those who remain in them unnecessarily do so at the peril of their soul's salvation."

This is why I want to encourage people to look to Jesus and His promises in faith, trusting Jesus to see them through the trying experiences they will pass through in the crisis ahead, when we'll all have to face the Sunday Law issue soon to break upon us! The choices and decisions we're making now will decide our destiny then! We need to be drawing closer and closer to Jesus and learning to depend more and more on Him and less and less on man. If we're crumbling now under the pressures of life, how will we expect to stand true to God and His seventh-day Sabbath when the real pressures will be brought against us during the Sunday Laws enforced upon us? Like it says in Jer. 12:5, "If thou hast run with the footmen, and they have wearied thee, then how canst thou contend with horses? And if in the land of peace, wherein thou trustedst they wearied thee, then how wilt thou do in the swelling of Jordon?"

"In every period of this earth's history, God has had His men of opportunity, to whom He has said, 'Ye are my witnesses.' In every age there have been devout men, who gathered up the rays of light as they flashed upon their pathway, and spoke to the people the words of God. Enoch, Noah, and Moses, Daniel, and the long roll of patriarchs and prophets, —these were ministers of righteousness. They were not infallible, they were weak, erring men; but the Lord wrought through them as they gave themselves to His service." *Gospel Workers*, (1915), p. 13.

These faithful witnesses gave the warning message for their time and I think of how God has used Ellen G. White to warn us, for our time we're living in today, to prepare us for the days of trial before us! May we, too, each one, choose to be God's faithful witness and be used of God to let our light shine in this dark sinful world so God can say of each of us, "Ye are my witnesses, saith the Lord, and my servant whom I have chosen: that ye may know and believe me, and understand that I am he; before me there was no God formed, neither shall there be after me." Isa. 43:10.

"The cities are to be worked from outposts. Said the Messenger of God, 'Shall not the cities be warned? Yes; not by God's people living in them, but by their visiting them, to warn them of what is coming upon the earth." *Country Living*, p. 30.

"As God's commandment-keeping people, we must leave the cities. As did Enoch, we must work in the cities but not dwell in them." *Country Living*, p. 30.

"Through the working of trusts, and the results of labor unions and strikes the conditions of life in the city are constantly becoming more and more difficult. Serious troubles are before us; and for many families' removal from the cities will become a necessity. The physical surroundings in the cities are often a peril to health. The constant liability to contact with disease, the prevalence of foul air, impure water, impure food, the crowded, dark, unhealthful dwellings are some of the many evils to be met. It was not God's purpose that people should be crowded into cities, huddled together in terraces and tenements. In the beginning He placed our first parents amidst the beautiful sights and sounds He desires us to rejoice in today. The more nearly we come into harmony with God's original plan, the more favorable will be our position to secure health of body, and mind, and soul." *Country Living,* p. 6.

"The angels of mercy hurried Lot and his wife and daughters by taking hold of their hands. Had Lot hastened as the Lord desired him to, his wife would not have become a pillar of salt. Lot had too much of a lingering spirit. Let us not be like him. The same voice that warned Lot to leave Sodom bids us, 'Come out from among them, and be ye separate… and touch not the unclean.' Those who obey this warning will find a refuge. Let every man be wide awake for himself, and try to save his family. Let him gird himself for the work. God will reveal from point to point what to do next… Lot trod the plain with unwilling and tardy steps. He had so long associated with evil workers that he could not see his peril until his wife stood on the plain a pillar of salt forever." *Country Living,* pp. 6, 7.

"Remember Lot's wife." Luke 17:32.

"The time is near when the large cities will be visited by the judgments of God. In a little while, these cities will be terribly shaken. No matter how large or how strong their buildings, no matter how many safeguards against fire may have been provided, let God touch these building, and in a few minutes or a few hours they are in ruins." *Country Living,* p. 7.

It makes me think of what Sister White wrote in *Testimonies for the Church*, vol. 9, p. 11–18, the chapter entitled, "The Last Crisis." In this article she brings out about the description of the two towers that was destroyed in New York City on Sept. 11, 2001. This terrible destruction that happened should be a wakeup call to us to get ready for these disasters and calamities that warn us of His soon coming!

"I am bidden to declare the message that cities full of transgression & sinful in extreme, will be destroyed by earthquakes, by fires, by floods… Calamities will come—calamities most awful, most unexpected, and these destructions will follow one after another. If there will be a heeding of the warnings that God has given, and if churches will repent, returning to their allegiance, then other cities may be spared for a time. But if men who have been deceived continue in the same way in which they have been walking, disregarding the law of God and presenting falsehoods before the people, God allows them to suffer calamity, that their senses may be awakened… There are reasons why we should not build in the cities. On these cities, God's judgments are soon to fall. The time is near when large cities will be swept away, and all should be warned of these coming judgments. O that God's people had a sense of the impending destruction of thousands on cities, now almost given to idolatry." *Country Living,* pp. 7, 8.

Urgent!

I was dreaming I had written an article entitled, "URGENT!" and it was 15 and 16 pages long and I was giving this article to someone to publish for me and to get it out to the people as soon as possible, and they were anxious to get it out to the public for me! I prayed and asked God to please help me write this article. This dream made me think of Bill and Mary publishing my book, ***Don't Be Trapped in the Cities!! Get Out Now!*** They've been putting my material on DVD's and getting it out to the people to help them realize the urgency of getting ready spiritually and physically for the crisis ahead of us when the Sunday Laws will be passed and we won't be able to buy or sell. We'll need to have our little ARKS of safety ready and set up for this time and have wells, trees, and our gardens and fruit trees and berry bushes producing so we can survive this time ahead of us. We'll also need to know our Bibles and what we believe and have our faith and trust in Jesus firmly established. We need to know Jesus and His power to save and have faith in His promises to us to care for us and protect us during the little time of trouble and then the great time of trouble when the plagues will be falling. Now is the time to be developing a Christ-like character. Now is the time to be obeying Jesus and all His requirements so we can have reform in our lives, which is the early rain and receive the Holy Spirit in the Latter rain so we can give the Loud Cry message of the third angel, because we have received the seal of God because we keep God's seventh day Sabbath holy and are true to all God's ten commandments. Revival and reformation is what we now need and the outpouring of the Holy Spirit power.

Sister White says, "A revival of true godliness among us is the greatest and most urgent of all our needs. To seek this should be our first work. There must be earnest effort to obtain the blessing of the Lord, not because God is not willing to bestow His blessing upon us, but because we are unprepared to receive it. Our heavenly Father is more willing to give His Holy Spirit to them that ask Him than are earthly parents to give good gifts to their children. But it is our work, by confession, humiliation, repentance, and earnest prayer, to fulfill the conditions upon which God has promised to grant us His blessing. A revival need be expected only in answer to prayer… I tell you that there must be a thorough revival among us. There must be a converted ministry. There must be confessions, repentances, and conversions. Many who are preaching the Word need the transforming grace of Christ in their hearts. They should let nothing stand in the way of their making thorough work before it shall be forever too late… A revival and a reformation must take place, under the ministration of the Holy Spirit. Revival and reformation are two different things. Revival signifies a renewal of spiritual life, a quickening of the powers of mind and heart, a resurrection from spiritual death. Reformation signifies a reorganization, a change of ideas and theories, habits, and practices. Reformation will not bring forth the good fruit of righteousness unless it is connected with the revival of the spirit. Revival and reformation are to do their appointed work, and in doing this work they must blend." *Last Day Events*, pp. 189, 190.

Also, on page 186 of *Last Day Events* Sister White says, "Before the final visitation of God's judgments upon the earth there will be among the people of the Lord such a revival of primitive godliness as has not been witnessed since apostolic times. The Spirit and power of God will be poured out upon His children… The work will be similar to that of the Day of Pentecost. As the former rain was given in the outpouring of the Holy Spirit at the opening of the gospel, to cause the upspringing of the precious seed, so the 'latter rain' will be given at its close for the ripening of the harvest… At that time the 'latter rain' or refreshing from the presence of the Lord, will come to give power to the loud voice of the third angel and prepare the saints to stand in the period when the seven last plagues shall be poured out."

This chapter in *Ministry of Healing*, pp. 161–169, makes me think of the experiences Jonathan and his dad and I are going through helping Jonathan to get well and off his addictions and coming back to Jesus. Sister White says on pp. 164, 165, "Mark how all through the Word of God there is manifest the spirit of urgency of imploring men and women to come to Christ. We must seize upon every opportunity, in private and in public, presenting every argument urging every motive of infinite weight, to draw men to the Saviour. With all our power we must urge them to look unto Jesus and to accept His life of self-denial and sacrifice. We must show that we expect them to give joy to the heart of Christ by using every one of His gifts in honoring His name."

It makes me think of my dream I had 4-17-13, "Only two years." There's an urgency here making us realize we must be about our Father's business. Here it is May 2014, and none of us are sure what may be in our future. Time is running out! This is not a date set for Jesus to come but to hurry and get ready. In two years, God helped me write my book, from 2013-2015, and ready for publication! Praise God! Also, a lot has happened making history in 2015 to let us know, time is running out!

This is why Sister White says in *Testimonies for the Church*, vol. 6, p. 61, 62, talking about "The Last Warning," "The Lord bids us: 'Show My people their transgression, and the house of Jacob their sins,' Isa. 58:1 The trumpet is to give a certain sound… Lift up the standard—the commandments of God and the faith of Jesus make this the important theme. Then, by your strong arguments, make it of still greater force. Dwell more on Revelation. Read, explain, and enforce its teachings. Our warfare is aggressive. Tremendous issues are before us, yea, and right upon us. Let our prayers ascend to God that the four angels may still hold the four winds, that they may not blow to injure or destroy until the last warning has been given to the world. Then let us work in harmony with our prayers. Let nothing lessen the force of the truth for this time. The present truth is to be our burden. The third angel's message must do its work of separating from the churches a people who will take their stand on the platform of eternal truth. Our message is a life-and-death message, and we must let it appear as it is, the great power of God. We are to present it in all its telling force! Then the Lord will make it effectual. It is our privilege to expect large things, even the demonstration of the Spirit of God. This is the power that will convict and convert the soul… The perils of the last days are upon us, and in our work we are to warn the people of the danger they are in. Let not the solemn scenes which prophecy has revealed be left untouched. If our people were half awake, if they realized the nearness of the events portrayed in the Revelation, a reformation would be wrought in our churches, and many more would believe the message. We have no time to lose; God calls upon us to watch for souls as they that must give an account… There will be times when we must stand still and see the salvation of God. Let Daniel speak, let the Revelation speak, and tell what is truth. But whatever phase of the subject is presented, uplift Jesus as the center of all hope, 'the root and the offspring of David, and the bright and morning Star.'" Rev. 22:16.

In *Last Day Events*, pp. 15–17, Sister White says, "There is need of a much closer study of the Word of

God; especially should Daniel and the Revelation have attention as never before… The light received from God was given especially for these last days… Let us read and study the 12th chapter of Daniel. It is a warning that we shall all need to understand before the time of the end… The unfulfilled predictions of the book of Revelation are soon to be fulfilled. This prophecy is now to be studied with diligence by the people of God and should be clearly understood. It does not conceal the truth, it clearly forewarns, telling us what will be in the future… The solemn messages that have been given in their order in the Revelation are to occupy the first place in the minds of God's people… Let the watchmen now lift up their voices and give the message which is present truth for this time. Let us show the people where we are in prophetic history… There is a day that God hath appointed for the close of this world's history: 'This gospel of the kingdom shall be preached in all the world for a witness unto all nations; and then shall the end come.' Prophecy is fast fulfilling. More, much more, should be said about these tremendously important subjects. The day is at hand when the destiny of souls will be fixed forever… Great pains should be taken to keep this subject before the people. The solemn fact is to be kept not only before the people of the world but before our own churches also, that the day of the Lord will come suddenly, unexpectedly. The fearful warning of the prophecy is addressed to every soul. Let no one feel that he is secure from danger of being surprised. Let no one's interpretation of prophecy rob you of the conviction of the knowledge of events which show that this great event is near at hand."

I have had dreams saying, "Hurry!" "Step Fast!" "URGENT!" "Get Ready! Get Ready! Get Ready!" "What thou doest, Do Quickly!" "Get Busy!" "Be in earnest to get things done!"

I have dreamed I saw charts showing the signs of the time of Christ soon coming and it said, "Step Fast!" David, my husband, has dreamed about the nearness of Christ's soon coming, and that things are almost over!

We are living in serious and solemn times in this world's history! God's prophet, E. G. White, for our day in which we are living NOW, said in *Testimonies for the Church*, vol. 5, p. 452, "God has revealed what is to take place in the last days, that His people may be prepared to stand against the tempest of opposition and wrath. Those who have been warned of the events before them are not to sit in calm expectation of the coming storm, comforting themselves that the Lord will shelter His faithful ones in the day of trouble. We are to be as men waiting for their Lord, not in idle expectancy, but in earnest work, with unwavering faith. It is no time now to allow our minds to be engrossed with things of minor importance. While men are sleeping, Satan is actively arranging matters so that the Lord's people may not have mercy or justice. The Sunday movement is now making its way in darkness." Read the whole chapter, "The Coming Crisis" *Testimonies for the Church*, vol. 5, pp. 449–454. Sister White says in *Country Living*, p. 21, "I see the necessity of making haste to get all things ready for the crisis."

I have had dreams of Sister White's quotes like the one in *Selected Messages*, book 2, p. 142, "The work of the people of God is to prepare for the events of the future, which will soon come upon them with blinding force," and *Testimonies for the Church*, vol. 8, p. 28, "Transgression has almost reached its limit. Confusion fills the world, and a great terror is soon to come upon human beings. The end is very near. We who know the truth should be preparing for what is soon to break upon the world as an overwhelming surprise."

In *Last Day Events*, p. 72, Sister White tells us, "We have nothing to fear for the future, except as we shall forget the way the Lord has led us, and His teachings in our past history." She goes on to say in *Last Day Events*, p. 72 and 73, "If there ever was a time when serious reflection becomes everyone who fears God, it is now, when personal piety is essential. The inquiry should be made, 'What am I, and what is my work and mission in this time? On which side am I working—Christ's side or the enemy's side?' Let every soul now humble himself or herself before God, for now we are surely living in the great Day of Atonement. The cases even now of many are passing in review before God, for they are to sleep in their graves a little season. Your profession of faith is not your guarantee in that day, but the state of your affections. Is the soul-temple cleansed of its defilement? Are my sins confessed and am I repenting of them before God that they may be blotted out? Do I esteem myself too lightly? Am I willing to make any and every sacrifice for the excellency of the knowledge of Jesus Christ? Do I feel every moment I am not my own, but Christ's property, that my service belongs to God, whose I am?... We should ask ourselves, "For what are we living, and working? And what will be the outcome of it all?... I have questioned in my mind, as I have seen the people in our cities hurrying to and fro with business, whether they ever thought of the day of God that is just upon us. Every one of us should be living with reference to the great day which is soon to come upon us… We cannot afford to live with no reference to the day of judgment; for though long delayed, it is now near, even at the door, and hasteth greatly. The trumpet of the Archangel will soon startle the living and wake the dead."

Sister White tells us in *Counsels to Parents, Teachers, and Students*, p. 249, "It should be the determination of every soul, not so much to seek to understand all about the conditions that will prevail in the future state, as to know what the Lord requires of him in this life. It is the will of God that each professing Christian shall perfect a character after the divine similitude. By studying the character of Christ revealed in the Bible, by practicing His virtues, the believer will be changed into the same likeness of goodness and mercy. Christ's work of self-denial and sacrifice brought into the daily life will develop the faith that works by love and purifies the soul. There are many who wish to evade the cross-bearing part, but the Lord speaks to all when He says, "If any man will come after me, let him deny himself, and take up his cross, and follow me. Matt. 16:24."

The Lord instructed Sister White to write these words found in *Fundamentals of Christian Education*, pp. 526, 527, "In the night season these words were spoken to me: 'Charge the teachers in our schools to prepare the students for what is coming upon the world....' Bear in mind that the Lord will accept as teachers only those who will be gospel teachers. A great responsibility rests upon those who attempt to teach the last gospel message. They are to be laborers together with God in the training of human minds. The teacher who fails to keep the Bible standard always before him, misses an opportunity of being a laborer together with God in giving to the mind the mold that is essential for a place in the heavenly courts."

Satan is Wroth!

Rev. 12:17, "And the dragon was wroth with the woman, and went to make war with the remnant of her seed, which keep the commandments of God, and have the testimony of Jesus Christ."

The Great Controversy, p. 36, Sister White says, "We cannot know how much we owe to Christ for the peace and protection which we enjoy. It is the restraining power of God that prevents mankind from passing fully under the control of Satan." Also, in *The Great Controversy*, p. 623, Sister White continues to tell us of the wrath of Satan, "Woe to the inhabitants of the earth and of the sea! for the devil is come down unto you, having great wrath, because he knoweth that he hath but a short time," Rev. 12:12. Fearful are the scenes which call forth this exclamation from the heavenly voice. The wrath of Satan increases as his time grows short, and his work of deceit and destruction will reach its culmination in the time of trouble."

As we've been trying to get God's last day message out to the world, to prepare for the soon coming crisis, by writing these articles for my book, ***Don't Be Trapped in the Cities!! Get Out Now!*** The devil has been trying in every way to get to us and try and stop us from warning God's people to prepare for the crisis and be ready! Satan has had our car break down so many times and overheat. Satan almost destroyed our car and us, when we were coming home late at night and a BIG deer walked right in front of our car and David slammed on the brakes and God removed the deer in time so we didn't ram into him at 60 miles per hour. How we praised the Lord! We always pray, for God's protection, when we get into the car. God was certainly there to spare our lives and our car! The Devil has had our son, Jonathan end up in emergency room several times and admitted to the hospital. Satan is trying to take his life! God has protected us from dangerous storms and our garden and our place, when Satan was out to destroy everything! Satan has tried to get us stung with wasps so many times, and even one time he had a wasp sting David, my husband, right beside his eye, but God kept it from stinging him right in the eyeball. Praise God! We all are feeling the attacks of Satan as we reach out to work for Jesus and to save souls. We know Satan is the destroyer like John 10:10 says, "The thief cometh not, but for to steal, and kill, and to destroy; I am come that they might have life, and that they might have it more abundantly." Praise God! Jesus is the restorer! Jesus is stronger than Satan and Jesus keeps watching over us!

In *The Great Controversy*, p. 560–562, Sister White writes "Because thou hast kept the word of my patience, I also will keep thee" (Rev. 3:10), is the Saviour's promise. He would sooner send every angel out of heaven to protect His people than leave one soul that trusts in Him to be overcome by Satan... Satan has long been preparing for his final effort to deceive the world... Little by little he has prepared the way for his masterpiece of deception in the development of spiritualism... Except those who are kept by the power of God, through faith in His Word, the whole world will be swept into the ranks of this delusion."

In *The Great Controversy*, p. 624, by Sister White, we are warned, "As the crowning act in the great drama of deception, Satan himself will personate Christ... Now the great deceiver will make it appear that Christ has come... The shout of triumph rings out upon the air 'Christ has come! Christ has come!' ... In gentle, compassionate tones he presents some of the same gracious, heavenly truths which the Savior uttered; he heals the disease of the people, and then, in his assumed character of Christ, he claims to have changed the Sabbath to Sunday, and commands all to hallow the day which he has blessed. He declares that those who persist in keeping holy the seventh day are blaspheming his name by refusing to listen to his angels sent to them with light and truth. This is the strong, almost overmastering delusion." On p. 625 of *The Great Controversy*, Sister White goes on to say, "But the people of God will not be misled... To all the testing time will come... Are the people of God now so firmly established upon His word that they would not yield to the evidences of their senses? Would they, in such a crisis, cling to the Bible and the Bible only? Satan will, if possible, prevent them from obtaining a preparation to stand in that day. He will so arrange affairs as to hedge up their way, entangle them with earthly treasures, cause them to carry a heavy, wearisome burden, that their hearts may be overcharged with the cares of this life and the day of trial may come upon them as a thief."

On pp. 632–634 of *The Great Controversy*, Sister White writes, "In the hour of peril and distress 'the angel of the Lord encampeth round about them that fear Him, and delivereth them.' Ps. 34:7... The precious Saviour will send help just when we need it... The eye of God, looking down the ages, was fixed upon the crisis which His people are to meet, when earthly powers shall be arrayed against them... But the Holy One who divided the Red Sea before Israel, will manifest His mighty power and turn their captivity" ... In the time of trouble He shall hide me in His pavilion; in the secret of His tabernacle shall He hide me." Ps. 27:5. In *The Great Controversy*, p. 621, Sister White says, "While Satan seeks to destroy this class, God will send His angels to comfort and protect them in the time of peril. The assaults of Satan are fierce and determined, his delusions are terrible; but the Lord's eye is upon His people, and His ear listens to their cries. Their affliction is great, the flames of the furnace seem about to consume them; but the Refiner will bring them forth as gold tried in the fire... The season of distress and anguish before us will require a faith that can endure weariness, delay, and hunger—a faith that will not faint through severely tried. The period of probation is granted to all to prepare for that time." On p. 622 of *The Great Controversy*, we read, "Those who exercise but little faith now, are in the greatest danger of falling under the power of satanic delusions and the decree to compel the conscience... We should now acquaint ourselves with God by proving His promises... We should rather dispense with selfish gratifications than neglect communion with God... We must take time to pray."

I recently had a dream that said, "Like everything else we have got to do, we have got to PRAY!"

Sister White goes on to say in *The Great Controversy*, p. 622, "If we allow our minds to be absorbed by worldly interests, the Lord may give us time by removing from us our idols of gold, of houses, or of fertile lands... The 'time of trouble, such as never was,' is soon to open upon us; and we shall need an experience which we do not now possess and which many are too indolent to obtain."

Also, in *The Great Controversy*, p. 623, Sister White tells us that, "Now, while our Great High Priest is making the atonement for us, we should seek to become perfect in Christ... Satan finds in human hearts some point where he can gain a foothold; some sinful desire is cherished, by means of which his temptations assert their power... Satan could find nothing in the Son of God that would enable him to gain the victory. He had kept His Father's commandments, and there was no sin in Him that Satan could use to his advantage. This is the condition in which those must be found who shall stand in the time of trouble. It is in this life that we are to separate sin from us, through faith in the atoning blood of Christ. Our precious Saviour invites us to join ourselves to Him, to unite our weakness to his strength, our ignorance to His wisdom, our unworthiness to His merits."

In *The Great Controversy*, p. 619 it says, "Satan endeavors to terrify them with the thought that their cases are hopeless, that the stain of their defilement will never be washed away. He hopes so to destroy their faith that they will yield to his temptations and turn from their allegiance to God."

In *The Great Controversy*, p. 586, we read, "Now that Satan can no longer keep the world under his control by withholding the Scriptures, he resorts to other means to accomplish the same object. To destroy faith in the Bible serves his purpose as well as to destroy the Bible itself." We read of something else Satan will do in *The Great Controversy*, p. 560, "Many will be confronted by the spirits of devils personating beloved relatives or friends and declaring the most dangerous heresies." On p. 612 of *The Great Controversy* it says, "Satan also works with lying wonders, even bringing down fire from heaven in the sight of men. (Rev. 13:13) Thus the inhabitants of the earth will be brought to take their stand… The publications distributed by missionary workers have exerted their influence, yet many whose minds were impressed have been prevented from fully comprehending the truth or from yielding obedience. Now the rays of light penetrate everywhere the truth is seen in its clearness, and the honest children of God sever the bands which have held them. Family connections, church relations, are powerless to stay them now. Truth is more precious than all besides. Notwithstanding the agencies combined against the truth a large number take their stand upon the Lord's side."

In the book *Country Living*, p. 32, Sister White warns, "It is no time now for God's people to be fixing their affections or laying up their treasures in the world. The time is not far distant, when, like the early disciples, we shall be forced to seek a refuge in desolate and solitary places. As the siege of Jerusalem by the Roman armies was the signal for flight to the Judean Christians, so the assumption of power on the part of our nation, in the decree enforcing the papal Sabbath, will be a warning to us. It will then be time to leave the large cities, preparatory to leaving the smaller ones for retired homes in secluded places among the mountain. And now, instead of seeking expensive dwellings here, we should be preparing to move to a better country, even a heavenly. Instead of spending our means in self-gratification, we should be studying to economize."

In *The Great Controversy*, pp. 35–38, Sister White writes, "By stubborn rejection of divine love and mercy, the Jews had caused the protection of God to be withdrawn from them, and Satan was permitted to rule them according to his will. The horrible cruelties enacted in the destruction of Jerusalem are a demonstration of Satan's vindictive power over those who yield to his control. We cannot know how much we owe to Christ for the peace and protection which we enjoy. It is the restraining power of God that prevents mankind from passing fully under the control of Satan…

Let men beware lest they neglect the lesson conveyed to them in the words of Christ. As He warned His disciples of Jerusalem's destruction, giving them a sign of the approaching ruin, that they might make their escape; so He has warned the world of the day of final destruction and has given them tokens of its approach, that all who will may flee from the wrath to come. Jesus declares: 'There shall be signs in the sun, and in the moon, and in the stars; and upon the earth distress of nations.' Luke 21:25; Matt. 24:29; Mark 13: 24–26; Rev. 6:12–17. Those who behold these harbingers of His coming are to 'know that it is near, even at the doors.' Matt. 24:33. 'Watch ye therefore,' are His words of admonition. Mark 13:35. They that heed the warning shall not be left in darkness, that that day should overtake them unawares. But to them that will not watch, 'the day of the Lord so cometh as a thief in the night.' 1 Thess. 5:2–5. The world is no more ready to credit the message for this time than were the Jews to receive the Saviour's warning concerning Jerusalem. Come when it may, the day of God will come unawares to the ungodly. When life is going on in its unvarying round; when men are absorbed in pleasure, in business, in traffic, in money-making; when religious leaders are magnifying the world's progress and enlightenment, and the people are lulled in a false security—then as the midnight thief steals within the unguarded dwelling, so shall sudden destruction come upon the careless and ungodly, 'and they shall not escape.'" 1 Thess. 5:3.

Following the Blueprint in Medical Missionary Work

Quotes from The Ministry of Healing

I had a dream and in the dream I was saying to someone, "I'm not that well acquainted with all the drugs out there and all their side effects. I don't waste my time on them. I spend my time studying and learning the herbs and all their benefits and the natural remedies."

In Sister White's *The Ministry of Healing*, p. 172, she lists the eight natural remedies: "Pure Air, Sunshine, Abstemiousness, Rest, Exercise, Proper Diet, the Use of Water, Trust in Divine Power—these are the true remedies. Every person should have a knowledge of nature's remedial agencies and how to apply them. It is essential both to understand the principles involved in the treatment of the sick and to have a practical training that will enable one rightly to use this knowledge."

I like these quotes given by Sister White in *The Ministry of Healing*, which I highly recommend everyone praying over and studying this marvelous book God inspired Sister White to write! The quotes are found on pp. 126 and 127. "A practice that is laying the foundation of a vast amount of disease and of even more serious evils is the free use of poisonous drugs... People need to be taught that drugs do not cure disease... Health is recovered in spite of the drug... By the use of poisonous drugs, many bring upon themselves lifelong illness, and many lives are lost that might be saved by the use of natural methods of healing... The only hope of better things is in the education of the people in right principles. Let the physicians teach the people that restorative power is not in drugs, but in nature. Disease is an effort of nature to free the system from conditions that result from a violation of the laws of health. In case of sickness, the cause should be ascertained. Unhealthful conditions should be changed, wrong habits corrected. Then nature is to be assisted in her effort to expel impurities and to re-establish right conditions in the system... Sister White goes on to say in *The Ministry of Healing*, p. 143, "Christ's method alone will give true success in reaching the people. The Saviour mingled with men as one who desired their good. He showed His sympathy for them, ministered to their needs, and won their confidence. Then He bade them, 'Follow Me.' "

Also, on p. 144 Sister White gives some valuable counsel, "We should ever remember that the object of the medical missionary work is to point sin-sick men and women to the Man of Calvary, who taketh away the sin of the world. By beholding Him, they will be changed into His likeness. We are to encourage the sick and suffering to look to Jesus and live. Let the workers keep Christ, the Great Physician, constantly before those to whom disease of body and soul has brought discouragement. Point them to the one who can heal both physical and spiritual disease. Tell them of the one who is touched with the feeling of their infirmities. Encourage them to place themselves in the care of Him who gave His life to make it possible for them to have life eternal. Talk of His love; tell of His power to save. This is the high duty and precious privilege of the medical missionary. And personal ministry often prepares the way for this. God often reaches hearts through our efforts to relieve physical suffering... If they are reached by the gospel, it must be carried to their homes. Often the relief of their physical needs is the only avenue by which they can be approached."

This next quote from Sister White, taken from *The Ministry of Healing*, p. 145, that makes me think of the Medical Missionary chapter in Isa. 58, "Many have no faith in God and have lost confidence in man. But they appreciate acts of sympathy and helpfulness. As they see one with no inducement of earthly praise or compensation come into their home, ministering to the sick, feeding the hungry, clothing the naked, comforting the sad, and tenderly pointing all to Him of whose love and pity the human worker is but the messenger—as they see this, their hearts are touched. Gratitude springs up. Faith is kindled. They see that God cares for them, and they are prepared to listen as His Word is opened."

Also, in *The Ministry of Healing*, pp. 146–160, Sister White has this advice to give us, "Whether in foreign missions or in the home field, all missionaries, both men and women, will gain much more ready access to the people, and will find their usefulness greatly increased if they are able to minister to the sick... All gospel workers should know how to give the simple treatments that do so much to relieve and remove disease... Gospel workers should be able also to give instruction in principles of healthful living. There is sickness everywhere, and most of it might be prevented by attention to the laws of health... They need to be impressed with the truth conveyed in the words of Holy Writ: 'Ye are the temple of the living God; as God hath said, I will dwell in them, and walk in them; and I will be their God, and they shall be my people.' 2 Cor. 6:16. Thousands need and would gladly receive instruction concerning the simplest methods of treating the sick—methods that are taking the place of the use of poisonous drugs. There is great need of instruction in regard to dietetic reform. Wrong habits of eating and the use of unhealthful food are in no small degree responsible for the intemperance and crime and wretchedness that curse the world. In teaching health principles, keep before the mind the great object of reform—that its purpose is to secure the highest development of body and mind and soul. Show that the laws of nature, being the laws of God, are designed for our good; that obedience to them promotes happiness in this life, and aids in the preparation for the life to come... Instead of looking upon an observance of the laws of health as a matter of sacrifice or self-denial, they will regard it, as it really is; as an inestimable blessing.

Every gospel worker should feel that the giving of instruction in the principles of healthful living is a part of his appointed work. Of this work there is great need, and the world is open for it... The Lord raised up as His representatives prophets and princes, the noble and the lowly, and taught them the truths to be given to the world... The church of Christ is organized for service. Its watchword is ministry. Its members are soldiers to be trained for conflict under the Captain of their salvation... Every church should be a training school for Christian workers... It is not the most brilliant or the most talented persons whose work produces the greatest and most lasting results. Men and women are needed who have heard a message from heaven. The most effective workers are those who respond to the invitation, 'Take My yoke upon you, and learn of me.' Matt. 11:29. It is heart missionaries that are needed... Taking his life in his hand, he goes forth, a heaven-sent, heaven-inspired messenger, to do a work in which angels can co-operate... God will take men who do not appear to be so richly endowed, who have not large self-confidence, and He will make the weak strong, because they trust in Him to do for them that which they cannot do for themselves. God will accept the wholehearted service, and will Himself make up the deficiencies. The Lord has often chosen for His co-laborers men who have had opportunity to obtain but a limited school education... As His blessing came to the captives in the courts of Babylon, so does He give wisdom and knowledge to His workers today... The secret of their success was their confidence in God. They learned daily of Him who is wonderful in counsel and mighty in power...

Nothing will so arouse a self-sacrificing zeal and broaden and strengthen the character as to engage in work for others... Doors of service are open everywhere.

All around us are those who need our help. The widow, the orphan, the sick and the dying, the heartsick, the discouraged, the ignorant, and the outcast are on every hand… It is of little use to try to reform others by attacking what we may regard as wrong habits… We must offer men something better than that which they possess, even the peace of Christ, which passes all understanding. We must tell them of God's holy law, the transcript of His character, and an expression of that which He wishes them to become. Show them how infinitely superior to the fleeting joys and pleasures of the world is the imperishable glory of heaven. Tell them of the freedom and rest to be found in the Saviour. 'Whosoever drinketh of the water that I shall give him shall never thirst,' He declared. John 4:14. Lift up Jesus, crying, 'Behold, the Lamb of God, that taketh away the sin of the world!' John 1:29. He alone can satisfy the craving of the heart and give peace to the souls of all people in the world, reformers should be the most unselfish, the most kind, the most courteous… As the dew and the still showers fall upon the withering plants, so let words fall gently when seeking to win men from error. God's plan is first to reach the heart. We are to speak the truth in love, trusting Him to give it power for the reforming of the life. The Holy Spirit will apply to the soul the word that is spoken in love…

Let us ever be channels through which shall flow the refreshing waters of compassion… Those who are fighting the battle of life at great odds may be strengthened and encouraged by little attentions that cost only a loving effort. To such the strong, helpful grasp of the hand by a true friend is worth more than gold or silver. Words of kindness are as welcome as the smile of angels… Sympathize with them in their trials, their heartaches, and disappointments. This will open the way for you to help them. Speak to them of God's promises, pray with and for them, inspire them with hope. Words of cheer and encouragement spoken when the soul is sick and the pulse of courage is low these are regarded by the Saviour as if spoken to Himself. As hearts are cheered, the heavenly angels look on in pleased recognition…

Be co-workers with Him. While distrust and alienation are pervading the world, Christ's disciples are to reveal the spirit that reigns in heaven. Speak as He would speak, act as He would act. Constantly reveal the sweetness of His character… Heavenly intelligences are waiting to co-operate with human instrumentalities, that they may reveal to the world what human beings may become, and what, through union with the Divine, may be accomplished for the saving of souls that are ready to perish. There is no limit to the usefulness of one who putting self aside, makes room for the working of the Holy Spirit upon his heart and lives a life wholly consecrated to God. All who consecrate body, soul, and spirit to His service will be constantly receiving a new endowment of physical, mental, and spiritual power. The inexhaustible supplies of heaven are at their command. Christ gives them the breath of His own spirit, the life of His own life. The Holy Spirit puts forth its highest energies to work in mind and heart. Through the grace given us we may achieve victories that because of our own erroneous and preconceived opinions, our defects of character, our smallness of faith, have seemed impossible. To everyone who offers himself to the Lord for service, withholding nothing, is given power for the attainment of measureless results. For these God will do great things. He will work upon the minds of men so that, even in this world, there shall be seen in their lives a fulfillment of the promise of the future state."

God gave me a dream, showing me in my dream, writing down quotes from *The Ministry of Healing* book. I feel God is pleased that I wrote these quotes down to encourage not only myself, as I bring our son, Jonathan, home from the care center he's at right now and help him off his drugs and nicotine and coffee and meat with God's help, help him walk again, and help him become a new creation in Christ, but I feel *The Ministry of Healing* quotes will be a help and a blessing to others who read them. I prayed and asked God to please help me pick the right quotations He wanted me to write down. I feel He's answered my prayers! Praise the Lord! Please pray for me and my son, Jonathan, as we step out in faith and trust the good Lord to see us through this experience ahead of us! Thank you!

A few helpful books to study by Sister White:
- The Ministry of Healing
- Counsels on Health
- Counsels on Diet and Foods
- Healthful Living
- Medical Ministry
- Testimonies for the Church, vols. 1–9
- The Place of Herbs in Rational Therapy

Three good books by Vance Ferrell:
- The Broken Blueprint
- The Medical Missionary Manual
- Natural Remedies Encyclopedia

Learning Natural Remedies

The following are experiences we have had to go through to prove to us how God, in answer to the prayers of faith has helped us while living out in the country having no doctor, no hospital, no medicines, just natural remedies. When we had any problem, whether medical or whatever, we learned to turn to God in prayer for help, just like the flower naturally turns to the sunshine. Phil. 4:19 promises to supply all our needs by Christ Jesus. Through these experiences God is teaching us faith and trust and dependence on Him and not man. So when the time comes when you can't buy or sell and all earthly support is cut off, we won't panic, but still keep looking and trusting in faith in God to sustain us and keep believing and trusting His promises to us and not crumble and give in when we face the Sunday Law crisis and the pressures brought upon us to keep the Sunday Law sabbath in place of God's true seventh day Sabbath. When this happens, we need to be settled in our mind that we will obey God and not man, as Acts 5:29 says. We need to be preparing our heart and mind for this moment and be determined what choice we will make then when we're faced with this Sunday Law issue. We need to be having our little Arks of safety all set up and prepared for this crisis when we won't go along with the Sunday Law enforced upon us. And when we'll be denied our privileges to be able to buy food and clothing, and we'll have no doctor or medicines, and our utilities will be cut off, and we'll have no computers, Internet, bank account, no jobs, and every earthly support will be cut off. There'll be no telephones, no washers and dryers, no hospital, no gas for your car or machinery, no postal service, no paychecks or Social Security checks. We will be totally cast out of the system because we refuse to obey man's Sunday Law. We need to be thinking about all this now and preparing now for the time when it finally happens. During this time, we'll have to trust wholly in God to care for us and our needs as we go through the early time of trouble when we'll be living out of our garden of vegetables and our fruit trees and berries and herb gardens that we have set up and prepared before all this crisis comes. Now is the time to be making the effort to learn how to garden and be out in the country where you'll be free from the interference of enemies and where you can have the safety of your little Ark, where you can raise your own provisions when you can't buy or sell. We now need to be making the effort to be learning how to do the natural remedies and know our herbs to use for our medicine and not drugs and learn now how to survive through these times soon to break upon us, as an overwhelming surprise.

Sister White says in *Counsels on Health*, p. 506, "As religious aggression subverts the liberties of our nation, those who would stand for freedom of conscience will be placed in unfavorable positions. For their own sake they should, while they have opportunity, become intelligent in regard to disease, its causes, prevention, and cure, and those who do this will find a field of labor anywhere. There will be suffering ones, plenty of them, who will need help, not only among those of our own faith but largely among those who know not the truth."

Counsels on Health, p. 533, Sister White says, "I wish to tell you that soon there will be no work done in ministerial lines but medical missionary work."

Sister White writes in *Vol. 1 Testimonies for the Church*, p. 486, "The health reform, I was shown, is a part of the third angel's message and is just as closely connected with it as are the arm and hand with the human body."

I had a dream on the Natural Remedies found in *Ministry of Healing*, p. 127, "Pure air, sunlight, abstemiousness, rest, exercise, proper diet, the use of water, trust in divine power—these are the true remedies."

Experiences

This is an answer to our prayers! This happened in the year 2013. David was down in our woods pulling up poison ivy by hand, with gloves on. It was wintertime and he thought maybe the poison ivy was dormant. As he was pulling a vine off the tree it hit him in his eye with his glasses on. He didn't think too much about it and kept working. His eye and his glasses were both okay. Then his eye began to itch and swell and he hurried to the house to tell me what happened. We have no doctor and no medical insurance so we prayed and asked God to please help us! God knew we had no money to go see a doctor. We knew the natural remedy for poison ivy was using gravel road dust from off the gravel road, and powder that on your poison ivy and keep it powdered on there until it cleared up. But you can't put gravel road dust in your eyes! But what to do? We rinsed it out over and over again with salt water, but it was getting worse. We had to do something and fast! David didn't want to lose his vision in his good eye. So we knelt down and prayed for God to please hear our prayers for HELP! God put it in my mind to cut up a raw smashed onion and place it over his eye. We did this and it worked! Praise the Lord! It cleared up the poison ivy in his eye with no complications!

This is why it's so important to learn our natural remedies now, so when the time comes, during the Sunday Laws, when you can't buy or sell, and you can't go see a doctor and buy any medicine or buy food or herbs, etc., you'll have learned how to care for yourself and your family and others who'll be needing help and you'll know what to do with the Lord's help and blessing. Now is the time to train up as gospel medical missionaries. Sister White writes in *Testimonies for the Church*, vol. 7, pp. 62–67, "We have come to a time when every member of the church should take hold of the medical missionary work."

Another experience we had we call it, "Lord! What Am I to Do?"

The morning began like always, having worship, working awhile, and then having breakfast. But this was going to end up being a different kind of day, unbeknown to us. Like the dream I had that said, "No one knows what tomorrow may bring!"

David, while eating breakfast in an extra big hurry, so he could get to town and take care of shopping for things we needed, he choked and coughed from his too big of bites and not thoroughly chewing his food like he should. He tried drinking some water and that didn't help. There was something lodged in his throat and it just wouldn't go down or come up, no matter what we tried. We prayed and asked God to please help him get this thing out that was stuck in his throat. He tried to vomit it up and that didn't work either. We just didn't know for sure what to do, but we prayed again, "Lord, what are we to do??!" He was breathing okay but it was irritating in his throat. He decided to go ahead and go on into town, and try and take care of business and maybe it would just slide on down while he did his shopping. But while he was in the store shopping he began to hear ringing in his ears and getting short of breath and becoming worried. So he drove on over to the emergency room in town and asked them what to do. We had no doctor and no medical insurance and no money. They suggested he sign himself in and be treated. He thanked them and left. He went on out to his car and prayed, "Lord! What am I to do??!" We always claim James 1:5 when we don't know what to do. I was at home praying for him. I had no idea what he was going through. We only had one little TracFone®, so he couldn't call me. He sat in his car praying, not knowing for sure what to do. Then it happened! The Lord put it in his mind to swallow something greasy. So he went to the store and bought some greasy peanut butter and ate a lot of that, and the thing that was stuck in his throat slid right on down. He was so thankful and relieved and he could breathe okay. He thanked and praised the Lord he was feeling okay now.

He decided to go back to the emergency room and let the nurse know and the receptionist know how he got his throat cleared out so they could know how to help others who suffered the same problem. He also saw in this experience an opportunity to leave *The Great Controversy* in their hands in the emergency room. When he gave the receptionist *The Great Controversy* book she was so happy to get the book and thanked him for it!

As David walked out to the car he thought to himself, this was God's way of getting *The Great Controversy* book in this lady's hands. If I hadn't had this happen to me, I never would have run across this person to give the book to, but God knows who the right people are who are interested and would read the book and be benefited by it. He was so glad he kept *The Great Controversy* books in his car to pass out. God supplied their spiritual need, while supplying David's physical need and seeing him through that experience so he could get *The Great Controversy* book into the right hands.

Praise God as we let Him direct and plan our every day and He's always working out things for our good as Rom. 8:28 promises, and also Ps. 32:8; Ps. 56:3; Ps. 55:16, 22.

This experience shows us how God will take care of us during the early time of trouble and supply our needs, when we'll be totally and completely dependent on God to take care of us when we can't buy or sell or get any medical help. Jesus will be right there to answer our prayers for help and watch over us and spare us and heal us. We need to be letting our faith in Jesus grow now. Jesus will be our Great Physician and take care of us and meet our needs so we can make it through the days ahead of us.

Sister White says in *Testimonies for the Church*, vol. 9, p. 10, "We have nothing to fear for the future, except as we shall forget the way the Lord has led us, and His teaching in our past history."

Read in Sister White's book, *Selected Messages*, book 2, chapters 28–31, and pp. 277–308. Here she gives statements on the use of drugs, and the use of remedies, E. G. White's use of remedial agencies, and personal experiences given. This will be most interesting to you and a real blessing and help.

Read in *Testimonies for the Church*, vol. 7, pp. 13–32 and pp. 62–67; *Testimonies for the Church*, vol. 9, pp. 11–29; 89–188.

In *Testimonies for the Church*, vol. 9, pp. 166–172, Sister White makes these comments, "Let us lift up the Man of Calvary by word and by holy living. The Saviour comes very near to those who consecrate themselves to God. If ever there was a time when we needed the working of the Spirit of God upon our hearts and lives, it is now. Let us lay hold of this divine power for strength to live a life of holiness and self-surrender… The Word of God is to be our lesson book. The Lord is our helper and our God. Let us look to Him to open the way for the carrying out of our plans… We are living in the last days. The end of all things is at hand. The signs foretold by Christ are fast fulfilling. There are stormy times before us, but let us not utter one word of unbelief or discouragement… He loves us with an everlasting love. Let us remember that we bear a message of healing to a world filled with sin-sick souls. May the Lord increase our faith, and help us see that he desires us all to become acquainted with His ministry of healing, and with the mercy seat. He desires the light of His grace to shine forth from many places… Henceforth medical missionary work is to be carried forward with an earnestness with which it has never yet been carried… Christ is no longer in this world in person, to go through our cities and towns and villages, healing the sick; but He has commissioned us to carry forward the medical missionary work that He begun… The Lord speaks to all medical missionaries saying: Go, work today in my vineyard to save souls. God hears the prayers of all who seek Him in truth. He has the power that we all need. He fills the heart with love, and joy, and peace, and holiness. Character is constantly being developed… If ever the Lord has spoken by me, He speaks when I say that the workers engaged in educational lines, in ministerial lines, and in medical missionary lines must stand as a unit, all laboring under the supervision of God, one helping the other, each blessing each… Christ, the great Medical Missionary, is our example. Of Him it is written that He "went about all Galilee, teaching in their synagogues, and preaching the gospel of the kingdom, and healing all manner of sickness and all manner of disease among the people." Matt. 4:23. He healed the sick and preached the gospel. In His service, healing and teaching were linked closely together. Today they are not to be separated…

Your light may be small, but remember that it is what God has given you, and that He holds you responsible to let it shine forth. Someone may light his taper from yours, and his light may be the means of leading others out from darkness… His methods of labor are to be followed today by those to whom He has left His work. We are to go from place to place, carrying the message. As soon as the truth has been proclaimed in one place, we are to go to warn others… Many will be called into the field to labor from house to house giving Bible readings and praying with those who are interested. Let our ministers, who have gained an experience in preaching the Word, learn how to give simple treatments and then labor intelligently as medical missionary evangelists."

Years ago God gave me a dream and it was the following quote from *Testimonies for the Church*, vol. 9, p. 172 by Sister White: "Workers—gospel medical missionaries—are needed now. You cannot afford to spend years in preparation. Soon doors now open to the truth will be forever closed. Carry the message now. Do not wait, allowing the enemy to take possession of the fields now open before you. Let little companies go forth to do the work to which Christ appointed His disciples. Let them labor as evangelists, scattering our publications and talking of the truth to those they meet. Let them pray for the sick, ministering to their necessities, not with drugs, but with nature's remedies, and teaching them how to regain health and avoid disease."

Sister White in *Testimonies for the Church*, vol. 7, p. 155, says, "The attention of the people must be arrested. Our message is a savor of life unto life or of death unto death. The destinies of souls are balancing. Multitudes are in the valley of decision. A voice should be heard crying: 'If the Lord be God, follow Him: but if Baal, then follow him.'" 1 Kings 18:21.

We have encouraging words given to us by Sister White in *Testimonies for the Church*, vol. 7, p. 214, "Place your mind and will where the Holy Spirit can reach them, for He will not work through another man's mind and conscience to reach yours. With earnest prayer for wisdom, make the Word of God your study. Take counsel of sanctified reason, surrendered wholly to God. Look unto Jesus in simplicity and faith. Gaze upon Jesus until the spirit faints under the excess of light. We do not half pray. We do not half believe. 'Ask, and it shall be given you.' Luke 11:9. Pray, believe, strengthen one another. Pray as you never before prayed that the Lord will lay His hand upon you that you may be able to comprehend the length and breadth and depth and height, and to know the love of Christ, which passeth knowledge, that you may be filled with all the fullness of God. The fact that we are called upon to endure trial proves that the Lord Jesus sees in us something very precious, which He desires to develop. If He saw in us nothing whereby He might glorify His Name, He would not spend time in refining us. We do not take special pains in pruning brambles. Christ does not cast worthless stones into His furnace. It is valuable ore that He tests. The blacksmith puts the iron and steel into the fire that he may know what manner of metal they are. The Lord allows His chosen ones to be placed in the furnace of affliction in order that He may see what temper they are of and whether He can mold and fashion them for His work."

Just a few more experiences we've had in learning natural remedies and herbs:

David and I had been studying and identifying wild herbs. One day David was in our woods and he saw a wild herb and he thought he'd try it. He tasted just a little bite of it, but found out it was a poisonous herb, and he got a bad reaction from it. We prayed for help and healing and he immediately took some activated charcoal stirred into a glass of water and it took away the bad effects. We praised God for His natural remedies! We always pray over our natural remedies, because it's really the power of God through prayer that actually does the healing. Jesus is the Great Physician we can always turn to.

One day David had been working in the woods cutting firewood, and he got a seed tick on him. You can use tea tree oil on it to help get the tick off of you. But he thought he'd try hand cream to see if it would smother the tick so he could pull him off, and it worked. Also, hand soap will help get the tick off you, too. David, also, found out that when you get a chigger bite that would make you itch for days, he found he could take a washcloth and get it real HOT with water, as hot as you can make it, without burning your skin, and place that on the chigger bite and hold it there awhile and it kills the chigger and it takes the itch away.

Another answer to prayer for healing came one time when David got something in his eye while cutting fire wood with our chainsaw. We prayed and asked God for help to please heal his eye. We flushed it out first with warm salt water and then I went out and picked some plantain herb in our yard and cleaned it off and put it in a little pan of water for a few minutes to boil it and then I mashed it up and let it cool down before I put the juice first in his eye to flush it out, then I applied the plantain poultice to his eye for about twenty minutes and thanks to the power of prayer and God's natural remedies, God,

the Great Physician, healed his eye. Praise God!

One time I sat down on our picnic table and unknown to me there was a nest of wasps under the seat and I got stung bad and I applied mud packs to the stings and prayed God would please take away the sting and the pain and swelling and praise God, our Great Physician, Jesus, healed me and in minutes I was okay.

David one time had a bug fly in his ear and he tried and tried to get that bug to come out of his ear. It was driving him crazy! He came to me to see if I could get it out. We prayed and asked God to please help us know what to do. I said to David, "Let me get the flashlight and shine it down in your ear. Bugs are drawn to light." So I did that and prayed God would help this natural remedy work and it did! The bug followed the light and came out of his ear! Praise God!

David was walking barefoot in the house at night and it was dark and his toes bashed into the coffee table and dislocated his little toe. We prayed and asked God to please help us with our problem. I got an ace bandage and wrapped it around his little toe I had tried to put it up close to the other toes and wrapped up his foot and he left it on all night and in the morning it was okay. It wasn't broken, just dislocated, but now back into place! We always pray and thank the good Lord for His answers to our prayers and give Him the glory!

One time while I was cooking, I god a bad burn. I have an aloe vera plant and I kept praying God would please heal this bad burn using His natural remedy by applying the juice of this plant to my burn and in not too much time it had healed up with no infection and no scar! Praise God, He did it again, in answer to prayer and the use of His natural remedy.

This happened years ago when we lived at another place. I was walking in the yard and the neighbor's dog had come over and was walking beside me. I didn't notice a rattle snake in the tall grass and I almost stepped on it. The neighbor's dog lunged at the snake and killed it, but he had gotten bit in the process and his face started swelling and he laid down and was weak and sick. I prayed and asked the Lord to please help me save the dog's life, that had taken the bite of the rattle snake for me. I thanked God for protecting me and then I immediately made up some activated charcoal with water and put some in his mouth and made a poultice and packed it all over his face and head and wrapped it with an ace bandage and prayed God would use this natural remedy to please heal the dog. Within a few hours he got up and was having no more problems! Praise God! Again God, the Great Physician, intervened to show His power of healing using God's natural remedies.

I could go on and on and on with experiences of how God in answer to prayer and using the natural remedies has helped us in our time of need and we know He'll do the same during the early time of trouble when we can't buy or sell or go see a doctor or go to a hospital, He'll look after us and protect us and care for our needs as we show faith in Him and His power to take care of all our problems at that time and care for us, too, when we'll be leaving our little Arks of safety and fleeing for our lives going out into the desolate and solitary places where God will supply our bread and water as Isa. 33:15 & 16 promises and will give His angels charge over us as Ps. 91 and Ps. 46 says. We need to be letting God develop our faith in Him and His promises now, so we'll be able to trust Him when all this takes place when the Sunday Laws will be enforced upon us. HAVE FAITH IN GOD! Heb. 11.

Some good books for reference to learn natural remedies and herbs are:

Natural Remedies Encyclopedia by Vance Ferrell, 1998, published by Harvestime Books

From the Shepherd's Purse by Max Barlow, 1990, Spice West Publications

All of Agatha Thrash's books by Agatha Thrash, Published Uchee Pines Institute

Nature's Healing Practices by Agatha Thrash, 2015, Published by TEACH Services, Inc.

The Place of Herbs in Rational Therapy Quotes of E. G. White, pamphlet published by M.E.E.T. Ministry

The Ministry of Healing by E. G. White, 1905, Published by Pacific Press Publishing Association

Instruction Relating to the Principles of Healthful Living by E. G. White, 1994, Published by TEACH Services, Inc.

Medical Ministry by E. G. White, 1932, Published by Pacific Press Publishing Association

Counsels on Diet and Foods by E. G. White, 1938, Published by Pacific Press Publishing Association

Counsels on Health and Instruction to Medical Missionary Workers by E. G. White, 1951, Published by Pacific Press Publishing Association

Prescription for Nutritional Healing by Phillis A. Balch, 2006, Published by the Penguin Group (U.S.A.) Inc.

The Divine Prescription & Science of Health & Healing by Gunther B. Paulien, Ph. D., 1997, Published by TEACH Services, Inc.

Today's Herbal Health by Louise Tenny, M.H., 2007, Published by Woodland Publishing

Plants & Health by A. C. SAS, 1990, Published by Eastern Publishing Association

Encyclopedia of Medicinal Plants, vols. 1 & 2, 2004, Published in Spain by Marpa

Encyclopedia of Foods, vols. 1–3, by George D. Pamplona-Roger, M.D., 2006, Editorial Safeliz

The Final Work by Vernon Sparks, M.D., 2004, Published by Home Bound Books

Back to Eden by Jethro Kloss, 1988, Back to Eden Books Publishing Co.

You can Survive by Jere Franklin, 2002, Remnant Publications

The Great Controversy Above Silver or Gold!

(I've read *The Great Controversy* book through eight times!)

The prophet of God, Ellen G. White, wrote in the book, *Colporteur Ministry*, pp. 120–130, the chapter entitled, "Books that Give the Message." On pages 127–138 she says, *"The Great Controversy* should be very widely circulated. It contains the story of the past, the present, and the future. In its outline of the closing scenes of this earth's history, it bears a powerful testimony in behalf of the truth. I am anxious to see a wide circulation for this book than for any others I have written; for in *The Great Controversy*, the last message of warning to the world is given more distinctly than in any of my other books… I am sure the Lord would have this work carried into all the highways and byways, where are souls to be warned of the danger so soon to come. I was moved by the Spirit of the Lord to write that book, and while working upon it, I felt a great burden upon my soul. I knew that time was short, that the scenes which are soon to crowd upon us would at the last come very suddenly and swiftly, as represented in the words of scripture: 'The day of the Lord so cometh as a thief in the night.'

The Lord has set before me matters which are of urgent importance for the present time, and which reach into the future. The words have been spoken in a charge to me, 'Write in a book the things which thou hast seen and heard, and let it go to all the people; for the time is at hand when past history will be repeated.' I have been aroused at one, two, or three o'clock in the morning with some point forcibly impressed upon my mind, as if spoken by the voice of God… I was shown… that I should devote myself to writing out the important matters for volume 4 [*The Great Controversy*] that the warning must go where the living messenger could not go, and that it would call the attention of many to the important events to occur in the closing scenes of this world's history. The book *The Great Controversy*, I appreciate above silver or gold, and I greatly desire that it shall come before the people. While writing the manuscript of *The Great Controversy*, I was often conscious of the presence of the angels of God…

But a much larger number who read it will not take their position until they see the very events taking place that are foretold in it. The fulfillment of some of the predictions will inspire faith that others also will come to pass, and when the earth is lightened with the glory of the Lord, in the closing work, many souls will take their position on the commandments of God as the results of this agency.

God gave me the light contained in *The Great Controversy* and *Patriarchs and Prophets* and this light was needed to arouse the people to prepare for the great day of God, which is just before us. These books contain God's direct appeal to the people. Thus He is speaking to the people in stirring words, urging them to make ready for His coming. The light God has given in these books should not be concealed…

Many will depart from the faith and give heed to seducing spirits. *Patriarchs and Prophets* and *The Great Controversy* are books that are especially adapted to those who have newly come to the faith, that they may be established in the truth. The dangers are pointed out that should be avoided by the churches. Those who become thoroughly acquainted with the lessons in these books will see the dangers before them, and will be able to discern the plain, straight path marked out for them. They will be kept from strange paths. They will make straight paths for their feet, lest the lame be turned out of the way…

They should be appreciated as books that bring to the people light that is especially needed just now. Therefore these books should be widely distributed. Those who make a careful study of the instruction contained in them, and will receive it as from the Lord, will be kept from receiving many of the errors that are being introduced. Those who accept the truths contained in these books will not be led into false paths."

Colporteur Ministry, p. 122, Sister White tells us, "I have been instructed that the canvassing work is to be revived.

Also, in *Colporteur Ministry*, p. 120, we read, "The Lord calls for workers to enter the canvassing field that the books containing the light of present truth may be circulated… The third angel's message is to be proclaimed with a loud voice. Tremendous issues are before us. We have no time to lose… The warning message is to be carried to all parts of the world. Our books are to be published in many different languages. With these books, humble faithful men are to go forth as colporteur evangelists, bearing the truth to many who otherwise would never be enlightened." On pp. 20–22 we read, "God calls for workers from every church among us to enter His service as canvasser evangelists. God loves His church. If the members will do His will, if they will strive to impart the light to those in darkness, He will greatly bless their efforts. In this closing work of the gospel there is a vast field to be occupied and, more than ever before, the work is to enlist helpers from the common people. Both the youth and those older in years will be called from the field, from the vineyard, and from the workshop and sent forth by the Master to give His message. Many of these have had little opportunity for education; but Christ sees in them qualifications that will enable them to fulfill His purpose. If they put their hearts into the work, and continue to be learners, He will fit them to labor for Him. There never was a time when more workers were needed than at the present. There are brethren and sisters throughout all our ranks who should discipline themselves to engage in this work… It is the duty of all to study the various points of our faith, that they be prepared to give a reason for the hope that is within them with meekness and fear.

Many are sad and discouraged, weak in faith and trust. Let them do something to help someone more needy than themselves, and they will grow strong in God's strength. Let them engage in the good work of selling our books. Thus they will help others, and the experience gained will give them the assurance that they are God's helping hand. As they plead with the Lord to help them, He will guide them to those who are seeking for light. Christ will be close beside them, teaching them what to say and do. By comforting others, they themselves will be comforted… Under divine guidance, go forward in the work, and look to the Lord for aid. The Holy Spirit will attend you. Angels of heaven will accompany you, preparing the way."

On p. 32 Sister White says, "Let not too much time be occupied in fitting up men to do missionary work.

Instruction is necessary but let all remember that Christ is the Great Teacher and the Source of all true wisdom. Let young and old consecrate themselves to God, take up the work, and go forward, laboring in humility under the control of the Holy Spirit. Let those who have been in school go out into the field and put to a practical use the knowledge they have gained… The education obtained in this practical way may properly be termed higher education."

God gave me a dream that said, "GO FORWARD!" God impressed me to go forward in faith and write the book, ***Don't Be Trapped in the Cities!! Get Out Now!*** God has allowed my husband David and me and our son Jonathan to go through some trying experiences that we should relate to try and encourage others that God will keep His promises to us in His Word and will see us through our hard times and trials in the crisis ahead of us all when we'll have to face the Sunday Law issue and have to decide which side we'll choose to be on, the Sunday side or God's true seventh day Sabbath side?

I had been praying and asking God to please help me find a particular E. G. White reference I wanted to quote and I just couldn't find it. Then one day in my morning worship I asked the Lord to please give me something to read from Him for my worship that morning. God had me turn to this quote I had been trying to find for so long, but couldn't find it. It was taken from *Testimonies for the Church*, vol. 6, p. 336, "Let those who gain such an experience in working for the Lord write an account of it for our papers, that others may be encouraged. Let the canvasser tell of the joy and blessing he has received in his ministry as an evangelist. These reports should find a place in our papers, for they are far reaching in their influence. They will be as sweet fragrance in the church, a savor of life unto life. Thus it is seen that God works with those who co-operate with Him."

Years ago God had given me a dream saying, "*The Great Controversy* is the book to get out to the people." So, we bought up a lot of paperback *The Great Controversy* books and began giving them out all over. We had so many exciting and thrilling experiences working with this book. I remember one time when we lived in the country at Wellsville, Kansas, there was a man who came to our door and said, "The strangest thing happens every time I pass by your place my car temperature gauge goes over to HOT. Do you think you could give me some water for my car?" I said, "Sure!" I got him water for his car and also gave him a *The Great Controversy* book. We never saw him again after God got *The Great Controversy* book in his hands.

One time we were traveling down the highway and right in front of a home our car temperature gauge shot over to HOT. We pulled off the highway and my husband went up to the home to ask for some water for our car and he had a *The Great Controversy* book in his back pocket to give to the people in that home. They gave us some water in a plastic milk jug and David gave them *The Great Controversy* book. When he went to put the water in the car, it didn't need any water and we drove off and our car wasn't showing HOT or overheating. We've had so many experiences getting *The Great Controversy* book out to people that the Lord lets our paths cross.

One time David stopped at a gas station to get gas and saw at the other gas pump a fellow who was dirty, unshaven with shabby clothes on and a voice in David's mind said, "Give that man a book." Then David thought, "No, he probably wouldn't read it anyway. He doesn't look like he'd be interested in reading a book like *The Great Controversy*. So David began to get into his car to leave and the voice in his mind said real loud, "Give that man a book!" So, David jumped out of his car and handed the man *The Great Controversy* and spoke encouraging words to him. The man was so happy to get the book and thanked David over and over and over for it!

We share with you these experiences that we've had, hoping they will encourage you to find the joy we've had in passing out this wonderful and powerful *The Great Controversy* book.

We've also had the privilege of passing out a lot of E. G. White's books by the hundreds door to door around a lot of towns and cities and different counties, books like *The Ministry of Healing*, *Steps to Christ*, *Christ's Object Lessons*, *The Great Controversy*, *The Desire of Ages*, *Patriarchs and Prophets*, *Daniel and Revelation*, and *The National Sunday Law* book. These were paperback books and David was doing self-supporting colporteuring on our own. One time David had a discouraging day going door to door with his paperback books and it just seemed no one was wanting to buy anything. He was beginning to feel a little discouraged and he kept praying as he kept on going door to door. Now we have a little sign we came up with ourselves that we decided whenever we'd see a beautiful red bird we'd take that as a sign that God was near. So, David said, "Lord, would you please send me a red bird and let him direct me to the home where someone will please give me some money for a book. You know our need of money to meet our expenses." Just then he saw a red bird ahead of him, so he began to follow it and it flew in front of him and flew off to the left down to another street and then up another street, always staying right in front of David so he could see where the red bird was going. Finally, the bird disappeared and so David knocked on the door of the house where the bird disappeared and the lady bought a *The Great Controversy* book from him and was so happy to get the book! David thanked the good Lord for hearing his prayers for help and for sending the red bird to direct him.

One time while David was again doing door to door canvassing on his own, as a self-supporting colporteur, we had wanted to go visit my mom, who was living in Arkansas at the time. This was back when our son, Jonathan, was ten years old. Jonathan's almost forty-four years old now. But we decided we'd all three go door to door to try and sell books to make enough gas money to go see my mom for a visit. We prayed God would please be with us and direct us and go before to the people and make their hearts receptive to want to buy a book. Jonathan was out on his own canvassing going door to door with two *The Great Controversy* paperback books in his hand. At one door an elderly lady came to the door and Jonathan told the lady he was selling books for gas money so he could go see his grandma, who lived in Arkansas. The lady gave him $10 for both of his *The Great Controversy* books he had in his hand. God must have let that elderly grandma know how he must feel wanting to get to see his grandma and felt sorry for him and God made her heart tender to give him $10 for his two books. This was back thirty-four years ago, so that was a lot of money back then. God did help us make enough gas money to get to go see Jonathan's grandma. Praise God! God always provided our needs as we trusted in Him.

In *Colporteur Ministry*, p. 88, we read, "The canvassers who are born again by the work of the Holy Spirit, will be accompanied by angels, who will go before them to the dwellings of the people, preparing the way for them."

And also on p. 89 Sister White says, "Canvassers should be able to give instruction in regard to the treatment of the sick. They should learn simple methods of hygienic treatment. Thus they may work as medical missionaries, ministering to the souls and bodies of the suffering. This work should now be going forward in all parts of the world. Thus multitudes might be blessed by the prayers and instruction of God's servants."

In *Colporteur Ministry*, p. 25, it says, "This is a work that should be done. The end is near. Already much time has been lost, when these books should have been in circulation. Sell them far and near. Scatter them like the leaves of autumn. This work is to continue without the forbiddings of anyone. The lost sheep of God's fold are scattered in every place, and the work that should be done for them is being neglected. From the light given me I know that where there is one canvasser in the field, there should be one hundred."

I remember an experience we had with *The Great Controversy* book last year when we were going to go visit our son, Jonathan, for his birthday in the care center he was at. We had bought him a pair of tennis shoes for his birthday and we had saved enough out of our Social Security check to get him a healthy loaf of homemade bread at the health food store on our way to go see him. We were short of money, because we had been having to buy a lot of building materials to keep building on the "Ark" we're building for the early time of trouble to be able to survive, eating out of our garden and berries and nut trees and fruit trees we had planted and were producing now. When we arrived at the health food store, my husband, David, ran in to get the loaf of bread we had saved enough money for and found out they had raised the price on it, about $1.79 more. David had already told the manager how much he liked his healthy bread with no chemicals and all natural. David took the loaf back and thanked the man and explained he wasn't able to get the loaf because the price had been raised and it was toward the end of the month and we didn't have that much to pay for that type of bread. David started walking out the door and the manager said, "Here you can have this loaf of bread." David thanked the man and shook his hand. He hurried out to the car to tell me all that had just happened and how God had let us get the loaf of bread free for Jonathan's birthday surprise! We were all excited as we drove off in our car in a hurry to see Jonathan and tell him how God had provided him with this free loaf of healthy bread for his birthday. We were praising and thanking the Lord for what He had just done for us and asking God to please bless this kind man for doing this for us. Then I said to my husband, "Honey, we forgot to give this man a *The Great Controversy* book! This man gave us a free loaf of bread, the staff of life, and we should freely give him the Bread of Life, Jesus Christ, in this truth-filled *The Great Controversy* book." So, we turned the car around and drove back to the health food store and we prayed he'd be receptive to *The Great Controversy* book as we presented it to him in appreciation of what he had done to help us. The man was so happy and excited to get the book and thanked David for the book. He said he was interested in books like that and would really enjoy studying it! Praise God from whom all blessings flow!

> "The book, *The Great Controversy*, I appreciate above silver or gold, and I greatly desire that it shall come before the people."
>
> *Colporteur Ministry,* p. 128

Stories

A CRISIS IS JUST UPON US!

We've had an interesting and exciting thing happen about our fruit trees. We've always said, "When the time is right the Lord will let our fruit trees produce big time, when God knows we'll need food to eat during the early time of trouble when you can't buy or sell.

Well, this year, 2014, our fruit trees have produced an overabundance until the branches are so overloaded they're hanging over and ready to break down from all the fruit! We just praise and thank the good Lord! Usually the raccoons come off the creek on our land and steal all our fruit and we hardly have anything left for us. This year as the raccoons start wiping out our fruit, we're picking them early and storing them down in our cool basement that God helped us build and get done in time to be able to have a place to store all our fruit and be able to enjoy and not the raccoons.

What's really strange about all this fruit on our trees is that our fruit trees didn't have hardly any blossoms on them this year, because of the HARP project up in Alaska that tries to control the weather. We've had early freezes and hail, no rain much in spring or summer, then late frosts, and 60 to 80 mile per hour winds to blow off whatever blossom may be left on the trees after all these happenings to destroy our fruit on our trees. As we examined our fruit trees through the summer, there was not much blossoms at all to make any fruit and we figured they were killed off through the different storms. Then in time of harvest they were overloaded and branches hanging down!! We were amazed and shocked and overjoyed and so thankful to God for Him blessing our fruit trees in spite of what the devil tried to do to wipe out our fruit production.

Then in a dream 8-5-14 I saw the raccoons in our apple trees and ruining the cantaloupes in the garden. I was so upset with them that I was looking around for a stick to knock them out of the trees. I was saying, "All that time and money and hard work and now the raccoons are destroying all the labor of our hands," as I saw the raccoons ruining dad's cantaloupes he had worked so hard to grow! The next day after having this dream we hurried and picked our fruit and stored it in the basement, along with garden things. This experience gives us a kind of foreboding feeling. It makes us think of Sister White's words warning us of what's coming! In *Last Day Events*, p. 11, she writes, "The present is a time of overwhelming interest to all living. Rulers and statesmen, men who occupy positions of trust and authority, thinking men and women of all classes, have their attention fixed upon the events taking place about us. They are watching the relations that exist among the nations. They observe the intensity that is taking possession of every earthly element and they recognize that something great and decisive is about to take place—that the world is on the verge of a stupendous crisis… The calamities by land and sea, the unsettled state of society, the alarms of war, are portentous. (Portentous means: Being a sign of something bad about to happen, ominous, amazing, and marvelous. Something that foreshadows a coming event. Omen—prophetic indications.) They forecast approaching events of the greatest magnitude. The agencies of evil are combining their forces and consolidating. They are strengthening for the last great crisis. Great changes are soon to take place in our world, and the final movements will be rapid ones."

Also, in *Last Day Events*, p. 38, Sister White says, "The angels of God in their messages to men represent time as very short."

Sister White continues to tell us in *Last Day Events*, p. 126, "Those who are making an effort to change the Constitution and secure a law enforcing Sunday observance little realize what will be the result. A crisis is just upon us."

Also, on p. 127 Sister White goes on to say, "As faithful watchmen you should see the sword coming and give the warning, that men and women may not pursue a course through ignorance that they would avoid if they knew the truth."

On p. 41 of *Last Day Events*, Sister White says, "…a great terror is soon to come upon human beings. The end is very near. We who know the truth should be preparing for what is soon to break upon the world as an overwhelming surprise." In the days ahead of us we will need a shelter in the time of storm. We'll need Jesus to care for us! Song, "A shelter in the Time of Storm."

Sister White writes in *Testimonies for the Church*, vol. 6, p. 407, "…The judgments of God are about to fall upon the world, and we need to be preparing for that great day."

In *Country Living*, p. 21, Sister White warns, "I see the necessity of making haste to get all things ready for the crisis."

In *The Great Controversy*, p. 622, Sister White tells us, "It is often the case that trouble is greater in anticipation than in reality; but this is not true of the crisis before us. The most vivid presentation cannot reach the magnitude of the ordeal."

In *Testimonies for the Church*, vol. 7, p. 83, Sister White says, "The time is near when the large cities will be visited by the judgments of God. In a little while, these cities will be terribly shaken." Again, in Sister White's writings we find in *Country Living*, p. 20, this counsel, "We are not to locate ourselves where we will be forced into close relations with those who do not honor God… A crisis is soon to come in regard to the observance of Sunday… And we are to be careful not to place ourselves where it will be hard for ourselves and our children to keep the Sabbath. If in the providence of God we can secure places away from the cities, the Lord would have us do this. There are troublous times before us."

Read the admonition of Sister White in *Country Living*, p. 21, "The Protestant world have set up an idol sabbath in the place where God's Sabbath should be, and they are treading in the footsteps of the Papacy. For this reason I see the necessity of the people of God moving out of the cities, into retired country places, where they may cultivate the land and raise their own produce. Thus they may bring their children up with simple, healthful habits. I see the necessity of making haste to get all things ready for the crisis."

May God's people heed the advice of Sister White given in *Country Living*, pp. 25–28, "Those who have felt at last to make a move, let it not be in a rush, in an excitement, or in a rash manner, or in a way that hereafter they will deeply regret that they did move out… Take heed that there shall be no rash movements made in heeding the counsel in moving from Battle Creek. Do nothing without seeking wisdom of God, who hath promised to give liberally to all who ask and who upbraideth not. All that anyone can do is to advise and counsel and then leave those who are convicted in regard to duty to move under divine guidance, and with their whole hearts open to learn and obey God… Let everyone take time to consider carefully, and not be like the man in the parable who began to build, and was not able to finish. Not a move should be made but that movement and all that it portends are carefully considered—everything weighed… To every man was given his work according to his several ability. Then let him not move hesitatingly, but firmly, and yet humbly trusting in God. There may be individuals who will make a rush to do something, and enter into some business they know nothing about. This God does not require. Think candidly, prayerfully, studying the Word with all carefulness and prayerfulness, with mind and heart awake to hear the voice of God… To understand the will of God is a great thing… and let the individual rely wholly upon God. Let there be much praying done, and even with fasting, that not one shall move in darkness, but move in the light as God is in the light… Let there be wise generalship in this matter, and all move under the guidance of a wise, unseen counselor, which is GOD… Submit all your ways to God's way and to God's will…

If everyone will come to Jesus in a teachable spirit, with contrition of heart, then he is in a condition of mind to be instructed and to learn of Jesus and obey His orders… We cannot have a weak faith now, we cannot be safe in a listless, indolent slothful attitude. Every jot of ability is to be used, and sharp, calm, deep thinking is to be done. The wisdom of any human agent is not sufficient for the planning and devising in this time. Spread every plan before God with fasting and with the humbling of the soul before the Lord Jesus, and commit thy ways unto the Lord. The sure promise is, He will direct thy paths. (Ps. 32:8) He is infinite in resources. The Holy One of Israel, who calls the host of heaven by name, and holds the stars of heaven in position, has you individually in His keeping…

I would that all could realize what possibilities and probabilities there are for all who make Christ their sufficiency and their trust. The life hid with Christ in God ever has a refuge; he can say, 'I can do all things through Christ which strengtheneth me.' (Phil. 4:13) I leave this matter with you, for I have been worried and troubled in regard to the dangers that assail all in Battle Creek, lest they shall move indiscreetly and give the enemy advantage. This need not be, for if we walk humbly with God, we shall walk safely."

It's now, 2015, and we can look back to, 2014, and see why God heavily produced fruit on our fruit trees and blessed our garden to produce well, so we'd have food to eat. God was looking out for our needs, because during the winter months, while the building materials costs were low, we used all our money we had and any money people sent us to buy building materials for the "ARK", and we were able to survive on all our food we had stored for the winter and put our food money on building materials. In September, 2015, the pope is going to Congress about the Sunday Laws. Things could soon begin to close up rapidly for us Seventh-day Adventists and we need to step fast and get set up and prepared for what's soon to break upon us with blinding force, as Sister White says in *Selected Messages*, book 2, p. 142, "The work of the people of God is to prepare for the events of the future, which will soon come upon them with blinding force." Also, read again in *Last Day Events*, p. 11, by E. G. White, "Great changes are soon to take place in our world, and the final movements will be rapid ones." We can see now how God, in the early time of trouble, can bless our garden and fruit trees to produce.

IT MUST HAVE BEEN AN ANGEL!

This experience happened a few years ago.

We had just purchased a much needed used car for $400, a 1987 Mazda, stick shift. We checked over everything and checked the oil and my husband and I and our son Jonathan were going to take a short trip in it. Although we weren't real acquainted with the car we had just purchased, the owner had assured us it was in good condition and safe to drive on a trip with our invalid son in a wheelchair. We had tested it out driving it before we purchased it, and felt everything was fine and safe. The Lord had answered our prayers to get the car at that low of price, $400. My husband and I had been working long and hard on the "ARK" and we were needing a much needed break. It was summer and nice weather and a trip seemed like fun, just to get away for a while and travel a little ways from home.

We packed the car with *10 Commandments Twice Removed* books we had purchased from 3ABN to pass out for one of their 10 Commandments weekends. We were going to pass them out as we traveled along. With hopes high and enjoying the drive and the pretty weather in our newly purchased car, we had gotten about 180 miles from home passing out a few books here and there, and the car was purring along and no problems. So we decided to pull into a Walmart and leave a few books there and get us something to eat in Walmart.

When we pulled into the parking lot, the unexpected happened! The gear shift had dropped out of the car! The stark reality hit us—we're stranded! It was evening and all the auto parts places were closed and the car mechanics had gone home. We only had a little money on us, not near enough to cover a major repair problem like this! Like always, when we're in trouble, like the flower naturally turns to the sun, we prayed and called on God to please help us! David jacked up the car on one side and saw the BIG major problem, but what to do about it, stranded here in the Walmart parking lot, 180 miles from home and we knew no one to call on to help us in our predicament that far from home and part places all closed and mechanics all gone home and no money to fix this big major car problem, and our invalid son in his wheelchair stranded in the car seat and we had nowhere to turn to but to the Lord!

David thought if maybe he bought some epoxy in the Walmart it might hold up the gear shift long enough to get us home. But that didn't work. While we were waiting to see if it would dry and hold, we kept praying and asking God to please help us. We were in a terrible situation and desperate and we needed help BAD and we needed it ___Now!___

We decided to pass out our *10 Commandments Twice Removed* books to the people who kept stopping by, seeing our car jacked up on one side in the parking lot and wanting to know what our problem was, but no one could help and no one had a solution! We'd thank them for being kind to stop and inquire about our problem. Then we'd give them a book. God kept bringing people after people and Jonathan and David and I were passing them out right and left until we had only one book left. The gear shift was still not fixed, and the car was still jacked up, and we were still sitting in the car perplexed and praying and wondering what we were going to do in our predicament. All we could do was pray to God to please help us!

That's when we saw a young man wearing a cowboy hat and he was driving a pickup truck and he pulled up beside us and said, "Are you having a problem?" We said, "Yes! We sure are! Our gear shift has fallen out of our car! We've tried epoxy and it didn't work. All the parts places and mechanics are closed up." By then he was out of his truck and looking under our car at the situation and he said, "Don't worry. I just happen to have just what you need that will work. This is a special bonding that will hold that up for you. I had some left over from the company I work for and I'm sure I'll have enough to do the job for you!" He was such a kind and gentle looking man and his eyes were so kind and tender looking. He was so friendly and nice and reassuring. He got down under the car and worked the gear shift back up into place and applied his "special bonding material" and braced it to stay in place while it dried. He said, "You'll have to wait a couple of hours before it will dry and hold, but you'll be okay. It will hold in place for you!" We happily thanked him and asked what we could pay him for his kindness and service to help us in our time of need?" He said, "No, you don't owe me anything. I'm just glad to be able to help you!" I said to him, "You're an answer to our prayers! We didn't know what we were going to do! Thank you so very much and God bless you!" I said to him, "Do you mind if we have prayer together and ask the Lord to bless you for helping us?" He said, "That's fine." We all held hands in a circle in the Walmart parking lot and each of us said a little prayer. His prayer was so tender and kind praying for us! Then I gave him our last *10 Commandments Twice Removed* book as he was getting into his pickup truck to leave and he smiled such a sweet smile and thanked me for the book. We waved goodbye to him as he smiled and drove off waving goodbye to us.

I said to David and Jonathan, as we just stood there amazed and awed at what had just happened, "It must have been an angel God sent us in answer to our prayers for help!! He knew just what to do, and he just happened to have just the right bonding material and just enough to fix our car problem."

While we sat in the car waiting for this special bonding material to dry before we could drive on home, we prayed and thanked the good Lord for helping us in our time of need and for looking out for us in our distress.

We then left that hallowed spot where we had met an angel coming to our rescue in answer to our earnest cries for help! As we drove back home in the dark I thought of Jer. 33:3, "Call unto me, and I will answer thee, and show thee great and mighty things which thou knowest not." I then thought of that beautiful Ps. 46 chapter that we should memorize for the time of trouble to be a source of strength and help and encouragement to us when we're going through that time of trouble and also, Ps. 91 and Ps. 40 and 2 Cor. 12:9, 10. God brought to my mind the quote found in *The Desire of Ages*, p. 356, "The Bible shows us God in His high and holy place not in a state of inactivity, not in silence and solitude, but surrounded by ten thousand times ten thousand and thousands of thousands of holy intelligences, all waiting to do His will… God is bending from His throne to hear the cry of the oppressed. To every sincere prayer He answers, 'Here am I.' He uplifts the distressed and downtrodden. In all our afflictions He is afflicted. In every temptation and every trial the angel of His presence is near to deliver… Not even a sparrow falls to the ground without the Father's notice."

I was also thinking of God's promise to His children found in *The Great Controversy*, p. 633, "The precious Saviour will send help just when we need it… The time of trouble is a fearful ordeal for God's people, but it is the time for every true believer to look up, and by faith he may see the bow of promise encircling him."

I like the precious words found in *The Ministry of Healing*, p. 481, 482, "Worry is blind and cannot discern the future; but Jesus sees the end from the beginning. In every difficulty, He has His way prepared to bring relief… Our heavenly Father has a thousand ways to provide for us of which we know nothing. Those who accept the one principle of making the service of God supreme, will find perplexities vanish and a plain path before their feet. The faithful discharge of today's duties is the best preparation for tomorrow's trials… Let us be hopeful and courageous. Despondency in God's service is sinful and unreasonable. He knows our every necessity… He has means for the removal of every difficulty, that those who serve Him and respect the means He employs may be sustained. His love is as far above all other love as the heavens are above the earth. He watches over His children with a love that is measureless and everlasting. In the darkest days, when appearances seem most forbidding, have faith in God. He is working out His will, doing all things well in behalf of His people. The strength of those who love and serve Him will be renewed day by day. He is able and willing to bestow upon His servants all the help they need."

I spoke up and said to Jonathan and David, as we continued our drive back home, "Apparently God had a lot of people in that area He wanted to get these *10 Commandments Twice Removed* books out to today, so He allowed us to be stranded there long enough to pass all our books out, and then He helped us with our problem by sending us an angel to take care of our problem, and to get us safely home with no more problems!!! Praise God!"

As a matter of fact, in all the time we owned that car, we never had any more problems with the gear shift. Whatever that 'special bonding material' was that the angel put on there worked! Praise God from whom all blessings flow!!!

I've often wondered, as I've thought back on this experience, "I wonder who the angel gave his *10 Commandments Twice Removed* book to that I had given to him?"

VISITED BY AN ANGEL IN DISGUISE!

This experience happened before we got the one dog that we now have.

It was getting toward evening and David was in town getting supplies, and i was home alone. It was cold, snowy winter weather so I had the house shut up to keep warm. It looked like no one was home. I heard a noise out in the driveway, and when I looked out the window, I saw an old, green pick-up truck that had gone around our gravel circle driveway, but hadn't stopped, and was headed back out onto the gravel road again. I couldn't tell who was in the truck. I watched where the truck went as it headed up the road to our neighbor's house. They were not home and the truck drove in and out of the driveway without stopping and getting out. This caused their dogs to start barking, and I thought to myself, "That's strange! I wonder who that could be, driving around like he's checking out everyone's place to see who's home and who's gone, and who doesn't have barking dogs?" The truck drove on up the hill and I didn't think any more about it.

Then one day David saw a big, white dog in the snow in our yard, and then he disappeared and we never saw him again and we never did see him anymore or dog footprints in the snow either.

Then I told David about the old green truck that circled our place and never stopped or got out and I never did see who it was. Our car was gone because David was in town, so it looked like we weren't home. Then they went on up to our neighbor's place and they weren't home, so they drove out and left, leaving the dogs barking. The truck headed on up the hill and I didn't think any more about it.

David said, "There's people being reported who go out to the country places and steal things and then they sell it for cash." He said, "I better go up and alert our neighbors what happened so they'll be on the lookout for thieves coming around looking for things to steal when no one is home and when there's no dogs around to bark and draw attention to what they're doing and chase them off."

I said, "We have no dogs to bark and discourage robbers from stopping and loading up what they want while we're gone. But we do pray every day and night for God's protection over the "ARK" that we're preparing for God's people during the early time of trouble when we'll be living off the land and out of our gardens, because we won't be able to buy or sell. We always pray and ask God to send His angels to watch over us and our place while we're gone or while we're sleeping. Even though we have no guard dogs to watch out for us and discourage intruders as thieves, we do have "The Angel of the Lord encampeth round about them that fear him, and delivereth them." Ps. 34:7.

When David went up to tell our neighbors about what happened the other day, the neighbor said, "Yes, just the other day someone broke into the millionaire's house up the hill and hauled off everything he had in the house. The millionaire doesn't stay out there in his country home all the time, but just visits it now and then, and he has no dogs to bark and scare them off like we have dogs to bark."

When David came home and told me about what had happened I said, "That's the same time I saw that old green truck circling our driveway and our neighbor's driveway and got their dogs to barking. I know now why we've been seeing dog footprints in the snow, all around our place and you saw a big white dog one day and then he just disappeared and didn't show up anymore after the robbery up the hill was over and we saw no more dog footprints in the snow in our yard. God must have let the driver of that old green truck see that big white guard dog here and its footprints all over the yard, and maybe he even heard the dog barking, too, and made him not want to get out of his truck and rob us or stop and get out and rob our neighbors with dogs.

We praised and thanked the good Lord for sending an angel in disguise of a watch dog to scare off the thieves and protect us and our place. The Lord is watching over us and protecting us, even when we have no idea what's happening. God knows when the thieves would be coming and He sent a big watch dog to scare them away. We each have a guardian angel watching over us day and night and never ceases His watchful care over us. In Sister White's book, *My Life Today*, p. 367 she says, "Not until the providences of God are seen in the light of eternity shall we understand what we owe to the care and interposition of His angels. Celestial beings have taken an active part in the affairs of men. They have appeared in garments that shone as the lightening, they have come as men, in the garb of wayfarers. They have accepted the hospitalities of human homes, they have acted as guides to benighted travelers. They have thwarted the spoiler's purpose, and turned aside the stroke of the destroyer."

In the book *Maranatha*, p. 270, by E. G. White, she writes, "During the night a very impressive scene passed before me. There seemed to be great confusion and the conflict of armies. A messenger from the Lord stood before me and said, 'Call your household. I will lead you; follow me.' He led me down a dark passage, through a forest, then through the clefts of mountains, and said, 'Here you are safe.' There were others who had been led to this retreat. The heavenly messenger said, 'The time of trouble has come as a thief in the night, as the Lord warned you it would come.'"

> "During the night a very impressive scene passed before me. There seemed to be great confusion and the conflict of armies..."
>
> *Maranatha*, p. 270

GOD OVERSAW IT ALL!

This experience happened almost forty-four years ago.

There was a time when my husband, David, was in the conference colporteur work, while I was pregnant with our son, Jonathan, soon to be delivered on April 21, 1970.

We were staying with my mom in Kansas City, Kansas, since my dad had passed away and she was living all alone and wanted us to please come and stay with her in her home while David canvassed.

We weren't selling a lot of books. People just didn't seem to have the money or the interest for religious books, and this type of work was all new to David.

We weren't covered with any medical insurance either, since David had just begun to work for the conference as a literature evangelist and had no benefits built up at this time.

It came time for Jonathan to be born, and I was admitted to the hospital and in filling out all the paperwork they wanted to know my occupation and my husband's occupation. I told them I wasn't employed, that I was just a housewife. I told them my husband's occupation was a religious book salesman.

I was twenty-seven years old when I delivered our son, Jonathan, natural child birth. I had been seeing my medical doctor regularly and the delivery went okay and Jonathan was fine. But, after the delivery serious complications arose for me. I wouldn't stop bleeding and everything they tried wouldn't stop my bleeding. I was growing weaker and weaker. I told the nurses I felt like I was dying! Finally, my doctor was called in and an OB/GYN specialist to discover the problem. I was taken back into surgery. My mom and my husband and I had prayer together before they rolled me back into surgery. We knew God was the Great Physician and He'd give the doctors the wisdom and knowledge they needed to know what to do to stop my bleeding. We claimed James 1:5. They found a small fibroid tumor that wouldn't stop bleeding, so they removed it and everything was okay. But, during the surgery, before they discovered the bleeding fibroid tumor, my blood pressure dropped so dangerously low and they began shooting me with medicines in my I.V. to revive me and giving me blood transfusions, because I almost died on the surgery table from the loss of so much blood and the exhaustion of being in delivery pains all night with no sleep and trying to give natural childbirth to our son, Jonathan.

When I came out from under the anesthesia, I heard myself singing the song, "Oh! That will be glory for me!" Then, when I revived enough to realize that that was me singing on the surgery table, and there were the doctors and nurses all around me and I was so embarrassed and I stopped singing!

The doctor then explained to me that they had removed a fibroid tumor and that had stopped the bleeding. He said that I'd be okay now. He said to me, "I'm going out to let your husband know what we found and that you're doing okay. Is there anything you want me to tell your husband?" I said, "Yes! Tell him I love him and that God is good!"

Everything went well after that and I and our dear precious baby was released from the hospital. I knew God had spared my life so I could raise our son for Jesus, that He had given me. Jonathan Paul means, "Little gift of God."

As time went on and my doctor kept checking me and my baby over, the baby was doing okay, I was nursing him. But the doctor noticed since I had lost so much blood in delivery and surgery that my blood count was so low I was anemic. He said, "You're going to have to do something to build your blood up fast; it's just too dangerously low." I didn't want to go the route he suggested because I like to do things the natural way.

So, David and I and my S.D.A. mom prayed and claimed James 1:5 and asked God for a natural remedy to build my blood up fast so I wouldn't have to go the doctor's route. I wanted to do it God's way. God helped us find the natural remedy we were looking for. In *Counsels on Diet and Foods*, p. 204, by Sister White, we read, "Get eggs of healthy fowls. Use these eggs cooked or raw. Drop them uncooked into the best unfermented wine you can find." (Grape juice) We did this and prayed God would please bless our natural remedy to stop me from being anemic.

I returned soon back to my doctor to have my blood work checked again. When he checked my blood work he exclaimed, "Everything in your blood work checks out fine! What did you do?!" He was so surprised when I told him what a simple natural remedy I had used. I thanked the good Lord and gave Him the glory!

After a long time I hadn't received any medical bills from anyone, so I called the OB/GYN specialist doctor and explained I hadn't received any bills from anyone after I was in the hospital delivering my baby and explained how the OB/GYN specialist had been called in on my complicated case, but I had never received any bills as yet from anyone for all they had done for me. The receptionist replied, "If you never get a bill from us, then that's because there's no bills to pay." I thanked her so very much for doing all this for us! Then I hung up and we praised and thanked the good Lord for overseeing all this for us! God is the best insurance to have and the best physician to have. God knew we had no insurance and no money to pay all these medical bills and He knew we were sacrificing all we had to work for Him as a literature evangelist and try and win souls for Him and get this wonderful and beautiful message out to a lost and dying world to warn the people of Christ's soon coming and so they could get ready! This was truly a blessing from God, as Phil. 4:19 says and Eph. 3: 8–21.

This makes me think of when the time will come and we'll have no way to pay for medical care or even receive any medical care or able to pay for the medicines we may be on now, because we'll be cut off from all earthly supports, because we won't go along with the Sunday Laws passed. Then we'll need to exercise faith in God to care for us and supply all our needs as Phil. 4:19 promises. We just need to be faithful to God and obedient to His commandments and move out of the wicked cities and get set up now for the crisis ahead and when God will oversee all these things for us at that time. I'm so thankful I serve such a wonderful and loving Saviour who sees all our needs and meets them. *The Ministry of Healing*, pp. 480–482.

Now is the time to train up as Gospel Medical Missionaries and learn how to care for ourselves and others when we'll have no doctors and no medicines to rely on, only God and the knowledge we've taken time to learn now for when we'll be cut off from every earthly support. *The Desire of Ages*, pp. 121, 122.

Testimonies for the Church, vol. 7, p. 63, "Let our people show that they have a living interest in medical missionary work. Let them prepare themselves for usefulness by studying the books that have been written for our instruction in these lines."

- Books like: *Counsels on Diet and Foods*, by E. G. White
- *The Ministry of Healing*, by E. G. White
- *Counsels on Health*, by E. G. White
- *Medical Ministry*, by E. G. White
- All the Agatha Thrash books
- *You Can Survive,* by Jere Franklin
- *Back to Eden,* by Jethro Kloss
- *Natural Remedies Encyclopedia*, by Vance Ferrell
  There are so many other books to study from.

PAPA, MAMA, BABY BEAR'S CHAIR, AND THE MYSTERY CHAIR!

One time when Jonathan, our son, came home for a visit from the care center he was staying at, he sat in our little lean-back recliner easy chair and tilted back in it and broke it down. He's 6-foot, 3-inches, and weighs around 300 pounds. So we began praying the good Lord would please help us find another big easy chair to replace it, since this one was non-repairable and we couldn't afford to buy one. The thrift store in Ottawa is so high priced on their furniture. They told us about a furniture place in Ottawa and when they have sales on things and what people trade in on their new furniture the furniture company just trashes out the trade-ins and leaves them at their dumpster to be picked up. They said that a lot of people come by and pick up things before the trash collectors come. We thanked them for their information and help and gave them a book.

So one day while my husband, David, was driving by this furniture company he happened to see a big beautiful soft cloth-covered recliner chair sitting out by the trash dumpster. So he stopped and sat down in the chair, and it was real comfortable, but one side had been broken down a little. He figured he could probably repair it, so he loaded it up in our little car's trunk, and brought it on home. We brought it in and began looking it over to see how we could possibly fix it. We prayed and asked God to please help us be able to figure out how to repair it. We claimed James 1:5. This was such a big beautiful and comfortable and fluffy soft recliner chair. It was just what we needed to replace our broken one. After much praying and claiming the promise in James 1:5–8, "If any of you lack wisdom, let him ask of God, that giveth to all men liberally, and upbraideth not; and it shall be given him. But let him ask in faith, nothing wavering. For he that wavereth is like a wave of the sea driven with the wind and tossed. For let not that man think that he shall receive anything of the Lord. A double minded man is unstable in all his ways." We kept studying the situation over and the Lord helped us figure out what to do to fix the chair and make it usable again. We thanked the good Lord for helping us and hearing our prayers to be able to fix the chair. David said, "Jonathan won't be able to sit in this chair when he comes home, because it's not all that strong and it won't hold his 300 pounds." Then David said, "This will be my chair to sit in and relax in since I don't weigh very much." I said, "But you know Jonathan will be coming home from the care center to stay and he'll need a large size recliner chair to relax in and put his feet up so they won't swell and so he can be with us in the front room to visit. We need to pray and ask the Lord to please supply Jonathan with a big comfortable oversized recliner chair for him when he comes home."

So we began praying and each time Dad went into Ottawa for supplies, he'd drive by the furniture company checking to see if they had put out any extra large size recliner chairs, sitting out by the dumpster to be picked up. Then one day he came back home from Ottawa with an extra-large brown leather-bound recliner chair that God had provided just for Jonathan to be able to sit in. We were so happy and excited and thankful God had heard our prayers for an extra big comfortable recliner chair for Jonathan to enjoy. Jonathan really did like the chair God gave him. Now daddy had his chair to relax in and enjoy and Jonathan had him an extra-large comfortable chair to relax in and enjoy. Then I said, "But I don't have a nice recliner chair for me to relax in and enjoy. Surely God has a chair for me, too. I'm going to start praying and asking God to please put a nice soft recliner chair out in the dumpster for me." Then, one day it happened. As dad came home from one of his trips to Ottawa town to pick up supplies, he came driving up in the driveway hauling in the trunk of our little car a medium size soft cloth comfortable recliner chair for me to relax in and enjoy. It was just the right size to fit into the spot I had prepared for it. Again we praised the Lord and thanked Him for supplying our needs for three nice recliner chairs, free of charge! God knew we had been putting all our Social Security checks on building the "ARK" and we never have any extra money for any luxuries to enjoy.

Now we all three have our mama and papa and baby bear chairs to relax in and enjoy, thanks to the good Lord who supplies all our needs as Phil. 4:19 promises and Eph. 3:14–21. If God will do this to supply us with three recliner chairs, we know He can and will supply us with all our needs during the time of trouble when we'll be totally dependent on God to take care of us and all our needs and trust in Him and His promises to us. This shows us, too, how God is interested in supplying us with even the little things in our lives that make us happy. God takes notice of our wants and needs and what makes us happy. And when we sit in our papa and mama and baby bear chairs, we're very grateful and thankful for these gifts from God to His little children. We know God put those chairs there in answer to our prayers, and kept anyone else from getting them. Since God likes to please His children here on earth and show His love and make us happy by giving us good gifts to those who ask Him, like Matt. 7:11 says, then we should want to please God and make Him happy by living a Christ-like life and having a Christ-like character like Enoch did in Heb. 11:5, 6, and be obedient to all His commandments so He can pour His Holy Spirit out on His children and place His seal on them so they'll be able to stand and go through the time of trouble soon to come upon us, when the Sunday Laws will be enforced by law as *The Great Controversy* says on p. 449 and read all chapter 25, "God's Law Immutable," pp. 433–450.

How much more God loves to do exceedingly abundantly above all that we ask or think as Eph. 3:20, 21 says, unto Him be glory! God did just that for us by providing us with not only three nice comfortable recliner chairs in answer to our prayers, but He supplied us with a fourth one that was in excellent condition with only a little 1-inch tear on it. Here's how it happened:

We were driving by the furniture company where we had picked up a lot of things God had provided for us to use to furnish our cabins on the "ARK" with, like mattresses, divans, tables and chairs, dresser drawers, etc. This particular day as we drove by we saw a real pretty white comfortable loveseat in excellent condition sitting by the dumpster. We got out and sat on it and it was so comfortable, but the only problem was it wouldn't fit in the trunk of our little car. So we took the cushions off and put them in our car and drove on home to get our old pickup truck and prayed all the way back that it would still be there. And lo and behold when we pulled into the furniture store and drove back where their dumpster was and where we had left the pretty loveseat we had come back for, we were so surprised to see a black big beautiful soft leather fluffy recliner chair in excellent condition sitting right there beside our beautiful white soft loveseat that God had kept there for us. But here was something exceedingly abundantly above all that we could ask or think, a fourth recliner chair! I jumped out and sat in the chair and it felt so relaxing and soft and comfortable and I leaned back in the recliner chair and said, "Praise the Lord! Thank you, Jesus!" We knew God had let the people see us wanting the loveseat and taking the cushions so no one else would want it without the cushions and leaving to go get our truck and while we were gone, they put the nice recliner chair out there for us! When we got both of them loaded onto the truck and drove past their window we could see a lady looking out the window smiling and we smiled back and waved to her. Later, as we were unloading the things when we got home, I said to David, "We should have given her a book." David said, "When I go into Ottawa again I'll stop by and thank her in person and give her a book.

Well, the time came and we made another trip to town and saw a double mattress sitting by the dumpster. We pulled in to get it and the owner came out and said, "I have a beautiful white thick soft double mattress like brand new you can have in a couple of days and you can come by and get it. Leave me your number and I'll let you know when you can pick it up." We thanked him and gave him a book. Then when the time came to pick it up, the owner wasn't there but his sister and brother work there, too, and they gave the mattress to David and he gave them both a book and told them we really do appreciate what you've done for us and God bless you! They were so nice.

Now as we sit in our papa and mama and baby bear chairs we look over at the empty chair God provided us with and wonder who God will bring to the "ARK" to sit in this fourth chair, the "mystery chair." One day I jokingly was saying to Jonathan, "Maybe God provided us with this fourth chair for your future wife, whenever she comes to the "ARK," when you get converted and are off all your drugs and are ready to marry the mate God has waiting somewhere for you!" I reminded him of the dream I had had that, "Some man was saying to me and David, 'God planned it to bring you two together to have Jonathan. He spoke well of Jonathan.'"

Only God knows who'll be filling this "mystery chair" and when. We'll just have to patiently wait and see what God's plans are and what He'll work out. God's will be done.

GOD PARTS THE RED SEA!

2011 was a terrible year for tornadoes!

With the tornado sirens blowing in both towns three miles on both sides of us, Quenemo and Pomona, we've had to seek shelter several times down in our little root cellar. But never has God let us be hit here on the "ARK." We have had tornado storms on both sides of the "ARK" going around us and we could see the treacherous storm clouds rolling and hear the loud roaring thunder and see the lightning flashing, but directly over our heads we could look up and see a beautiful clear blue sky! It made us think of how God parted the Red Sea for the Children of Israel so they could pass through safely on dry ground. We have witnessed so many times God's loving and caring and protective hand over this place that has been built and dedicated to Him and His people for going through the time of trouble ahead of us.

Just like Noah built his ark as God directed him to do so he and all who obeyed God could go safely through the flood God was sending. It took faith for Noah to build that ark on dry ground. Heb. 11:5–10 It will take faith for God's people to build little Arks of safety while God is still holding the four winds of strife until His people are sealed as Rev. 7:1–4 says. These little Arks will have to be prepared before the Sunday Laws are passed because we'll need them to go through the time of trouble when we can't buy or sell because we won't go along with keeping man's Sunday sabbath in place of God's true seventh day Sabbath. We will then need to be able to grow our own food in our own gardens out in the country like Sister White says in *Country Living*, p. 21, "The Protestant world have set up an idol Sabbath in the place where God's Sabbath should be, and they are treading in the footsteps of the Papacy. For this reason I see the necessity of the people of God moving out of the cities into retired country places, where they may cultivate the land and raise their own produce. Thus they may bring their children up with simple, healthful habits. I see the necessity of making haste to get all things ready for the crisis."

We praise God for all He's done to help us and protect us and care for us and supply all our needs! We realize as we walk in God's will He'll be with us and direct our paths as we move forward in faith as the Children of Israel did through the Red Sea. He'll do the same for all those who put their faith and trust in the Lord and want to obey Him like Prov. 3:5,6 promises: (5)"Trust in the Lord with all thine heart; and lean not unto thine own understanding. (6) In all thy ways acknowledge Him, and He shall direct thy paths." Also, God's promise in Ps. 37: 3–5: (3) "Trust in the Lord, and do good; so shalt thou dwell in the land, and verily thou shalt be fed. (4) Delight thyself also in the Lord; and He shall give thee the desires of thine heart. (5) Commit thy way unto the Lord; trust also in Him; and He shall bring it to pass."

Sister White says in *Last Day Events*, p. 254, "The season of distress and anguish before us will require a faith that can endure weariness, delay, and hunger—a faith that will not faint, though severely tried. The 'time of trouble such as never was' is soon to open upon us; and we shall need an experience which we do not now possess, and which many are too indolent to obtain. It is often the case that trouble is greater in anticipation than in reality; but this is not true of the crisis before us. The most vivid presentation cannot reach the magnitude of the ordeal."

Also, Sister White wrote in her great and wonderful book, *The Great Controversy*, p. 622, "Those who exercise but little faith now, are in the greatest danger of falling under the power of satanic delusions and the decree to compel the conscience. And even if they endure the test they will be plunged into deeper distress and anguish in the time of trouble, because they have never made it a habit to trust in God… We should now acquaint ourselves with God by proving His promises… We must take time to pray."

I SAW DAVID'S GUARDIAN ANGEL!

It was many years ago, during the summer that this experience happened, when my husband was doing self-supporting canvassing work on his own. We were canvassing in the big city. David was selling paperback books like: *The Great Controversy*, *Steps to Christ*, *Patriarchs and Prophets*, *Christ's Object Lessons*, *The Ministry of Healing*, *National Sunday Law*, etc. He canvassed, asking only for donations, for his books he was selling. We were in need of gas and food money. Our car gas tank was on empty and so were our stomachs. We didn't even have enough gas left in the car to drive back home, which was around 55 miles away, and our pocketbook was empty of money, too.

David had canvassed all day and hadn't sold anything. We kept praying and asking God to please open up the hearts of the people to feel their need of the truth we were wanting to share with them. We knew God had the right people out there who needed what we had and we desperately needed the money they had for the book. We knew God would prepare the way before us as He promised in *Colporteur Ministry*, p. 22, "Angels of heaven will accompany you, preparing the way." Also, the promise in *Colporteur Ministry*, p. 124, "They contain the very message the people must have, the special light God had given His people. The angels of God would prepare the way for these books in the hearts of the people."

God knew we needed to make a sale to be able to make it home or we'd have to spend the night in our little car. We knew we were fighting Satan, head on, who didn't want these truth-filled books to get to the souls he had in his snare. We were in a real battle, fighting as real soldiers in war to rescue these precious souls for Jesus!

We kept praying and claiming God's promise in Phil. 4:19, "But my God shall supply all your need according to His riches in glory by Christ Jesus." We, also, repeated the promise in Phil. 4:13, "I can do all things through Christ which strengtheneth me." We repeated the promise in Ps. 34:6–9, "This poor man cried, and the Lord heard him, and saved him out of all his troubles. The angel of the Lord encampeth round about them that fear him, and delivereth them. O taste and see that the Lord is good: blessed is the man that trusteth in him. O fear the Lord, ye his saints: for there is no want to them that fear Him." We, also, claimed Ps. 91:11, "For he shall give his angels charge over thee, to keep thee in all thy ways." We knew we needed the protection and care of the angels as it was getting late and David wouldn't be able to canvass after dark, because people would be fearful of someone knocking on their door at night, and could maybe call the police.

David began to become discouraged and began to murmur and complain and said, "God isn't going to sell anything for me! I'm just not a good salesman!" I said to him, "David, don't talk like that! That doesn't please the Lord! You have to have faith in what you pray for and show faith in God's promises we just claimed! Remember, without faith it is impossible to please Him! Then I quoted the promise to him in Heb. 11: 6, 'But without faith it is impossible to please him: for he that cometh to God must believe that he is, and that he is a rewarder of them that diligently seek him.' God has the right person out there and at the right time God will bring you two together. God will be with you and direct you and protect you and help you and hold you up! You just have to persevere like a strong soldier for Christ and His cause and don't give in to the devil trying to discourage you and stop you! Jesus is stronger than Satan!"

I knew my husband was hot out there walking in the heat, and hungry and making no sales.

I thought of how Elijah in 1 Kings 18 & 19 became discouraged but the Lord came to him and fed him and spoke to him in a still small voice. I thought of what Sister White wrote in *The Ministry of Healing*, p. 481, "In every difficulty He has His way prepared to bring relief… Our heavenly Father has a thousand ways to provide for us of which we know nothing. Those who accept the one principle of making the service of God supreme, will find perplexities vanish and a plain path before their feet." I took one of *The Ministry of Healing* books and read that on pp. 481–482 and prayed for my husband out there tired from fighting the mean dogs and people and under pressure to make a sale to meet our needs. I asked God to please forgive us of our sins, so our prayers will be answered and I thanked Him for all His many blessings He had given us in the past and knew He wouldn't fail us in our time of need now.

When he came back to the car, it was late and dark, and he had made only a little sale, but not near enough for gas money to make it home. We bought a little food to eat and thanked God for supplying us with something to eat. Then, we found a quiet place to park the car and tried to settle down to sleep in our little car. We prayed for God's protection over us and prayed for His power to help us make a sale tomorrow for gas money to make it home.

The next morning, after a miserable night spent in the car, we had our worship and presented our predicament to the Lord, again reminding Him of our need for gas and food money. We thanked Him for protecting us during the night in the big wicked city.

Then, David started out again canvassing and made very little from donations. Not near enough for food and gas money. So he kept canvassing.

He couldn't find too many people home in the daytime. They were either at work, or school, or out shopping, or not answering their doors. It just seemed the devil was on his trail. We both still kept praying. We both felt miserable from trying to sleep all crunched up in our little car through the long hot buggy summer night. I read my Bible and prayed that God would lead David to the Divine appointments He had for him that day. And poor David kept walking, walking door to door not selling hardly anything. The day wore on and the evening was coming on again, and we still hadn't made enough money for gas and food. We both were hot and tired, but we kept praying and asking God for help and we knew God would work all things out for the good, as Rom. 8:28 promises. Only God knew why we hadn't sold enough to meet our needs yet. In 1 Thess. 5:18 it says, "In everything give thanks: for this is the will of God in Christ Jesus concerning you."

It was now beginning to get darker and where I was parked in the car, I could look up a couple of blocks or less, and see the town lights come on. I saw David, with his canvassing case of books, and he was walking on the sidewalk through downtown and he crossed the street and headed toward me in the car. There was a tall man walking beside him on David's right side. The man was head and shoulders taller than David and the man was wearing an all-white tennis outfit. They were both walking side by side and headed toward the car and got closer and closer. I thought, "Oh! No! Who is David bringing with him to the car right now when my hair is a mess and I'm so hot and tired from trying to sleep all night in this car?!

Then I noticed they both turned together and crossed the street to the other side of the business street and passed the bar and the fellow with him stayed right at his right side and in perfect step with David. He walked like he was David's bodyguard or something. Then they disappeared out of my sight, as they passed through a group of teenagers standing outside the bar.

It was dark and late when David finally returned to the car and had made enough money for gas to get us back home and food money so we could eat. We praised and thanked the good Lord for what He had done for meeting our needs and the needs of the people David had met these last two days. He had given away a lot of books and pamphlets and sold books, too. God is so good! We both were so happy and so grateful for what all David and the Lord did in getting this beautiful message out to God's other sheep, not of this fold yet, as, John 10:10 & 16 says.

Then, on our drive home I said to David, "Who was that fellow with you, that you were out canvassing with?"

He said, "I didn't have anyone with me." I said, "But I saw you with your case, coming toward the car, with a real tall fellow dressed in all white like a tennis outfit and walking on your right side and keeping right in step with you, and when you turned and walked across the street past the bar he stayed right at your side."

David said, "Yes, that was me and I was walking up there by the bar and when I crossed the street in front of the bar there were a lot of teenagers all hanging around outside the bar all around the sidewalk that I was on. I thought, as I approached them there on the sidewalk in the dark, that they might think I was a salesman carrying my case with a lot of money on me, and might attack me for my money. So, I just prayed and kept walking toward them and they all just parted and let me go by with no problem! But I didn't have anyone with me."

I said, "David, that had to have been your guardian angel walking with you that I saw. The Lord let me see your guardian angel and those teenage kids in front of the bar all hanging around on the sidewalk must have seen him, too, and they parted and let you go by with no problem!"

We both prayed and thanked the good Lord for His loving and protective care, and also for the wonderful and joyful experience this eventful experience we had just gone through turned out to be for us! Thank you, Jesus!

What testing and trying experiences a colporteur can have as he walks and works for God in trying to get the truth-filled books to the people in need of the

Saviour, Jesus, and how the devil tries to stop the truth from getting to these precious souls out there needing help! We're in a real battle like real soldiers fighting for souls for Jesus! But what a privilege and honor it is to be in companionship with angels and the Holy Spirit as we do God's colporteur work!

Read in *Testimonies for the Church,* vol. 5, pp. 132–137, the chapter entitled, "Laborers for God." Also, read in *Colporteur Ministry*, pp. 4, 32, 38, 88, 110. On page 110 it says, "In working for perishing souls you have the companionship of angels." In *Colporteur Ministry*, p. 110, Sister White says, "Those who labor for the good of others are working in union with the heavenly angels. They have their constant companionship, their unceasing ministry. Angels of light and power are ever near to protect, to comfort, to heal, to instruct, to inspire. The highest education, the truest culture, and the most exalted service possible to human beings in this world are theirs."

We each have a guardian angel that is always with us. Someday if we remain faithful we'll get to meet our guardian angel. Read *Last Day Events*, pp. 298–299, by E. G. White.

Elder Robert Pierson, one of our late General Conference Presidents, he tells of a story of a colporteur named, Jens Horland, who relates his difficult task in crossing over a dangerous mountain range to be able to canvass the people on the other side. He tells how he had to remove his shoes, because the path was so steep, then finally his socks, so he could get a better grip on the treacherous path that clung to the side of the mountain. Seeing how dangerous this journey was getting to be, he prayed and asked God to please send His angel to help him be safe. When he reached the valley safely, he canvassed the first place he came to where an elderly couple lived. The husband asked him, "Where is your companion?" The Literature Evangelist replied, "I have no companion. I'm all by myself." The old man answered, "There was someone with you. My wife and I saw someone helping you down that steep mountain." Then the colporteur remembered his prayer to God to send His angel to help him and of the promise in God's Word in Ps. 34:7, "The angel of the Lord encampeth round about them that fear Him, and delivereth them."

Two songs make me think of the kind of work the colporteur is doing for the Lord, "Throw Out the Lifeline" and "Rescue the Perishing."

With the coming of the Lord so near, may we each be about our Father's business. Luke 2:49, "And he said unto them, How is it that ye sought me? Wist ye not that I must be about my Father's business?"

Colporteur Ministry, p. 91, Sister White writes, "… Sometimes you will find it very trying to do work of this kind… We may enjoy the companionship of the heavenly angels. We may not discern their forms, but by faith we may know that they are with us." Read the Chapter 17, "Accompanied by Angels," in *Colporteur Ministry*. Also, read Chapter 3, "A Call for Colporteur Evangelists." Sister White says on p. 25, "From the light given me I know that where there is one canvasser in the field, there should be one hundred."

Is God calling you to be a Literature Evangelist? Purchase a *Colporteur Ministry* book and read over it and pray and fast over it and let the Lord impress you what He wants you to do. Claim God's promises found in: Ps. 32:8; Ps. 37:3-7; Prov. 3:5-8; James 1:5,6; Phil. 4:13, 19; Rom. 8:28; John 15:16.

LED BY GOD'S PROVIDENTIAL GUIDANCE!

This experience happened years ago when we drove a 1994 Ford Escort:

David had taken off in our old 1994 Ford Escort car that had 238,000 miles on it. He was all excited about being able to attend his 50th year Alumni at Indiana Academy. But about 70 miles from home the car just stopped running and he pulled over to the side of the highway. He checked over the car and couldn't seem to see any problem. He prayed and asked God to please help him with his problem. He thought maybe it might just be the fuel filter plugged up. He had just filled up with gas a couple of miles back. He didn't have much money on him, except enough gas money to get him to his Alumni in Indiana and then back home. We hadn't had enough money to allow for any car trouble expenses. He decided to use some of his gas money to buy a fuel filter.

A real nice highway patrolman had stopped to give him a ride clear into town, when he saw his parked car at the side of the highway, and David walking on the highway in the heat of the day. David had taken a lot of *The Great Controversy* books with him to pass out as he traveled along, so he stuck one in his back pocket, as he began the walk into town to buy a fuel filter. David said a prayer that he'd get this *The Great Controversy* book into the right hands. When the cop stopped and picked David up they talked about world events and David gave him *The Great Controversy* book. The cop was really thankful and happy to get ahold of a book like *The Great Controversy*. David thanked him for the ride, and bought his part and started on his long hot journey back to his car running and walking, always praying the right person would stop and give him a ride. A truck driver this time stopped and gave him a ride and they talked about world conditions and when David got out where his car was parked he thanked the man for the ride and got a *The Great Controversy* book out of the car and gave it to the man. The truck driver was so thrilled to get this *The Great Controversy* book and thanked David for giving it to him!

David soon found out that the trouble with the car wasn't the fuel filter. He checked over other things and just couldn't figure out what had happened to make the car just stop and not start up again. Many people had stopped to see if they could help David and he thanked them and gave them a *The Great Controversy* book. It was beginning to get late in the evening now. When he saw he couldn't get the car started and it was getting darker and darker, he decided to call me to drive our 1989 pickup Chevy truck to pull him home. All I had in the truck was just enough gas, hopefully to get where he was, and no money to buy any gas, because he had taken what little money we had with him for gas money to get to his Alumni and money for gas to get back home. He said he'd buy gas for the truck when I got there. The gas gauge on our old truck didn't work. I had to drive by faith that I had enough gas to get there in the dark. I can't see well in the dark either to be driving at night. David told me to round up the old chain to be able to pull the car home and to get a flashlight. He told me approximately where he was stranded on the highway and that he'd be watching for me to wave me down. We knew we had no money to pay for a tow truck to pull us 70 miles back home and our insurance wouldn't cover the cost either. This was the only way we could get our car home. We both prayed together on the phone. I was a nervous wreck getting things rounded up and heading out in the dark and can't see good and not knowing if I had enough gas in the truck to get 70 miles and the gas gauge doesn't work and there were other things wrong on this old 1989 pickup truck, too. Like the back brakes didn't work; just the front brakes worked. I knew, too, I was going to have to pull the car in the dark 70 miles with David steering the car and me driving the truck and using only a 5-foot old rusty chain! How I prayed for help as I drove nervously along in the dark, hoping I could find where David was stranded by the highway. I claimed the promise in Ps. 56:3, "What time I am afraid, I will trust in Thee." I knew God would help us!

David continued to pass out *The Great Controversy* books while waiting for me to come and find him and people kept stopping to help him.

It was real late and dark when I finally located him and the car. We both prayed for God's help and safety as we got the chain hooked up in the dark to the truck and the car. We got the car turned around and headed for home and stopped and got gas in the truck. We took off again and prayed for help and safety and that no cop would stop us. I sure did pray as I drove the truck pulling my precious husband in the car behind me, with just a 5-foot old rusty chair between us.

We had to rattle over a railroad crossing track and when we did, the chain came loose and fell off his car and it came to a stop right on the railroad tracks! I hurried and turned the truck around and went back to where the car was stranded on the railroad tracks! We frantically prayed that no train would come while we were trying to hurry in the dark with a dim flashlight to get the chain hooked up again to the car! We prayed earnestly that the chain would hold on while we had to go 70 miles through towns and stop lights and traffic and that I could see okay with all the bright headlights in my eyes and that God would help David steer the car safely behind me, as we were driving around 40–50 miles per hour up and down hills and other train tracks to bounce over.

When the good Lord finally got us safely home and we had pulled safely into our driveway and parked, the chain just dropped off on its own!! How we prayed and thanked the good Lord for holding that chain on for us, so we could get safely home with no problems! What a terrible and terrifying experience that was! But God is developing our faith and trust in Him through these trying experiences He's allowing us to go through, so during the crisis ahead of us with the Sunday Law, when we can't buy or sell, because we'll keep God's true seventh day Sabbath and not go along with man's Sunday sabbath, we will have to depend on God to care for all our needs and see us through all our trials then. Have faith in God!

Before we went to bed that night David said, "In the morning we'll do a compression check on the car and see how the cylinders are."

During the night David had a dream. He dreamed he wouldn't be able to check the fourth cylinder on the car.

The next morning, he told me what he had dreamed. He said, "Let's get busy and do the compression check and see if what I dreamed is right."

So, we proceeded to check out the first cylinder and then the second cylinder. They weren't checking out too good. While checking the third cylinder, the starter motor went out and quit working. So, we couldn't check the fourth cylinder, just like the dream had said! We had been noticing for some time that the car had been losing its power and we had thought maybe it was starving for gas. We knew something wasn't right about the car, but no money to have it checked out and fixed. We decided to park the car and use it for parts and asked the Lord to please help us find another 1994 Ford Escort to match parts with the one we just junked out. We knew a junk car mechanic but he didn't have any 1994 Ford Escort for sale.

We kept praying and looking and watching the papers for a reasonably priced Ford Escort 1994 to match parts. We knew a gas saver car like this would be expensive, with gas prices high. We had no money saved to buy a car with and we knew we'd have to find someone who'd take payments.

We kept praying and looking and several months went by and we went back to our mechanic friend at the junk yard and asked if he could fix us up a junk car reasonably, and make payments? He said his wife had a car she wasn't driving anymore because there was a lot wrong with it and she had bought her another car. He said he could fix up her old car and sell it to us. So, we agreed. He said it would take him some time to get it in shape to sell and not to stop by for a while. So, we waited a month and checked back and he hadn't been able to work on it, yet. We waited another month and he still hadn't been able to fix it. When we checked back the third time he said his wife had sold it for twice the amount we were going to pay for it and it hadn't even been repaired yet! He felt bad about what happened, but it was his wife's car and she knew nothing about what we had decided about her husband selling her car to us, when he got a chance to repair it for us. We told him we understood and it was okay. So, we kept praying and asking God to please find us another 1994 Ford Escort we could drive and then use our junked out 1994 Ford Escort for parts. Time went on and nothing showed up. So, we kept praying and asking God to guide and direct.

We were in a bind, needing money, so David had gone out canvassing that day in a little town not too far from home. He happened to run across a mechanic in that little town where in God's providential guiding, God led him to this mechanic who had a 1994 Ford Escort parked in his yard, along with other cars. David explained to him our predicament and he said he was in the process of fixing it up, but it would be awhile before he got it ready. He quoted a price and David got his telephone number and said he'd call back and see how he was doing on the car. The man didn't want to buy any of the books David had for sale, but he handed David a $10 bill. He was a very well-to-do man. David thanked him for his help. David told him he'd be back, that he'd like to buy the car when the man got it ready.

After several months the car was ready and David drove it and it checked out okay. The man let us make payments on it. Praise God! I left a *National Sunday Law* book on his front porch, since he hadn't wanted to buy any books, but had been so kind to give us $10. He was an answer to our prayers for help in our time of need. So, I wanted to leave him a book to help him find the truth and be saved.

We drove that car for a long time and was so thankful for a gas saver car and that it matched parts with our car we had to junk out. We were so thankful God helped us get it paid off and free of debt. God is always working behind the scenes to answer our prayers for help, when we can't even see how He will do it. I love the promise of God found in *The Ministry of Healing*, p. 481, where Sister White says, "Our heavenly Father has a thousand ways to provide for us of which we know nothing. Those who accept the one principle of making the service of God supreme, will find perplexities vanish and a plain path before their feet." Read Rom. 8:28 and 2 Cor. 12:9, 10.

In *The Great Controversy*, p. 623, Sister White says, "God's providence is the school in which we are to learn the meekness and lowliness of Jesus. The Lord is ever setting before us, not the way we would choose, which seems easier and pleasanter to us, but the true aims of life. It rests with us to co-operate with the agencies which heaven employs in the work and conforming our characters to the divine model. None can neglect or defer this work but at the most fearful peril to their souls."

As we look back now on these things, we can see how God was testing our faith and trust in Him and His power to see us through our trying times, helping our faith and trust in Him to grow. Heb. 11:6 says, "But without faith it is impossible to please Him…"

We can see how we were being led by God's providential guidance. God didn't let us get that one car that belonged to the junk yard man's wife, because it wouldn't have matched parts with our 1994 Ford Escort that we had to junk out. We can look back, too, and see how God impressed David to canvass that little town where God knew that 1994 Ford Escort was there for sale and how in our time of need God impressed the man to give us $10. Always God's providential leading is working for our good, as we let the Lord plan for us. In *The Ministry of Healing*, p. 479, Sister White tells us, "He (Christ) accepted God's plans for Him, and day by day the Father unfolded His plans. So should we depend upon God, that our lives may be the simple outworking of His will. As we commit our ways to Him, He will direct our steps." Prov. 3:5, 6 says, "Trust in the Lord with all thine heart: and lean not unto thine own understanding. In all thy ways acknowledge Him, and He shall direct thy paths."

We know, too, that God had plans for all those *The Great Controversy* books to get passed out to the right people, that day when God allowed David to get stranded on the highway, on his way to his 50th Alumni. Why David wasn't able to make it to the Alumni is one of those questions we'll have to ask God when we get to heaven, when He'll make all things plain to us then.

Testimonies for the Church, vol. 9, p. 286, Sister White makes this comment, "All that has perplexed us in the providences of God will in the world to come be made plain. The things hard to be understood will then find explanation. The mysteries of grace will unfold before us. Where our finite minds discovered only confusion and broken promises, we shall see the most perfect and beautiful harmony. We shall know that infinite love ordered the experiences that seemed most trying. As we realize the tender care of Him who makes all things work together for our good, we shall rejoice with joy unspeakable and full of glory."

When we were going through this experience of needing a car, David's sister, Hilma, and her husband, Tom, came down from Chicago for a few days visit. Tom isn't a Seventh-day Adventist and every worship time we'd all meet together for morning and evening worship and David and I would share our experiences of how God had cared for us and our needs and He'd supply in answer to our many prayer requests for help and how God would work miracles a lot of times to answer our prayers. We shared how our car had broken down and we had been praying for an exact kind of car to match parts with our old 1994 Ford Escort that was junked out. We told Tom and Hilma that we knew God could do the impossible like Luke 1:37 promises, "For with God nothing shall be impossible" and we trusted God to supply us with the exact car we needed, at a reasonable price we could afford, since our income was so low, and that we could make payments. Tom is a rather skeptic person and I don't think he really believes there's a God. But he listened to our experiences we shared, how God was with us to help us in all our trials and troubles and supplied all our needs in answer to our earnest prayers.

When it came time for them to go back home to Chicago and they were getting in their van to leave, Tom said to me, "Well, I'm really curious to see how God is going to answer this prayer of yours for the car you need to match parts with your car that broke down and one you can afford and be able to make payments on."

When the time finally came, we were so happy to be able to share this car experience with Tom, how God answered our prayers for just the car we needed to match parts and one we could afford and make payments on and we're free of debt of a car. Praise the Lord! God is always seeing us through our trials and troubles in His own way and time, as we trust in the Lord to supply all our needs as Phil. 4:19 promises. We give God all the praise and glory and thank Him for hearing and answering our prayers for help! We had also been able to use the new tires off our old junk car, 1994 Ford Escort, and we used old parts off of it, too, that saved us a lot of money!

Friends, are you finding yourself in perplexing situations? Are worries weighing you down? Are you going through trials and troubles right now that you seem you just can't handle and they're overwhelming you and you don't know what the future holds for you?

Turn your eyes upon Jesus and turn your life over to Jesus and let Him handle your life's perplexities and worries and trials and troubles and let Him plan for you! Take time with Jesus through prayer and Bible Study and get acquainted with Jesus and His love for you and His will for you. (Read Ps. 121 and John 3:16 and 1 Peter 5:7 and Ps. 34 and Ps. 37 and Prov. 3 and Ps. 50:15 and Ps. 55:22. Read books by Sister White, like *The Desire of Ages*, *Steps to Christ*, etc. I like this quote of Sister White in the book, *Steps to Christ for a Sanctified Life*, p. 54 & 55 & 57, " Then do not fear to trust Him…even though you do not see the immediate answer to your prayers. Rely upon His sure promise, 'Ask, and it shall be given you.' If we take counsel with our doubts and fears, or try to solve everything that we cannot see clearly, before we have faith, perplexities will only increase and deepen… We must pray always if we would grow in faith and experience. 'In everything by prayer and supplication with thanksgiving let your requests be made known unto God.' Phil. 4:6… There is necessity for diligence in prayer; let nothing hinder you. Make every effort to keep open the communion between Jesus and your own soul… We should pray in the family circle, and above all we must not neglect secret prayer, for this is the life of the soul. It is impossible for the soul to flourish while prayer is neglected. Those whose hearts are open to receive the support and blessing of God will walk in a holier atmosphere than that of earth and will have constant communion with heaven… Let the soul be drawn out and upward, that God may grant us a breath of the heavenly atmosphere. We may keep so near to God that in every unexpected trial our thoughts will turn to Him as naturally as the flower turns to the sun. Keep your wants, your joys, your sorrows, your cares, and your fears before God. You cannot burden Him; you cannot weary Him. He who numbers the hairs of your head is not indifferent to the wants of His children. 'The Lord is very pitiful, and of tender mercy.' James 5:11. His heart of love is touched by our sorrows and even by our utterances of them. Take to Him everything that perplexes the mind. Nothing is too great for Him to bear, for He holds up worlds. He rules over all the affairs of the universe. Nothing that in any way concerns our peace is too small for Him to notice. There is no chapter in our experience too dark for Him to read; there is no perplexity too difficult for Him to unravel. No calamity can befall the least of His children, no anxiety harass the soul, no joy cheer, no sincere prayer escapes the lips, of which our heavenly Father is unobservant, or in which He takes no immediate interest. 'He healeth the broken in heart, and bindeth up their wounds.' Ps. 147:3. The relations between God and each soul are as distinct and full as though there were not another soul upon the earth to share His watch care, not another soul for whom He gave His beloved Son… We should keep in our thoughts every blessing we receive from God, and when we realize His great love we should be willing to trust everything to the hand that was nailed to the cross for us."

I just hope and pray these experiences God has put us through and brought us safely out of, that I'm sharing with you, will help you and strengthen your faith in God to trust your future in His loving care! Jesus loves you! Like the dream I had said, "God can do anything!" Mark 10:27; Luke 1:37; Phil. 4:13.

LOST IN THE WOODS

This experience happened many years ago, when we made a visit to Grandma's place in Arkansas:

It was a beautiful fall day and we had Jonathan living at home with us. He had moved home from the care center he had been staying at. Jonathan said he'd like to take a trip to Arkansas. We hadn't been there for a long time, so we thought we'd like to take a little break from all our hard work and run down there for a few days' vacation, which we all needed. So we packed our things and headed out. It was about 400 miles down there, so when we arrived in the early hours of the morning, we all were exhausted, and went right to bed. It was a cold night. The next morning David said he wanted to go and plant a few persimmon seeds and paw-paw seeds down by the creek in the forest. We prayed before he left that God would protect him and watch over him down in the big forest. I knew he'd be gone a long time, so I finished up my work and laid down to rest and read awhile. It was getting dark outside.

Many hours later David came home and told me he had gotten lost in the deep forest while planting seeds. He had gotten all turned around and lost all sense of direction while he was following the creek and planting the seeds. Then, the creek forked several times and when he was through planting it was late and he started back home, but couldn't decide which way was home. All he knew, it was getting late, and he couldn't find his way out of this big forest. He tried to follow the creek back out to find home, but it kept coming to forks so many times, and got him all turned around and lost even more. He'd go one way and get deeper in the woods. He'd try another way and nothing looked familiar that way, so he'd try another direction, and he was becoming desperate to know which way to turn or what to do! It was getting later and darker and cold and all he had was a light jacket and a flashlight, but no water or food with him. He was thirsty and tired and he knelt down and prayed and asked the Lord to please help him find his way home!

While he was praying he heard a noise and it sounded like a car out on a gravel road, so he headed toward the sound of the car, hurrying and crashing through the woods, hoping to reach the car before it passed him by. When he reached the road the car had already gone past him, they hadn't seen him! Now, what to do? He was on a road, but which direction was home? It was dark and hard to see his way, but he chose to go to the left, the way the car had gone. Nothing looked familiar, so he headed the other direction on the road. He prayed again and asked God to please help him out of his distress. He prayed and asked God to please help someone to come in a car and find him and help him home. It was cold and dark and as he walked along the road trying to find his way in the dark, he remembered what people had told him about the bears and the snakes in the woods. Then, he heard a sound coming up behind him! It was a car, the same car that had passed him by before, and he thought they hadn't seen him. It was an elderly couple on their way to church. When David had flagged them down, he explained to them he had been planting seeds in the forest by the creek and had gotten all turned around and didn't know which way was home.

He told them he was from Kansas and wasn't familiar with the forest. They asked him where home was, that he was trying to find, and they would drive him back to his home. When David mentioned where home was, they told him he was headed in the wrong direction. They told him there's not too many homes out here to ask directions in this deep forest! They drove him to his driveway and David wanted to give them a book, but they refused. David thanked them for their help and kindness and told them they were an answer to his prayers. We certainly prayed and thanked the good Lord for protecting him and getting him safely home in answer to his prayers for help. We both wondered if maybe God had sent angels to help him get safely home, or had sent someone to be right there at the right time to help him in his time of trouble he was going through, trying to find his way back home through the deep forest and at night, in answer to his prayers for help.

Sometimes in life people can get lost and off the straight and narrow path and find it hard to get back on track and find their way back to Jesus and back on the path to heaven. There's so many things out there to distract us away from Jesus and His ideal for us. And Satan does have a thousand traps just waiting for us to fall into. Then, when we pray and ask God for His help and guidance, He's always right there to hear our cries for help and to direct our steps and bring us back into His arms of love and put our feet back on the path leading to heaven. But we must search for Him with all our heart like Jer. 29:11 says, and like David searched and prayed with all his heart to God for help in finding his way back home.

David said to me, "I'm going to have to know how to find my way in the woods, so when we have to flee for our lives, in the Great Time of Trouble, I won't get lost. I'll have to have me a compass." I said, "Yes, it's good to know how to follow a compass. But we'll have to depend on God to be our compass and guide then, because He has promised to be with us as Ps. 46 & Ps. 34 & Ps. 91 promises. It would be well to be memorizing these promises now, so we can claim them then. We need not be fearful and worry when this time comes, because we've learned to lean on Jesus and put our faith and trust in Him and His promises to guide and direct us through our trials and troubles ahead of us, when we'll be seeking the Lord for direction in our lives, as to where to go and when and how. God will hear our cries for help and will direct our paths as Ps. 32:8 promises. And when our time comes to flee for our life into desolate and solitary places during the Great Time of Trouble, God will send angels to guide and direct us and protect us and be our shelter and provide us our bread and water as Isa. 33:15, 16 promises. Read E. G. White's book *Maranatha*, pp. 270–275, about angelic protection in the time of trouble. We need to be learning NOW to have faith and trust in His promises and prove Him and His word, so we'll have faith and trust, that it will take then, to rely on Him to care for us and all our needs as Phil. 4:19 promises and claim Ps. 56:3, "What time I am afraid, I will trust in Thee."

God will, if we're faithful and true to Him, hear our prayers for help now and in the early Time of Trouble and in the Great Time of Trouble and when the seven last plagues are falling, He'll hear our cries and call for help then. God, too, can use us, right now, if we'll let Him, to be an answer to someone's cry for help that is lost and perishing out there in the world of sin. Someone who has strayed from God's fold and is lost and wondering which way to turn for help to be able to come back to Jesus and His truth and get back on the right path that leads to God's heavenly home. God wants to use our hands and feet and voice and money and time and talents to be able to save these precious and lost and dying souls out there in sin, not knowing what to do to be saved from Satan and all his snares. I think of that song, "Rescue the Perishing, Care for the Dying."

Let's just pray we can stay in tune with Jesus, so He can direct our paths and use us to be soul winners for Him and let the Holy Spirit guide and direct our steps, so we'll be in the right place, at the right time, doing the right thing, so God can use us to be a help and a blessing to those God lets cross our path. Like God directed Philip to go to Gaza, where the Ethiopian eunuch was searching the scriptures about Jesus, the Lamb of God, but he didn't understand what he was reading. God used Philip to explain the truth of the Scriptures and to baptize the Ethiopian eunuch. Then, the Spirit of the Lord caught Philip away to other places to witness and work for Him. (Acts 8:26–40)

Jesus is soon to come and we haven't much time to get ready and help our loved ones and others God directs us to help, to be ready to meet Jesus.

It's like a recent dream I had that said, "We haven't much time to warn our loved ones."

Our time here is short and we must be about our Father's business and put our priorities straight and earnestly pray for victories in our own lives, through the power of the Holy Spirit and receive the latter rain. Things are closing up fast, and the last movements will be rapid ones! Sister White says in *Last Day Events*, pp. 38 & 39 & 42, "The angels of God in their messages to men represent time as very short… Christ is waiting with longing desire for the manifestation of Himself in His church. When the character of Christ shall be perfectly reproduced in His people, then He will come to claim them as His own… May the Lord give no rest, day nor night, to those who are now careless and indolent in the cause and work of God. The end is near. This is that which Jesus would have us keep ever before us—the shortness of time."

Soon the Sunday Law will be upon us! What are you going to do then? It depends on what you're doing right now, what you will do then. We need to be examining ourselves now. The judgment hour is going on right now. How will you and I stand? 2 Cor. 13:5; Rev. 14:6–12—the three angel's messages.

Recently, I heard that the pope contacted the President Obama and said he wanted a National Sunday Law passed! God's People! Wake Up!!

Sister White says in *Last Day Events*, p. 126, "Those who are making an effort to change the Constitution and secure a law enforcing Sunday observance little realize what will be the results. A crisis is just upon us!" Friends, let us not be lost in the maze!

"Keep your wants, your joys, your sorrows, your cares, and your fears before God..."

Steps to Christ for a Sanctified Life, p. 55

THE MYSTERIOUS CLOUDS!

One day I was riding my bicycle around our circle driveway and I looked up in the sky and I saw that the clouds had formed into the perfect form of three angels with their wings spread out like they were flying in the midst of heaven. (Rev. 14:6–12) There was the cloud form of another fourth angel coming some distance flying behind the other three angels. I hurried and called my husband, David, out to see this strange phenomenon. He, too, was so amazed at how much these cloud formations looked so much like three angels flying in heaven right over our place and the fourth angel coming from behind the other three angels. We know we as Seventh-day Adventists are to give the final warning message to a perishing world, through the three angels' messages.

Sister White in her book, *Last Day Events*, pp. 45 & 46 says, "The Lord has made us the depositaries of His law; He has committed to us sacred and eternal truth, which is to be given to others in faithful warnings, reproofs, and encouragement…. Seventh-day Adventists have been chosen by God as a peculiar people, separate from the world. By the great cleaver of truth He has cut them out from the quarry of the world and brought them into connection with Himself. He has made them His representatives and has called them to be ambassadors for Him in the last work of salvation. The greatest wealth of truth ever entrusted to mortals, the most solemn and fearful warnings ever sent by God to man, have been committed to them to be given to the world… In a special sense Seventh-day Adventists have been set in the world as watchmen and light bearers. To them has been entrusted the last warning for a perishing world. On them is shining wonderful light from the Word of God. They have been given a work of the most solemn import—the proclamation of the first, second, and third angels' messages. There is no other work of so great importance. They are to allow nothing else to absorb their attention."

Another experience I had with a strange cloud formation phenomenon was not long after I saw the cloud formation of the angels flying in heaven. I had dreamed I saw snow on the tree branches. We hadn't had our first snow yet. That morning we had our first snow with only a little snow on things. The weathermen that day were forecasting a freeze with 3–5 inches of snow or more. I had also dreamed that night the word, "Freeze." The next morning we hadn't gotten any snow, just a flurry, but a terrible freeze down to 2 degrees! We were having 55 mile per hour winds, too, and it was so cold! As it warmed up, David decided to go to town and get some groceries, in case we got some really bad weather and we got snowed in or a freezing rain. While he was gone I went out to do my running around our circle driveway. David and I and Jonathan had been praying for God's protection over us during these winter forecasts. While I was running I saw over my head up in the clear blue sky over our place a mysterious and strange looking white cloud formation that looked like the pillar of cloud over the Children of Israel as they journeyed in the wilderness and God sent a pillar of cloud over them by day and a pillar of fire over them at night to protect them from the hot sun in the daytime and the cold nights He placed a pillar of fire over them to keep them warm. I thanked God for His sign in the pillar of cloud that he'd protect us from the storms passing by us and see us through whatever may come upon us and not to fear but trust in Him to take care of us in the days ahead of us! I thought of Isa. 4:5,6, "And the Lord will create upon every dwelling place of mount Zion, and upon her assemblies, a cloud and smoke by day, and the shining of a flaming fire by night: for upon all the glory shall be a defense. And there shall be a tabernacle for a shadow in the daytime from the heat, and for a place of refuge, and for a covert from storm and from rain."

In *A Dictionary of the Holy Bible*, p. 96, they give a definition of, "cloud," "The pillar of cloud, the miraculous token of the divine presence and care, Num. 12:5, 6, which guided the Israelites in the desert; it was a means of protection and perhaps of shade by day, and gave them light by night. Exod. 13:21, 22. By it God directed their movements. Num. 9:15–23 & Deut. 1:33." (Read Neh. 9:19–21.)

When David came home from town with our groceries, I told him of the pillar of cloud formation over "the ARK," our place. I said, "God is wanting us to know He's looking out for us like He cared for the Children of Israel, and we have nothing to fear."

David then told me what he had heard in town while shopping. A lady told him about a 6-foot snow New York had gotten and how peoples' roofs were caving in from the weight of the snow. What a terrible disaster!

We prayed for our Seventh-day Adventist people there and the others who were suffering from all this calamity!

We praised and thanked the good Lord for looking after us!

"Seventh-day Adventists have been chosen by God as a peculiar people, separate from the world."

Last Day Events, p. 454

A TEST OF FAITH!

This is the continued story of what the outcome was for our 1992 Honda car that broke down on I-35 Highway and David and I towed it home with our old 1989 Chevy truck, using only a 5-foot old rusty chain and our truck having no back brakes.

The car stayed parked for a long time in our yard, with no money to fix it. We only had our old 1989 Chevy truck to drive and it had no back brakes, and no window on the passenger's side and the old truck refused to start when it got too cold. It needed carburetor work done on it, but no money to fix it either. We had our winter propane to buy and our taxes were due and we needed God to help us with all these financial issues we were facing. So we kept praying for God to please help us out of our financial problems! Only God knew how desperate we were for money—repair the car and truck and keep up with our bills and needing food and gas money. The old truck was a gas hog. The propane tank was emptying fast and the due date for paying our taxes was staring us in the face. How was God going to get us out of this dilemma we were in?! We weren't even sure our car was repairable. We had no idea what was wrong with it. How earnestly we prayed to the good Lord for help to see us through this hard time we were going through! We had been putting our money on building on the "ARK" trying to get things done before the terribly cold winter weather hit and we'd have to stop building outside. We had, also, been out money fixing our water line leak under our house trailer and getting tin skirting up to keep the pipes from freezing and other repairs needed on the place, before the weather kept us from getting these urgent things done. We knew God was testing our faith to trust Him to see us through our predicament. So, as naturally as the flower turns to the sun, we just as naturally turned to God for His help and guidance as to know what we were to do to supply our need for help. We always claim God's promises that He stands behind, like Phil. 4:19 and James 1:5 and Matt. 21:22. We knew God wouldn't fail us!

We decided to ask our junk yard mechanic friend if he could please take a look at our 1992 Honda and see what he thought the problem might be and we'd be glad to pay him for his services, when we got the money. It hadn't been too long back that he had repaired our car when it needed it and we had gotten the $250 bill paid to him for that. He drove out to our place and looked the car over and towed it back to his place and checked the books over and said that it could be possibly twenty-seven different things why it wouldn't start. He had it at his place for over two months. We really needed our gas saver car because our gas hog truck was taking so much gas and we had to drive it to different places. We feared our mechanic friend was going to charge us A LOT of money to be trying to figure out the problem with our car. We kept praying it wouldn't cost us a lot of money to repair and that it was repairable. During this time, his wife had gone down in her back and was in a lot of pain and on pain pills. We had explained to him some natural remedies that could help his wife's problem. We prayed for her. He was having problems of his own, he said, and we prayed for that, too, with him.

Finally, one day he came up our driveway driving our 1992 Honda. We were so happy to see our car was repaired! We asked him what he found the problem to be and he said it was in the key switch. He had gone to another junk yard to get the part to see if that was the problem and it worked! We thanked him and praised the Lord and him for getting our car running! We then asked the fearful question, "What do we owe you?" We were so shocked when he said, "You don't owe me anything!" We offered to pay him and he said, "No." We told him he was an answer to our prayer that we had no idea where we were going to get the money to pay him right away because we had taxes to pay and winter propane to get and money for food and gas. I said to him, "Let's pray." David and I took his hands and held them in our hands and prayed that God would bless him for his kindness shown to us in answer to our prayers in being able to not have to pay him and also, be able to meet all our other expenses! We prayed for his wife to get well and for God to help him with his problems he was having personally, and also, the water problem they were having at their home, too. We thanked him again and gave him a hug and I went into the house and got him a book by Sister White, *Steps to Christ*, which had been put in a book called, *Shelter in the Time of Storm* with true story experiences shared in it and lots of Bible promises.

We talked about the world events and how Jesus is soon to come and the most important thing in life is to give our heart to Jesus and live to please Him and be ready for Jesus' soon coming! David reminded him to be sure and read *The Great Controversy* book he had given him some time back. Again we offered to pay him for his services and he said, "No, you don't owe me anything!"

David drove him home in our car and when David returned home, we just praised the Lord and thanked Him for seeing us through this trial we had just gone through! We were able to have food and gas money and propane tank filled up, by writing a pre-dated check for them to hold till we got our November Social Security check on the 3rd. Now, when we get our December Social Security check we'll be able to pay on our taxes! Praise the Lord from whom all blessings flow! This experience God allowed us to go through has strengthened our faith in God's promises to see us through our trials and troubles now and know He'll not fail us when the real test comes over the Sunday Law crisis, God will see us through that time, too, as we put our faith and trust in Him to help meet our needs then!

Friends, are you allowing Jesus to see you through the trials and troubles you're facing right now?! Are you letting the Lord test your faith and trust in Him, so it will grow and see you through the great issue ahead of each one of us over which day we will keep when the Sunday Law will soon be passed?! Are you getting yourself and your dear family and friends ready for the decisions that will have to be made ahead of us all?! Are we loving and obeying Jesus and His commandments now so we'll be faithful to Him and His true seventh day Sabbath then?! These are life and death decisions we'll each have to face in the near future! How are we each preparing for this final event?! Let's pray God will open our eyes to see the storm coming and prepare our hearts and lives for it!

Sister White writes in *Last Day Events*, p. 38, "For forty years did unbelief, murmuring, and rebellion shut out ancient Israel from the land of Canaan. The same sins have delayed the entrance of modern Israel into the heavenly Canaan. In neither case were the promises of God at fault. It is the unbelief, the worldliness, unconsecration, and strife among the Lord's professed people that have kept us in this world of sin and sorrow so many years."

Again, on p. 127, Sister White has this to say, "As faithful watchmen you should see the sword coming and give the warning, that men and women may not pursue a course through ignorance that they would avoid if they knew the truth."

Again, on p. 64, Sister White tells us, "The storm is coming, the storm that will try every man's faith of what sort it is. Believers must now be firmly rooted in Christ or else they will be led astray by some phase of error… It would be well for us to spend a thoughtful hour each day in contemplation of the life of Christ… Unless we become vitally connected with God, we can never resist the unhallowed effects of self-love, self-indulgence, and temptation to sin."

On p. 85, Sister White gives this advice, "Those who are watching and waiting for the appearing of Christ in the clouds of heaven will not be mingling with the world in pleasure societies and gatherings merely for their own amusement."

On p. 80–82, Sister White speaks and says, "I wish to tell you that soon there will be no work done in ministerial lines but medical missionary work… The health reform, I was shown, is a part of the third angel's message and is just as closely connected with it as are the arm and hand with the human body… True temperance teaches us to dispense entirely with everything hurtful and to use judiciously that which is healthful… pure air, sunlight, abstemiousness, rest, exercise, proper diet, the use of water, trust in divine power—these are the true remedies… Whatever injures the health not only lessens physical vigor but tends to weaken the mental and moral powers. Indulgence in any unhealthful practice makes it more difficult for one to discriminate between right and wrong and hence more difficult to resist evil… God is trying to lead us back, step by step, to His original design—that man should subsist upon the natural products of the earth. Among those who are waiting for the coming of the Lord meat eating will eventually be done away; flesh will cease to form a part of their diet. We should ever keep this end in view and endeavor to work steadily toward it… Greater reforms should be seen among the people who claim to be looking for the soon appearing of Christ. Health reform is to do among our people a work which it has not yet done. There are those who ought to be awake to the dangers of meat eating who are still eating the flesh of animals, thus endangering the physical, mental, and spiritual health. Many who are now only half converted on the question of meat eating will go from God's people, to walk no more with them."

Listen to the words of God's prophet, Sister White, when she says in *Last Day Events*, p. 22 & 23, "Gluttony and intemperance lie at the foundation of the great moral depravity in our world. Satan is aware of this and he is constantly tempting men and women to indulge the taste at the expense of health and even life itself. Eating, drinking, and dressing are made the aim of life with the world. Just such a state of things existed before the flood. And this state of dissipation is one of the marked evidences of the soon close of this earth's history… We know that the Lord is coming very soon. The world is fast becoming as it was in the days of Noah. It is given over to selfish indulgence. Eating and drinking are carried to excess. Men are drinking the poisonous liquor that makes them mad… In the days of Noah the overwhelming majority was opposed to the truth, and enamored with a tissue of falsehoods. The land was filled with violence. War, crime, murder was the order of the day. Just so will it be before Christ's second coming… The labor unions are quickly stirred to violence if their demands are not complied with… In every mob wicked angels are at work, rousing men to commit deeds of violence… Very soon the wickedness of the world will have reached its limit and, as in the days of Noah, God will pour out His judgment… The terrible reports we hear of murders and robberies, of railway accidents and deeds of violence, tell the story that the end of all things is at hand. Now, just now, we need to be preparing for the Lord's second coming."

Read what Sister White warns on p. 28, "God has a purpose in permitting these calamities to occur. They are one of His means of calling men and women to their senses… They are among the agencies by which He seeks to arouse men and women to a sense of their danger."

Reading on, we find these words penned by Sister White on pp. 188 & 189, "The convocations of the church, as in camp meetings, the assemblies of the home church, and all occasions where there is personal labor for souls, are God's appointed opportunities for giving the early and latter rain… A revival of true godliness among us is the greatest and most urgent of all our needs. To seek this should be our first work."

Sister White continues her counsel in the book *Last Day Events*, p. 208, "When the storm of persecution really breaks upon us then will the message of the third angel swell to a loud cry, and the whole earth will be lightened with the glory of the Lord… A crisis is right upon us. We must now by the Holy Spirit's power proclaim the great truths for these last days. It will not be long before everyone will have heard the warning and made his decision. Then shall the end come." This is why I'm so urgent to get my book out to the people to warn them! Also, on pp. 211 & 213 we read, "There will be an army of steadfast believers who will stand as firm as a rock through the last test… Soon the last test is to come to all inhabitants of the earth. At that time prompt decisions will be made. Those who have been convicted under the presentation of the Word will range themselves under the bloodstained banner of Prince Emmanuel."

Again, Sister White writes in her book, *Last Day Events*, p. 254, 257, 259, & 266, "The season of distress and anguish before us will require a faith that can endure weariness, delay, and hunger—a faith that will not faint, though severely tried… The time of trouble such as never was is soon to open upon us; and we shall need an experience which we do not now possess, and which many are too indolent to obtain. It is often the case that trouble is greater in anticipation than in reality; but this is not true of the crisis before us. The most vivid presentation cannot reach the magnitude of the ordeal… As Nebuchadnezzar the king of Babylon issued a decree that all who would not bow down and worship this image should be killed, so a proclamation will be made that all who will not reverence the Sunday institution will be punished with imprisonment and death… Let all read carefully the thirteenth chapter of Revelation, for it concerns every human agent, great and small… The time of trouble is about to come upon the people of God. Then it is that the decree will go forth forbidding those who keep the Sabbath of the Lord to buy or sell, and threatening them with punishment, and even death, if they do not observe the first day of the week as the Sabbath…

If the people of God will put their trust in Him and by faith rely upon His power, the devices of Satan will be defeated in our time as signally as in the days of Mordecai… 'And at that time shall Michael stand up, the great Prince which standeth for the children of thy people; and there shall be a time of trouble, such as never was since there was a nation even to that same time: and at that time thy people shall be delivered, every one that shall be found written in the book.' (Dan. 12:1). When this time of trouble comes, every case is decided; there is no longer probation, no longer mercy for the impenitent. The seal of the living God is upon His people. This small remnant, unable to defend themselves in the deadly conflict with the powers of earth that are marshaled by the dragon host, make God their defense. The decree has been passed by the highest earthly authority that they shall worship the beast and receive his mark under pain of persecution and death. May God help His people now, for what can they then do in such a fearful conflict without His assistance…

Could men see with heavenly vision, they would behold companies of angels that excel in strength stationed about those who have kept the word of Christ's patience. With sympathizing tenderness, angels have witnessed their distress and have heard their prayers. They are waiting the word of their Commander to snatch them from their peril... The precious Saviour will send help just when we need it."

In *Early Writings*, p. 72, by E. G. White, we read, "True faith rests on the promises contained in the Word of God, and those only who obey that Word can claim its glorious promises." Read Mark 11:24; John 15:7; John 3:22.

> **"The season of distress and anguish before us will require a faith that can endure weariness, delay, and hunger - a faith that will not faint, though severely tried..."**

Last Day Events, p. 254

THE LOST BILLFOLD

This experience happened some time ago, while Jonathan, our son, was in a care center living. He's living at home with us now. Praise the Lord!

Well, what started out to be a good day, getting to go visit our son, Jonathan, at the care center where he was staying, it ended up being a nightmare to us.

Jonathan was all excited and happy we were coming to see him, and we were all excited and happy to get to see him, too.

We had gotten ready to go and had the car loaded up with some good healthy home cooked food to give Jonathan. When we got into the car, as we always do, we pray first for a safe trip and no accidents or car trouble. David tried to start the car, but nothing happened. We prayed again and asked God to please let the car start. Nothing happened! It was a dead battery! We had been having problems with it, but no money to buy another one right now. We had been putting all our money on building materials to try and get things done on the "ARK" before the cold, and snowy, and windy, winter weather set in and we couldn't work outside anymore.

We put the battery charger on the battery for the rest of the day. I called Jonathan to let him know we were not able to come and see him, because of the bad battery. We both were terribly disappointed! He understood. We had prayer together on the phone. I said, "Maybe tomorrow we'll come."

In the meantime David sat out on our front porch steps and cracked us some walnuts to eat for supper. That evening, the battery had taken a charge, so David ran into town to pick up our mail at the post office. The next day, Daddy went to get his billfold and car keys, but he couldn't find his billfold! He knew he had the billfold on him when we were planning to go see Jonathan. But where was it now?! We prayed and asked God to please help us to find it! We looked the car over and all through the house and the easy chairs David had sat in, but no billfold! We thought maybe when he had gone into town to get the mail yesterday, it might have dropped out of his pocket when he was getting out of the car. So he decided to see if it had been found in town outside the post office. We prayed the car battery would start again and prayed we'd please find Daddy's lost billfold. The Lord answered our prayers for the car to start, but when he checked with the post office lady she said, "No billfold has been found." Daddy thought, maybe someone found it in the parking lot at the post office and kept it, thinking there was money and credit cards in it. But there was no money or credit cards in it. We were so thankful we had no credit cards to worry about being lost. We were so thankful we were free of debt like Sister White says to be in *Counsels on Stewardship*, p. 257 "Deny yourself a thousand things rather than run in debt… Avoid it as you would the smallpox… Pay your debts and then owe no man anything if you live on porridge and bread… Deny your taste, deny the indulgence of appetite, save your pence and pay your debts. When you can stand forth a free man again, owing no man anything, you will have achieved a great victory."

David came home with no billfold being found. So, we prayed again and began searching the house all over again and the car. I kept saying to David, "There has to be a reason why the Lord is allowing this to happen. God is always working for our good as, Rom. 8:28 promises! God must be testing our faith like Matt. 21:22 says, "And all things, whatsoever ye shall ask in payer, believing, ye shall receive!" So we kept praying and looking all over for the lost billfold and claiming Mark 10:27, "And Jesus looking upon them saith, With men it is impossible, but not with God, for with God all things are possible."

Now I had to call Jonathan again and let him know the battery was charged up and doing okay, right now, but Daddy has lost his billfold and we can't drive without his driver's license. Again he was disappointed and so were we, but he understood. Again we prayed together on the phone.

That night I prayed, "Lord, if it's your will please give me a dream showing me what happened to David's billfold. Or, maybe Lord you could please send an angel to put it somewhere where I can see it and find it?! Thank you, Lord, for helping us with our problem!" All through the night we both prayed. We knew if it wasn't found soon, we'd have to call and report David's driver's license was lost.

The next day was October 22, 2013. I said, to David, "This is a special day for us Seventh-day Adventists. Remember, October 22, 1844, the judgment hour began?! Maybe God will help us find your billfold today?!" We prayed and began searching all over the place again, praying the Lord would please put it where we would find it, since I had had no dream where David's billfold was.

We pulled David's bed out to see if it maybe had slipped out of his pocket while he read on his bed and studied his Bible. But all we found under his bed was a piece of paper where I had written the dream down that I had had some time ago. David had been reading the dream in bed and had fallen asleep reading it and it must have fallen down between the wall and the bed and was lost and forgotten about.

This is the dream on the piece of paper found: (Linda's dream): I was explaining to someone that the people in Noah's day didn't believe Noah, God's prophet then, that there would be a flood and they were destroyed. So, today, there's people who don't believe God's prophet He has for us today, Ellen G. White, that gives us warnings to prepare for Christ's soon coming! God had prophets all through the Bible times and so He has His prophet for our time today, too, and we need to heed her writings just as much as the Bible prophets, because she's as much a prophet of God as was Noah and all the other Bible prophets. 2 Chron. 20:20. See where the people ended up in Noah's day by not believing God's prophet sent to warn them—dead and lost! Let this be a warning to us not to reject God's prophet for our day, Ellen G. White, and her writings and warnings to us in our day. Read the chapter, "In the Holy of Holies" in *The Great Controversy*, by E. G. White, especially p. 431, "Men cannot with impunity reject the warning which God in mercy sends them. A message was sent from heaven to the world in Noah's day, and their salvation depended upon the manner in which they treated that message. Because they rejected the warning, the Spirit of God was withdrawn from the sinful race, and they perished in the waters of the flood… But Christ still intercedes in man's behalf, and light will be given to those who seek it."

Also, in *Testimonies for the Church*, vol. 8, p. 298, we read what Sister White, God's prophet for our day, says, "Perilous times are before us. Everyone who has a knowledge of the truth should awake and place himself, body, soul, and spirit under the discipline of God. The enemy is on our track. We must be wide awake, on our guard against him. We must put on the whole armor of God. We must follow the directions given through the Spirit of Prophecy. We must love and obey the truth for this time. This will save us from accepting strong delusions.

God has spoken to us through His word. He has spoken to us through the testimonies to the church and through the books that have helped to make plain our present duty and the position that we should now occupy. The warnings that have been given, line upon line, precept upon precept, should be heeded. If we disregard them, what excuse can we offer?… Christ is waiting to kindle faith and love in the hearts of His people."

When we had read this dream, David said, "Wow! That's really an important dream you had! Maybe that's why I lost my billfold and we had to search diligently for it so we could find this lost and forgotten dream under my bed that God gave you awhile back. Now you can share it with others to help them see how important it is to believe in God's prophets and our prophet for our day, in Sister White. Maybe now God will help us find my lost billfold?!"

I said to David, "You know that dream we just read makes me think of the dream I had of Sister White's quotes found in *Selected Messages*, book 2, p. 142, where she says, "The work of the people of God is to prepare for the events of the future, which will soon come upon them with blinding force." I, also, think of my other dream what Sister White said in *Testimonies for the Church*, vol. 8, p. 28, where she warns us with these startling words, "Transgression has almost reached its limit. Confusion fills the world, and a great terror is soon to come upon human beings. The end is very near. We who know the truth should be preparing for what is soon to break upon the world as an overwhelming surprise." Again, we prayed for help in being able to find David's lost billfold, trusting God to do what He knew was best and His will be done in His own way and time.

David said, "I'm going to go pawpaw hunting and walnut hunting down in our woods, do you want to go with me?" I said, "No, I'm going to keep looking for your billfold outside." So, I went outside searching and praying and asking God to please send an angel to put the billfold where I could see it and find it and please put it in my mind where to go look for it to find it. So, as I walked around praying, I thought, "Now where did David go and what was he doing the day he lost his billfold?" I remembered he had sat out on the front porch steps and cracked walnuts for us to eat that night for supper. So, I prayed and went over by the steps and looked down on the ground. There lay David's lost billfold! What a beautiful sight to my eyes! What a prayer of praise and thanksgiving to God for answering my prayer to send an angel to put it where I could see it and find it! It was right there in plain sight! I was so happy and excited and I kept saying, "Thank you, Jesus! Thank you, Jesus!"

Now I could hardly wait to share the good news with daddy, when he came back from the woods! I thought of that text in Dan. 6:22 where Daniel said, "My God hath sent his angel, and hath shut the lions' mouths." I knew God had answered my prayer and had put David's billfold where I could see it and find it in plain sight.

When David came back from hunting paw paws and walnuts in our woods, I met him at the door with his lost billfold in my hands and I said, "SURPRISE!!" "Praise the Lord!" I gave him a big hug and said, "Praise the Lord, He found it in answer to our prayers!" David said, "Praise the Lord! You have made my day! Where did you find it?!" Then, I proceeded to tell him how the angel put it in plain sight by the steps so I could see it, in answer to my prayers! He said, "But I've been back and forth there and up and down those steps so many times and I didn't see it!" We both prayed and thanked the good Lord for hearing our earnest prayers for help to find David's billfold!

David went outside to work with the walnuts and paw paws he'd found in the woods. While he was outside, I prayed and asked God to please help me write out this experience so it could be a help and a blessing and encouragement to others as to the power of God to do His will in our lives and trust Him as He allows us to go through these trying experiences in our lives and allow God to work all things for our good and allow God to let our faith grow. I thought of the story recorded in Dan. 6 of Daniel's experience in the lions' den and how God allowed Daniel to go through that trying experience, but God was with him and brought him through it all. The story is found in *Prophets and Kings*, pp. 539–548, by E. G. White, Chapter 44, "In the Lions' Den."

Also, in Dan. 3 is the story of Shadrach, Meshach, and Abednego and the golden image they refused to bow down to and were thrown into the fiery furnace and how Jesus was with them to deliver them in their terrible experience. The story is found in *Prophets and Kings*, pp. 503–513, chapter 41, "The Fiery Furnace." Daniel and his three friends had their faith tested but they proved strong and their faith grew more and more in Jesus and His power to save and sustain them. Read in *Prophets and Kings*, pp. 567–581, chapter 46, entitled, "The Prophets of God Helping Them."

I like the paragraph on pp. 576 & 578, "To His children today the Lord declares, 'Be strong… and work: for I am with you.' The Christian always has a strong helper in the Lord. The way of the Lord's helping we may not know; but this we do know: He will never fail those who put their trust in Him. Could Christians realize how many times the Lord has ordered their way, that the purposes of the enemy concerning them might not be accomplished, they would not stumble along complaining. Their faith would be stayed on God, and no trial would have power to move them. They would acknowledge Him as their wisdom and efficiency, and He would bring to pass that which He desires to work out through them…" Hag. 2:23 says, "In that day, saith the Lord of hosts, will I take thee, O Zerubbabel, my servant, the son of Shealtiel, saith the Lord, and will make thee as a signet: for I have chosen thee, saith the Lord of hosts…" Now the governor of Israel could see the meaning of the providence that had led him through discouragement and perplexity; he could discern God's purpose in it all. This personal word to Zerubbabel has been left on record for the encouragement of God's children in every age; God has a purpose in sending trial to his children. He never leads them otherwise than they would choose to be led if they could see the end from the beginning, and discern the glory of the purpose that they are fulfilling. All that He brings upon them in test and trials comes that they may be strong to do and to suffer for Him."

May God help us to learn to leave everything in His hands and trust our future in His keeping day by day. For in the near future our faith and trust in God is going to be severely tried and tested when the Sunday Law will be passed and we can't buy or sell because we won't go along with keeping Sunday as the Sabbath, but will remain true to God's seventh day Sabbath and trust God and His promises to take care of us and our needs as Phil. 4:19 promises and Ps. 91 and Ps. 46 promises.

I look back on these experiences God has allowed us to go through testing our faith and trust in God and learning to rely on Him and His promises. I can see now that if we hadn't let God take us through these experiences of testing our faith and letting it grow stronger in Him, we never would have the faith and confidence we have developed in God and that we're now trying to encourage others to have in God and His promises. Without these trials and troubles we've gone through, we'd never been able to write the book God wanted me to write, ***Don't Be Trapped in the Cities!! Get Out Now!***

Oh! Yes! We eventually got a new battery and was able to go see and enjoy our son, Jonathan! Praise God! Maybe Satan was planning for us to have a bad accident or something when we were planning to go see Jonathan the day the car wouldn't start and Daddy lost his billfold. So God delayed our trip for a while to protect us from Satan's trap. All we can do is trust God day by day and let Him plan for our future. God always knows best and is always working things out for our good, as we allow Him to lead in our plans and decisions. "Have Faith in God!"

> "Transgression has almost reached its limit. Confusion fills the world; and a great terror is soon to come upon human beings..."
>
> *8T, p. 28*

A CHRISTMAS STORY

Actually, this Christmas story began at Thanksgiving of 2014.

We were praying and asking the Lord for money for food. Our dear friend, Sandie, from New Jersey, sent us $60 for Thanksgiving, for us to have money to buy groceries for Thanksgiving! She knows and understands our situation of trying to build the "ARK" on our little income and still keep up with all our other expenses. So, periodically, through the year, she'll send us money she has saved in a jar, she has designated for the "ARK." She and her daughter have shown an interest in wanting to come and be with us on the "ARK," when the time comes. It seems the Lord impresses her to send her money from her "ARK" jar, just when we really are in great need! She's been such a help and a blessing! God bless her! She is so appreciated!

Also, I have a cousin, Nancy, from Florida, and she periodically sends us a $100 bill to help us with building materials for the "ARK," or to use as needed. What a help and blessing she has been to us, too! May God bless her, too.

It seems like just when we're in a time of need and praying God would please send us some money, Nancy or Sandie or my cousin Diane and her husband Larry, or Hilma, David's sister, or Kathy, David's cousin, and Cynthia from New York will send us some money! God has been faithful to answer our prayers right on time as He uses people to supply our needs for money! Praise the Lord! We've even had total strangers hand us money, as God has impressed them to give to us! Only God, knowing our great need for help, at just the right time, ALWAYS comes through.

Well, this little Christmas story was one of those times we were in need and how God came to our rescue! This time He used my cousin, Nancy. We had been trying to keep building on the "ARK" and buy winter propane and pay our taxes and still keep up with all our expenses, too. We had, with the Lord's help, taken care of everything, praise God! But, there was just one thing we badly needed, and that was food!

We were just fifteen days from Christmas, and we had a long time to go before we got our next Social Security check. They were forecasting a freezing rain and possibly snow, and we knew we had to get some groceries in before we couldn't get out in this bad weather coming in that evening! What were we going to do?! We did what we always do—WE PRAYED!!! We prayed God would please send us some money in the mail, so we could hurry into town before the storm hit and get some much-needed groceries! We claimed Jer. 33:3, "Call unto me, and I will answer thee, and show thee great and mighty things, which thou knowest not..." We, also, claimed, Phil. 4:19, "But my God shall supply all your need according to his riches in glory by Christ Jesus." Also, we repeated the promise in Luke 1:37, "For with God nothing shall be impossible." So, as we continued to pray and claim God's promises we watched our mailbox and waited for the mailman to come and prayed there would please be money in the mail, so we could hurry into town and get our groceries in before the storm hit! We watched the storm clouds gathering, as we waited and prayed for money from the Lord, in the mail!

There it was! A letter from Nancy, with a $100 bill in it, wishing us a "Merry Christmas!" Wow! What a Merry Christmas she made for us!! We praised the Lord and thanked Him for seeing us through another time of need and asked God to please bless Nancy for what she had done for us, by letting the Lord use her to answer our prayer for help! Praise God from whom all blessings flow! God is so good!

We paid our $10 tithe and David took our grocery list and hurried into town to get our much needed food, and gas in the car, before the weather got bad.

When David got up to the cashier, to check out his groceries, he didn't have enough money to buy the big ten pounds of pinto beans, along with his other groceries, so he had the cashier put the beans aside and he paid for the rest of the groceries he had gotten. He headed on out to the car and was putting things in the car and the cashier lady came running out the door over to David's car and said, as she handed him his ten pound bag of pinto beans, "Here! You can have your bag of beans!" David said, "Is this for real?! I don't have the money to pay for them!" She said, "The lady that was behind you in line wanted you to have them, and so she paid for them! The beans are yours!" David thanked her and offered her a book and she refused it. Then David said, "Who's the lady that paid for my beans? I want to thank her and give her a book, if you don't want it? I have others." She said, "No thank you." David said, "Where's the lady at, that paid for my beans?" The cashier lady said, "She's in the car parked right next to your car!" David looked over to the big beautiful van parked next to him and saw a middle aged lady sitting in the driver's seat with her window rolled down, so she could see and hear everything going on! David walked over and thanked her for what she had done to help him out and how very much he appreciated it! He handed her a *The Desire of Ages* book and said, "I want to give you this book, as a gift, to thank you for what you have done for me. I used to sell these books, and I know you'll be blessed as you read this book." She thanked him and accepted the book. David thanked her again for paying for his beans.

When he went back to his car, to get into the car to leave, right by the driver's side of the car on the parking lot, lay a Texas Sweet Grapefruit. He picked it up and brought it home to me. He knew I'd been hungry for Texas grapefruits, my favorite, but they're so expensive, so we hadn't been able to buy any, until they come down in price.

When David got home and unloaded the groceries he said, "Let me tell you the story behind this big bag of pinto beans, and this grapefruit." When he told me and Jonathan how God had supplied our beans to eat and my grapefruit, that was so delicious and so much appreciated, and he told how God helped him get *The Desire of Ages* book into her hands, I said, "…Silver and gold have I none; but such as I have, give I thee…", Acts 3:6. We prayed and thanked the good Lord for how He had helped us to get the money from Nancy to get the groceries, and how He impressed that lady to buy our beans for us, and someone had been impressed to leave a grapefruit by the driver's side of the car door for David to see it. Only God knew how very much I'd been wanting a Texas Sweet Grapefruit!! I said to David and Jonathan, "Now unto him that is able to do exceeding abundantly above all that we ask or think, according to the power that worketh in us. Unto him be glory in the church by Christ Jesus throughout all ages, world without end. Amen." Eph. 3:20, 21. We all three bowed our heads and thanked God for all He had done to supply all our needs! He even held off the ice storm! It didn't hit us till the next morning, but we were safe and warm and had food to eat! Thanks to the good Lord!!

We each one are going to have to allow God to test our faith in Him and His promises, so our faith will grow, to get us through the trying and testing times ahead of us, when our faith will be severely tested and tried during the Sunday Law and to get us through the early time of trouble, when all we'll be able to do will be to trust in the Lord to care for us and supply all our needs, and then get us through the Great Time of Trouble and the seven last plagues. Sister White says in *Last Day Events*, p. 64, "The storm is coming, the storm that will try every man's faith of what sort it is. Believers must now be firmly rooted in Christ or else they will be led astray by some phase of error."

You know, the greatest Christmas story that was ever written was the story of Jesus, leaving heaven and coming down to this dark cruel world where Satan reigned over man and held man captive in their sins! But Jesus came to our rescue, to free us from Satan's hold on us! As a little baby, he was born in a manger, because there was no room for Him in the inn! Through the years He lived a sinless life, as an example as to how to overcome Satan. Jesus came to this world as our Saviour! He loved us enough to go through terrible temptations and troubles and trials that Satan poured upon Him, to try and stop Jesus' mission to save fallen man! But, Jesus endured and never gave up, even willing to lay down His life and die on the cruel cross to free us from Satan's power! We now serve a risen Saviour who has gained the victory over Satan in our behalf! Jesus gave His all for us and sacrificed all for us, that we can be saved! But, if we don't accept His free offer of salvation, then, what more can He do?! The best gift we can give to Jesus to show our love and appreciation for His great sacrifice made for us, is to give Him our heart this Christmas and surrender our lives over to Him and part company with the devil! This will bring such joy to Jesus and the angels in heaven! Enoch had this testimony, before his translation, that he pleased God! (Heb. 11:5, 6)

Sister White tells us in *Last Day Events,* p. 71, "Now Enoch was a representative of those who will be upon the earth when Christ shall come, who will be translated to heaven without seeing death." Sister White says on p. 65 of *Last Day Events*, "Christ and Him crucified should be the theme of contemplation, of conversation, and of our most joyful emotion… Never will the human heart know happiness until it is submitted to be molded by the Spirit of God. The Spirit conforms the renewed soul to the model, Jesus Christ." Read the Christmas story of Jesus in Matt. 1 and Matt. 2 and Luke 2. Friends, Jesus loves You! John 3:16

FOR HE SHALL GIVE HIS ANGELS CHARGE OVER THEE!

"For he shall give his angels charge over thee, to keep thee in all thy ways. They shall bear thee up in their hands, lest thou dash thy foot against a stone."

Ps. 91:11, 12

"The angel of the Lord encampeth round about them that fear him, and delivereth them. O taste and see that the Lord is good: blessed is the man that trusteth in him… He keepeth all his bones: not one of them is broken."

Ps. 34:7, 8, 20.

The following experience happened some time ago, while building on the "ARK."

We were beginning to have cold wintery weather and unable to work outside much. It had turned out to be a nice day and so my husband, David, and I decided it would be a good day to build on the "ARK." We got out all our tools and ladders and as we always do, we pray for God's help and protection as we build and claim James 1:5, "If any of you lack wisdom, let him ask of God, that giveth to all men liberally, and upbraideth not, and it shall be given him."

We decided to continue building on the roof we'd been working on and try and finish that up before the cold freezing rains came in that they were forecasting that night.

We were trying to hurry along and were making good time, and then it happened! David lost his footing on the ladder and came falling down, off the high ladder, to the ground and landed on his side on a 2x4 board! He laid there awhile thinking, "Did I break a bone, or am I hurt?!" He got up and found out he was okay and nothing was broken and he wasn't even hurt! We said, "Praise the Lord! We prayed and thanked the good Lord for sparing his life and for protecting him from serious injuries! We realized falling from such a height could have been very serious and even fatal, especially in our old age! We thought of those texts in Ps. 91:11, 12; and Ps. 34:7, 8, and 20.

We knew David's guardian angel had certainly caught him in his hands and gently brought him down to the ground so he wouldn't injure himself. We were so very grateful and thankful for the angel's watchful care! The same way David's guardian angel had caught him when he fell, coming out the front door of our house trailer, one day in winter. He slipped on our icy slippery ramp and his feet went flying up in the air and he came crashing down backwards on the hard concrete ramp, hitting the back of his head, with no hurt or injury!

Praise the Lord! We know the devil is wroth with us and trying in every way to stop our work on the "ARK" any way he can, because we are trying to hurry and get all things ready for the crisis that is soon coming! Like Sister White says what God's people are to be doing, found in *Country Living*, pp. 9-12, "In harmony with the light given me, I am urging people to come out from the great centers of population. Our cities are increasing in wickedness, and it is becoming more and more evident that those who remain in them unnecessarily do so at the peril of their soul's salvation…

The time is fast coming when the controlling power of the labor unions will be very oppressive. Again and again the Lord has instructed that our people are to take their families away from the cities, into the country, where they can raise their own provisions; for in the future the problem of buying and selling will be a very serious one. We should now begin to heed the instruction given us over and over again: Get out of the cities into rural districts, where the houses are not crowded closely together, and where you will be free from the interference of enemies…

The trade unions will be one of the agencies that will bring upon this earth a time of trouble such as has not been since the world began…

The work of the people of God is to prepare for the events of the future, which will soon come upon them with blinding force. In the world gigantic monopolies will be formed. Men will bind themselves together in unions that will wrap them in the folds of the enemy. A few men will combine to grasp all the means to be obtained in certain lines of business. Trade unions will be formed, and those who refuse to join these unions will be marked men…

The trades unions and confederacies of the world are a snare. Keep out of them, and away from them, brethren. Have nothing to do with them. Because of these unions and confederacies, it will soon be very difficult for our institutions to carry on their work in the cities. My warning is: Keep out of the cities. Build no sanitariums in the cities. Educate our people to get out of the cities into the country, where they can obtain a small piece of land, and make a home for themselves and their children…

But erelong there will be such strife and confusion in the cities, that those who wish to leave them will not be able. We must be preparing for these issues. This is the light that is given me…

These unions are one of the signs of the last days. Men are binding up in bundles ready to be burned. They may be church members, but while they belong to these unions, they cannot possibly keep the commandments of God; for to belong to these unions means to disregard the entire Decalogue…

Those who claim to be the children of God are in no case to bind up with the labor unions that are formed or that shall be formed. This the Lord forbids. Cannot those who study the prophecies see and understand what is before us?"

Read Heb. 11:7. We praise God that He is helping us to build the "ARK," and to protect us and those who will be with us on the "ARK," in the near future. And that He'll care for us from the attacks of Satan while we're doing God's will and will provide for each one who will step out in faith and begin to prepare their own little Arks of safety, too, for the serious times ahead of us that love and obey all God's ten commandments, including His seventh day Sabbath and not the Sunday sabbath, that will soon be enforced upon us, preventing us from buying or selling.

Read Rev. 13 chapter, especially verse 17, "And no man might buy or sell save he that had the mark, or the name of the beast, or the number of his name."

I like the promise given to those who will be going through the Great Time of Trouble, after the close of probation, and during the seven last plagues: Isa. 33:15 & 16, "He that walketh righteously, and speaketh uprightly; he that despiseth the gain of oppressions, that shaketh his hands from holding of bribes, that stoppeth his ears from hearing of blood, and shutteth his eyes from seeing evil; He shall dwell on high: his place of defense shall be the munitions of rocks: bread shall be given him: his waters shall be sure." I like, also, Ps. 91 and Ps. 46.

There's a question W. D. Frazee asks in his book entitled, *ANOTHER ARK TO BUILD*, p. 162, "Now my question is this, friends, if there is coming a time before the close of probation when you cannot buy anything to eat, of what help is it going to be to you to have a promise that angels will feed you at some later time in a cave, if you starve to death before that? Is that a practical question?" On p. 163 W. D. Frazee goes on to say, "Who told Noah the flood was coming? God did. And he told him to preach. But He also said, Build an ark. Noah was to practice what he preached. He was to preach what he was practicing. It was all tied up together. Hear this wonderful statement from *Story of Redemption*, p. 63: 'He was not only to preach, but his example in building the ark was to convince all that believed what he preached… Every blow struck upon the ark was preaching to the people. Noah directed, he preached, he worked, while the people looked on in amazement and regarded him as a fanatic.' You see, Noah preached with his hammer as well as his vocal cords!" W. D. Frazee goes on to say in his book, *Another Ark to Build*, p. 163, "Now, I wonder if God has given you and me any hammering to do while we are preaching and warning people about that storm of persecution that is coming? Is there some practical work involved in preparing for that awful boycott when thousands will be confronted on the one side with the seal of God and on the other with the mark of the beast? I believe there's an answer to that. I find part of it in *Selected Messages*, book 2, on p. 141, the servant of the Lord says: 'The time is fast coming when the controlling power of the labor unions will be very oppressive. Again and again the Lord has instructed that our people are to take their families away from the cities, into the country, where they can raise their own provisions; for in the future the problem of buying and selling will be a very serious one.'"

Yes, my dear friends, I'm so thankful for the care of the angels and how they watch over us and protect and supply our needs. Sister White writes in the book, *Sons and Daughters of God*, pp. 35, 36, "Angels are ever present where they are most needed, with those who have the hardest battle with self to fight, and whose surroundings are the most discouraging. In all ages, angels have been near to Christ's faithful followers. The vast confederacy of evil is arrayed against all who would overcome, but Christ would have us look to the things which are not seen, to the armies of heaven encamped about all who love God, to deliver them. From what dangers, seen and unseen, we have been preserved through the interposition of the angels, we shall never know, until in the light of eternity we see the providences of God. Then we shall know that the whole family of heaven was interested in the family here below, and that messengers from the throne of God attended our steps from day to day… The angels' work is to keep back the powers of Satan… Angels, who will do for you what you cannot do for yourselves, are waiting for your co-operation. They are waiting for you to respond to the drawing of Christ."

Now is our time to develop a personal relationship with Jesus and have faith in His promises and learn to rely on His power to see us through what's coming upon everyone who remains true to God's Sabbath.

> **"But erelong there will be such strife and confusion in the cities that those who wish to leave them will not be able…"**

Country Living p. 11

GOD WILL PROVIDE!

Sister White writes in Last Day Events, p. 72, "We have nothing to fear for the future, except as we shall forget the way the Lord has led us, and His teaching in our past history."

This experience happened many years ago, but it is still fresh in our minds.

"But my God shall supply all your need according to His riches in glory by Christ Jesus," Phil. 4:19

Well, we were at the end of the month again, and not much money left from our small Social Security check, to make it to the end of the month. Maybe some of you can relate to that?!

We had spent our money on building materials to be able to keep building on the "ARK." As we worked, we ran out of some screws we were needing and had to make a trip to town to get them. Then, David noticed we had a flat tire on the car. While he put the spare tire on, I walked around while waiting, and then I noticed a flat tire on our old Chevy truck. We counted our money and remembered flats used to be $8 to fix. We prayed God would help us please have enough to supply our needs and claimed, Phil 4:19. We left for town to purchase the screws needed and then drove over to get the two flat tires fixed. The old truck tire looked like it could be a dry rot tire, and we'd not have enough to buy a used tire for it, so we prayed the old tire would be repairable, and that we'd have enough money to fix both flat tires needed on our car and truck. As we drove in to have the two flats fixed, I said to David, "Ask them what they charge to fix a flat tire, and I'll be counting how much money we have left over after buying the screws."

David carried our little tire in from our car first and asked what it would cost to fix the flat? As he was coming out to tell me, to see if we had enough money to fix the two flats, the guy started fixing the small tire's flat.

David told me it cost $10.51 to fix a flat tire. We saw we didn't have enough to fix two flat tires at that price. So, we paid for the flat tire already fixed and when the man brought it out to the car David asked him if he would please look at our old truck tire and see if he thought it was in good enough condition to even be fixed. As the man walked off carrying the truck tire into the shop to check it out, David told him to please wait on fixing it, if it was a good enough tire, because we had to take some screws back to the store that we had purchased so we'd have enough to pay for the tire to be repaired. The fellow took a look at it and said the tire was still in good condition and he said it just needs a valve stem that's leaking. He fixed it for only $3. We thanked him and I gave him a National Sunday Law book by Jan Marcussen. He was happy to get it! I told him he was an answer to our prayers, to be able to have enough money to fix our two flat tires and still be able to keep the screws we had gotten from the store. David said to the man, "It's the end of the month and things are kinda rough." The man said he understood.

When we drove off, we were thanking the Lord for hearing our prayers to help us to have enough money to take care of our needs. David spoke up and said, "Now we still have just enough money left over to buy us that watermelon we have been wanting to buy and eat so bad!"

It made me think of that promise found in Eph. 3:20, 21, "Now unto him that is able to do exceeding abundantly above all that we ask or think, according to the power that worketh in us, Unto him be glory in the church by Christ Jesus throughout all ages, world without end. Amen."

We had, also, been praying for rain for our garden, since it had been so long without rain. Everyone was needing rain, it was like a drought. A lot of peoples' gardens and farmers' crops had failed. We had well water we had been watering our garden with to keep it going, until God sent us a much needed rain. Then, in answer to prayer we had gotten a 1-inch rain!

We found out the fellow that fixed our flat tires was a farmer and he said he had put in $200 worth of corn seed and it failed, because of the bad drought. David saw a puddle of water at the place where the farmer had fixed our flat tires and David asked him how much rain they had gotten there in town and he said, "Not very much, only 1/5 inch of rain. David said to him that we had gotten a whole inch of rain. The fellow said, "Where do you live?!" David said, "About twenty miles away, out in the country." We told him we'd been praying for rain and that was just what our garden needed to keep it alive and we were so thankful for it!

These experiences we're going through, right now, is like being in boot camp training, like what soldiers in army training go through, to prepare them for the battles ahead of them, so they will be strong and courageous and endure the hardships and trials and troubles ahead of them when the pressures against them will be strong and fierce and they won't give up or give in to the enemy. This is what God is trying to do for His people, to make them strong in faith, so when their resources are cut off, and when the Sunday Law is passed, they have learned to lean on Jesus and rely on Him to take care of them and their needs and trust in Him to help them.

Sister White tells us in her book, *The Ministry of Healing*, pp. 470, 471, "Many who sincerely consecrate their lives to God's service are surprised and disappointed to find themselves, as never before, confronted by obstacles, and beset by trials and perplexities… Trials and obstacles are the Lord's chosen methods of discipline and His appointed conditions of success… Often He permits the fires of affliction to assail them that they may be purified. The fact that we are called upon to endure trial shows that the Lord Jesus sees in us something precious which He desires to develop… The Lord allows His chosen ones to be placed in the furnace of affliction to prove what temper they are of and whether they can be fashioned for His work."

Also, in *Country Living* book by Sister White we find this advice and counsel, on p. 28, "We cannot have a weak faith now; we cannot be safe in a listless, indolent, slothful attitude… Spread every plan before God with fasting, [and] with the humbling of the soul before the Lord Jesus, and commit thy ways unto the Lord. The sure promise is, He will direct thy paths. He is infinite in resources. The Holy One of Israel, who calls the host of heaven by name and holds the stars of heaven in position, has you individually in His keeping… I would that all could realize what possibilities and probabilities there are for all who make Christ their sufficiency and their trust. The life hid with Christ in God ever has a refuge; he can say, 'I can do all things through Christ which strengtheneth me.'"

David and I, through all the experiences God has put us through, to teach us faith and dependence in God, helps us to see why we're to, "In everything give thanks." 1 Thess. 5:18. And, also, in the promise in Rom. 8:28, "And we know that all things work together for good to them that love God, to them who are the called according to his purpose." We can see how God directs us to the right people to witness to them and share the truth with them, as we are going through our trials and troubles and letting God help us get through our obstacles, as we pray in faith. Like, before we drove clear into the large city of Ottawa to get our two flats fixed, we decided to check in our little town, just 3 1/2 miles from us and see what they charge to fix a flat. We found out that they charged over $10 to fix a flat and so we decided to go on to Ottawa, where we thought we would be charged only $8 a flat. But before we left we thanked the man and David offered him a *National Sunday Law* book, but he refused it. David began telling the man about the world conditions and what it all meant and what is ahead and what's behind the pope's agenda for pushing for a Sunday Law, using the U.S.A. to get it passed and what that will mean to those of us who won't go along with the plan for this one world power and that Jesus is soon to come and how important it is to be ready.

The fellow said, "Let me have that book! That sounds interesting!" So, David gave him the book and we left. This made us think of the text in John 10:16, "And other sheep I have, which are not of this fold: them also I must bring, and they shall hear my voice; and there shall be one fold, and one shepherd." David felt impressed to get this man's interest in the book, so he'd want it, so he could see the truth and accept it and be saved. We thought of all the thousands of books we've given out and what Sister White says in *Last Day Events*, p. 90, "As long as probation continues there will be opportunity for the canvasser to work."

In Sister White's book called *The Publishing Ministry*, we find this quote of Sister White on page 3, "As the preaching of Noah warned, tested, and proved the inhabitants of the world before the flood of waters destroyed them from off the face of the earth, so the truth of God for these last days is doing a similar work of warning, testing, and proving the world. The publications which go forth… bear the signet of the Eternal. They are being scattered all through the land, and are deciding the destiny of souls."

Also, on p. 213 of *Last Day Events*, Sister White writes, "The seed has been sown, and now it will spring up and bear fruit." We could now see how God is using those of us Seventh-day Adventists who choose to get the light of truth out to these precious souls Jesus has out there in the world, that He's wanting to use our hands, and feet, and voice to witness for Jesus and tell and share of His power to save. We are so thankful for the privilege to be used of God to rescue the perishing and care for the dying, no matter what we have to go through to do it. Even though we are out of money, we know we're in good hands and have peace of mind knowing that God will provide.

GOD IS ALWAYS RIGHT ON TIME

The Desire of Ages, p. 32, by Sister White, we read: "But like the stars in the vast circuit of their appointed path, God's purposes know no haste and no delay."

Little did we know that long before Christmas, my cousin Diane and her husband Larry had sent us $100 for Christmas. It was at a time when we were changing our mailing address and their money and letter got sent back to them, and we knew nothing about it. Then, when they got their mail sent back to them she wrote and said, "I sent you $100 for Christmas and it was returned to us. When I hear from you as to where to send this money, I'll mail it back to you." I wrote back and thanked them for sending the money and gave them our new mailing address. As I sent the letter, I prayed a prayer that they would feel impressed to send us more than $100 because we so much needed to buy paint for the 4x8 boards we were putting up in our meeting place, and we had no money for this project.

We have always turned to the Lord in prayer to meet our needs and claim Phil. 4:19, "But my God shall supply all your need according to his riches in glory by Christ Jesus." Also, *The Ministry of Healing*, p. 481, by Sister White, "Worry is blind and cannot discern the future; but Jesus sees the end from the beginning. In every difficulty He has His way prepared to bring relief. 'No good thing will he withhold from them that walk uprightly.' Matt. 11:30; Ps. 84:11. Our heavenly Father has a thousand ways to provide for us of which we know nothing. Those who accept the one principle of making the service of God supreme, will find perplexities vanish and a plain path before their feet."

As I mailed the letter to Diane and Larry, I began to fast and pray over my request to God, to please have Diane and Larry to feel impressed, by the Holy Spirit, to send us more money than the $100 they had sent earlier. I was fasting and praying over a lot of prayer requests I had presented to God, like the conversion of my son and our loved ones, etc. Day by day I kept praying over these prayer requests. I kept watching the mail to see what God would do to supply our need for being able to buy paint to paint our walls in our meeting place.

Finally, after many days, the day arrived when Diane and Larry sent their money gift with a letter. Here's what she wrote: "This morning Larry and I went out to "Denny's" for breakfast and right next to where we parked the car I saw something on the ground and I picked it up and it was a $20 bill. There was no one around at all so I decided I would just send it on to you since I couldn't find the owner. So that is why the extra $20 is enclosed."

Praise God! Little did Diane and Larry know that they were helping to answer my prayer request for money to buy paint. I feel they have found the owner to that $20 bill, "us." I feel God sent an angel in answer to our prayer, to place that $20 bill right where Diane would see it there on the ground beside their car and impressed her to send it to us to help supply our need we had been praying and fasting over. God bless them richly for their love and kindness and help to us in helping us to be able to keep working on the "Ark" we're preparing for when the Sunday Laws are passed and people, God is calling to come to our place, the "Ark," for a refuge when they need a place because they won't go along with keeping Sunday as the Sabbath, but will obey Jesus' commandments to keep God's seventh day Sabbath as taught in God's Word in Exod. 20:1–17. So, people who follow God and not man, will not be able to buy or sell, and during this time when we're eating out of our gardens and living out of the cities, we'll be drawing together and trusting God to take care of us through this early time of trouble that will be going on all around the world happening to God's faithful and true followers who'll be suffering for Christ's sake and His truth. NOW, is the time to be preparing for those days ahead of us.

In, *Last Day Events*, by Sister White, on p. 141 are these words recorded, "The adherents to truth are now called upon to choose between disregarding a plain requirement of God's Word or forfeiting their liberty. If we yield the Word of God and accept human customs and traditions, we may still be permitted to live among men, to buy and sell and have our rights respected. But if we maintain our loyalty to God it must be at the sacrifice of our rights among men, for the enemies of God's law have leagued together to crush out independent judgment in matters of religious faith and control the consciences of men…"

In Acts 5:29 it says, "Then Peter and the other apostles answered and said, 'We ought to obey God rather than men.'"

In *The Ministry of Healing*, by Sister White, on pp. 159, 160 we are told by God's prophet, "There is no limit to the usefulness of one who putting self aside, makes room for the working of the Holy Spirit upon his heart and lives a life wholly consecrated to God. All who consecrate body, soul, and spirit to His service will be constantly receiving a new endowment of physical, mental, and spiritual power. The inexhaustible supplies of heaven are at their command. Christ gives them the breath of His own Spirit, the life of His own life. The Holy Spirit puts forth its highest energies to work in mind and heart. Through the grace given us we may achieve victories that because of our own erroneous and preconceived opinions, our defects of character, our smallness of faith, have seemed impossible. To everyone who offers himself to the Lord for service, withholding nothing, is given power for the attainment of measureless results. For these God will do great things. He will work upon the minds of men so that, even in this world, there shall be seen in their lives a fulfillment of the promise of the future state."

God is always right on time and is always working out things for our good as Rom. 8:28 says, "And we know that all things work together for good to them that love God, to them who are the called according to his purpose." God works on the hearts of people to be a help and a blessing to those in need. God has His helping hands to do His service. Praise God! God used Diane and Larry to be at the right place at the right time to find that $20 to be used to answer our prayer request for money to buy paint for our meeting place. God has only our eyes, hands, and feet and voice and ears for Him to work through to do His will in answering people's prayers and supplying their needs. Praise God! Thank you Jesus for answering our prayer request through Diane and Larry. Thank you Diane and Larry for listening to the Holy Spirit for sending us this money we so much needed and was praying for in faith that God would answer our prayer, because we were using it in doing God's work here on the "Ark." God knew the right time to get their money through the mail to us, right when we were needing money to buy paint. Friends, are you letting God use you to be a help and a blessing to others in need?

Read Isa. 58:6, 7, "Is not this the fast that I have chosen? To loose the bands of wickedness, to undo the heavy burdens, and to let the oppressed go free, and that ye break every yoke? Is it not to deal thy bread to the hungry, and that thou bring the poor that are cast out to thy house? When thou seest the naked, that thou cover him; and that thou hide not thyself from thine own flesh?"

Matt. 7:12, "Therefore all things whatsoever ye would that men should do to you, do ye even so to them: for this is the law and the prophets."

In *The Desire of Ages*, p. 640, written by Sister White, she says, "In doing as Jesus did when on earth, we shall walk in His steps."

THROUGH THE MAIL WITH AN ANGEL!

We were wanting to get started on building on our 24' x 44' greenhouse, as soon as the good weather started. We were praying and asking God to please supply us with the money we'd need to buy building materials. I knew my birthday was coming up and that I was praying for money to come in the mail, so I could use it for buying building materials. David asked me what I wanted for my birthday and I said, "I'm praying for money to buy building materials for the greenhouse."

I checked the mail each day in hopes there would be money in the mail. Nothing. Then I began to pray and fast for money to come in the mail and I also fasted and prayed for my son, Jonathan, who was going through a rough time and needed extra prayers and fasting done for him, and there were others who needed my prayers and fasting done for them, too.

Then one day I walked out to the mailbox and there in the mailbox was a birthday card from my cousin, Nancy, from Florida. She had remembered my birthday with a pretty card and a $100 bill cash inside the card, along with a little, "Pass it on message card" that read, "RELAX! It's all in God's hands." and a verse from Ps. 3:5, "I laid me down and slept; I awaked; for the Lord sustained me." I praised the Lord and thanked Him for hearing my prayers for money in the mail and asked God to please bless Nancy for remembering my birthday with a $100 bill. There was a very unusual thing about this birthday card in the envelope. The envelope had not been licked and sealed securely shut and was wide open! I could see the $100 bill cash and the little pass it on message card inside the birthday card inside the envelope, that was wide open, as it traveled all that way from Florida to Kansas through the mail with no one taking out the money, or the money not sliding out through all the miles it traveled in the mail to get to me in answer to my prayers and fasting for money I so badly needed for materials for our greenhouse. God had watched over that money for me and kept it from falling out or from being stolen! Like the little pass it on message card said, "RELAX! It's all in God's hands!" I just praised and thanked God for doing this for me. We, as Christians, need to learn to RELAX and trust the Lord to care for our needs and see us through things we can't understand or figure out and leave it all in God's hands and let Him do what He knows is best, remembering and trusting in His promises that He can do anything and that nothing is impossible with God! Like Luke 1:37 says, "For with God nothing shall be impossible." And, also, like the promise in Mark 10:27 says, "And Jesus looking upon them saith, with men it is impossible, but not with God: for with God all things are possible." Dan. 6:22, "My God hath sent his angel and hath shut the lions' mouths…" (God sent His angel to shut the flap on the envelope to protect my $100 bill.) This experience is certainly something to praise the Lord for as Ps. 9:1 says, "I will praise thee, O Lord, with my whole heart; I will show forth all thy marvelous works." Truly Nancy's birthday card and money came through the mail with an angel watching over it! Praise the Lord! It's all in God's Hands!

GOD BROUGHT US THROUGH!

I know everyone has an allergy to something. Some allergies are worse than others. Like David has allergies that make him itch real badly. But one time he ate a lot of alfalfa sprouts and he had no idea he was allergic to alfalfa. He broke out all over in hives and finally had to end up in the emergency room it got so dangerously bad! The doctor said it could have killed him if he had waited any longer to get medical help! They gave him Benadryl medicine and it cleared up the bad hives. Praise the Lord! God brought us through that terrible experience!

Another time David had gotten a small tick on the back of his knee and didn't discover it for a while until he broke out with hives all over his body and again we rushed him to the emergency room and they gave him Benadryl medicine and it cleared up the bad hives. We always pray and ask God for help when we don't know what to do and we claim James 1:5 and we always thank the good Lord when He brings us through our terrible problems! I said to David, "We're going to have to keep some Benadryl medicine on hand for these emergencies you go through and save money running to the emergency room for Benadryl medicine. So, we purchased a little bottle over the counter and kept it on hand in our first aid kit. It sat there for many years.

Then, one night I woke up and saw David's light on in his bedroom. I went in to check and see that he was okay. He was sitting in his chair eating raw squash. Now, he had eaten raw squash before when he would eat something he was allergic to and it made him itch and he found out the raw squash would help his itch. But this time he was broke out all over his body with big hives and itching! I said, "Daddy, why didn't you let me know you were having a problem?" He said, "I didn't want to bother you." The raw squash wasn't helping much. Jonathan said, "Dad, you better get to the emergency room, that looks BAD!" Then, I remembered the Benadryl medicine in the first aid kit and I went and got a couple pills for him to take and we prayed. After some time he wasn't much better. The raw squash wasn't helping and the Benadryl medicine wasn't doing much for the hives either. We prayed again and I gave him two more Benadryl pills for allergies. He ate a bunch of raw garlic with some food. Nothing seemed to help much. Then, God impressed David to notice a small seed tick on his neck and it had a white spot on the tick's back. David noticed his mouth and jaw and lips were all swollen up as he looked in the mirror and saw the tick on his neck. It had been on him for some time and was sunk down in the skin and he couldn't pull him off, so he put hand soap on him and that smothered it and then he got him pulled off. I gave him some activated charcoal tablets we had and we prayed God would please heal Daddy, now that that tick was off of him and not shooting poison into his system anymore!

Finally, the hives started going away and the itch wasn't bad and the swelling on his face was going away and he was feeling much better and continued to improve. Praise the Lord! God brought us through again, through another terrible experience that could have been fatal, but God stepped in and healed Daddy and saved us having to go to the emergency room for help. We just praised and thanked the good Lord he got well and no complications from the tick bite, like Lyme's Disease! I thought of Ps. 46, especially verse 1, "God is our refuge and strength, a very present help in trouble..." Read the rest of the chapter and also Ps. 91. It made me think, in the time of trouble when all earthly support will be cut off and we won't be able to buy or sell and no medical help will be available and no medicines can be bought and no food, all we'll have is the Lord to care for us and bring us through our hard times we'll be going through then and will have faith in His power and in His promises to take care of all our problems and supply us with all our needs as Phil 4:19 says.

It's tick season again and we're more careful to check for ticks on us and prevent this from happening again! We have faith that God can bring us through anything that's ahead of us! Praise God! Read Ps. 92:1

The time is coming in the near future when all we'll have is Jesus to supply all our needs. But Jesus is really all we need. Makes me think of the song, "Take the World, But Give Me Jesus," and the song, "I'd Rather Have Jesus than Anything."

TRAPPED!

(Only God Can Help!)

Once upon a time there was a happy little bluebird living free in the country and enjoying life. As she freely flew around enjoying all the bugs to eat, she kept passing by this chimney wood stovepipe that looked so inviting. She kept thinking, "What a nice place that stovepipe would make for a house."

It had the little chimney cap on it and it would make a good shelter to be under that covering and would make a cozy little home to raise her young in. She got so curious one day, so she flew closer and closer to the cap on the stovepipe and landed on it and felt perfectly safe. So, she flew under the stove cap to get a better look and check it out. But as she flew under the stovepipe's cap, she felt like she was dropping down lower and lower into the stovepipe and she couldn't do anything about it! She kept dropping lower and lower and she couldn't spread her wings to fly and get out of the TRAP she found herself in! She finally grew weary of struggling to get out of her "trap," and she just gave up and dropped down to the bottom and landed on a big bunch of papers and she was in total darkness and in a big cast iron box, all enclosed with no way out! She chirped and fluttered for a while but finally grew tired of trying to get out of the mess she was in and just gave up to die, thinking there was no help for her. Our son, Jonathan, sits about ten feet from our wood stove and he said he heard some noise coming from the wood stove. I said, "It's probably a bluebird got trapped in there. Every year a bluebird thinks that cap on our stovepipe would make a good place to nest and they get caught in the stovepipe and drop down into the big cast iron wood stove.

Usually, we open the front door and open the wood stove door and the trapped bird flies out and flies on out the open front door. But our front door is broken and we can't open it now." We didn't know what we were going to do. I said, "If we open the wood stove door the bird will fly out and go all over the house flying all over and pottying on everything. But, we hate to let it stay in there for days dying away. I said, "We may just have to start the fire up in the wood stove and let the smoke and fire kill her fast, so she won't torture for days, just slowly dying." So we prayed and asked the Lord to please help us know what to do?! We sat down to eat breakfast, and we could hear the little bird chirping out for help and fluttering around, trapped, and not knowing how to get out of the mess she was in! As we ate, I saw the little bird's tail feathers stick out under the crack in the door. I prayed, "Lord, please help this little bird stay real still so when I open the door she won't fly out into the house, but will let me rescue her by not flying away, but will let me lift her up into my hands and carry her outside the house and set her free from the trap she's in, thank you!"

So, I put a glove on my hand and opened the door slowly and reached down and picked up her still little body and took the quiet frightened little bird outside and sat her gently onto the grass and thought maybe she was so weak and quiet and was ready to die. But, no, as soon as she was free she took off flying high in the air and took off flying home. I hoped she had learned her lesson and wouldn't return back to this trap again! I thanked and praised the Lord for answering my prayers to be able to free the little bluebird from her frightful trap. I was so glad I didn't have to burn her and destroy her in the fire. I felt so good the little bird had a chance to live and enjoy life again!

This experience with the bluebird makes me think of how we humans sometimes let ourselves get trapped in our sins and as Prov. 5:22 says, "His own iniquities shall take the wicked himself, and he shall be holden with the cords of his sins." So many times we think we can venture onto Satan's ground, maybe out of curiosity, and think we can be safe just this once, or it's not all that bad, or I'll be alright, but we find ourselves in Satan's TRAP and held in the cords of our sins! You give Satan an inch, and he'll take a mile. We find ourselves in Satan's snare and we can't get out!

Only Jesus has the power to save us from our sins and free us from the death trap we're in! Too many of us want to manage things the way we want them and not surrender all to Jesus and ask Him to please come into our lives and give us victory from our sins, and we just keep struggling in our own strength with no power to free ourselves from Satan's hold on us, until we call out to Jesus with all our heart to save us from destruction!

Then, Jesus comes to rescue us from the TRAP we're in and give us freedom to live a new life in Christ and free to live a joyful peaceful life for Jesus, free of Satan's hold on us!

It's like our son, Jonathan. Satan keeps trying to get him lured back into the nursing home where all the temptations to sin are and get back into Satan's traps, that Jesus has given him deliverance from by coming home and all those drugs he was on, and smoking and the poor unhealthy diet of pork, coffee, meat, and dairy foods, sweets, and junk foods, and the bad TV programs and devil music and the many temptations there are out in the world of sin. Here at home he's free of all those Satan traps when he chose to leave the nursing home and come home and be free of all those things, with God's help! Satan is still trying to tempt him to return back to the nursing home, where he can do those things he used to do that was killing him spiritually and physically. What he needs is a converted heart and a love for Jesus more than for the pleasures of the world of sin. How earnestly we pray for our son, that he'll choose to cut loose totally and completely from Satan's hold on him! Please pray for our son, too! Thank you! Only God can help him from Satan's hold on him!

So many of us are like this: Jesus delivers us from Satan's hold on us, but like the dog wanting to return back to his vomit, like 2 Peter 2:19–22 says, "While they promise them liberty, they themselves are the servants of corruption: for of whom a man is overcome, of the same is he brought in bondage. For if after they have escaped the pollutions of the world through the knowledge of the Lord and Saviour Jesus Christ, they are again entangled therein, and overcome, the latter end is worse with them than the beginning. For it had been better for them not to have known the way of righteousness, than after they have known it, to turn from the holy commandment delivered unto them. But it is happened unto them according to the true proverb, the dog is turned to his own vomit again; and the sow that was washed to her wallowing in the mire."

In *Desire of Ages* book by E. G. White, on pp. 130, 131 we read, "Christ declared to the tempter, 'Get thee behind me, Satan: for it is written, Thou shalt worship the Lord thy God, and Him only shalt thou serve.'... So we may resist temptation, and force Satan to depart from us. Jesus gained the victory through submission and faith in God, and by the apostle He says to us, 'Submit yourselves therefore to God. Resist the devil and he will flee from you. Draw nigh to God, and He will draw nigh to you.' James 4:7, 8. We cannot save ourselves from the tempter's power; he has conquered humanity, and when we try to stand in our own strength, we shall become a prey to his devices; but, 'the name of the Lord is a strong tower: the righteous runneth into it, and is safe.' Prov. 18:10. Satan trembles and flees before the weakest soul who finds refuge in that mighty name.

After the foe had departed, Jesus fell exhausted to the earth, with pallor of death upon His face. The angels of heaven had watched the conflict, beholding their loved commander as He passed through inexpressible suffering to make a way of escape for us. He had endured the test, greater than we shall ever be called to endure. The angels now minister to the Son of God as He lay like one dying. He was strengthened with food, comforted with the message of His Father's love and the assurance that all heaven triumphed in His victory. Warming to life again, His great heart goes out in sympathy for man, and He goes forth to complete the work He has begun; to rest not until the foe is vanquished, and our fallen race redeemed. Never can the cost of our redemption be realized until the redeemed shall stand with the Redeemer before the throne of God. Then as the glories of the eternal home burst upon our enraptured senses we shall remember that Jesus left all this for us, that He not only became an exile from the heavenly courts, but for us took the risk of failure and eternal loss. Then we shall cast our crowns at His feet, and raise the song, 'Worthy is the Lamb that was slain to receive power, and glory, and blessing." Rev. 5:12. Read in *The Desire of Ages* book by E. G. White, chapter 12, "The Temptation" and also, chapter 13, "The Victory," pp. 114–131.

On 11-28-11 God gave me this dream: I was trying to win this person to the Lord (like Jonathan.) I finally admitted, "I can't do it! It's the Holy Spirit that can change a person's life. I can live a good example for them and pray for them, but it's the Holy Spirit that does the work of changing people. I can encourage them, but can't do the changing for them. Only the Holy Spirit can try and help the person, but it's still the power of the Holy Spirit that will do the converting. We need the power of the Holy Spirit in our own life to be a success."

Sister White says in *Manuscript* 31, 1890, "We can enlighten the people only through the power of God. The canvassers must keep their own souls in living connection with God. They should labor praying that God will open the way, and prepare hearts to receive the message He sends them. It is not the ability of the agent or worker, but it is the Spirit of God moving upon the heart that will give true success."

Also, in *Testimonies for the Church*, vol. 6, p. 325, Sister White says, "Connect firmly with Christ, and present the truth as it is in Him. Hearts cannot fail to be touched by the story of the atonement. As you learn the meekness and lowliness of Christ, you will know what you should say to the people; for the Holy Spirit will tell you what words to speak. Those who realize the necessity of keeping the heart under the control of the Holy Spirit will be enabled to sow seed that will spring up unto eternal life. This is the work of the evangelistic canvasser."

"We can enlighten the people only through the power of God."

Manuscript 31, 1890

CAMP MEETING DREAM

Linda's Dream: On June 2, 2015, I had a dream. I was saying to my husband, David, "Camp meeting starts tonight," and it was June 13, Saturday that was in my dream for camp meeting to begin for us. I was saying to David something about how people can meet someone at camp meeting time.

When I woke up from the dream I looked on the calendar and sure enough, June 13 was on a Saturday, like my dream had said! David and I would have liked to have attended a place for camp meeting, but we couldn't afford it, and our son didn't want to go, and with the medicines he's on, he can't overheat and it would be hard on him and his paralyzed legs and in a wheelchair, and it would make it hard on all of us. But God knew our heart, that we would love to go to a camp meeting and have our boy anointed for conversion and healing and freedom from his addictions like his medicines and nicotine, and Satan's hold on him! Please pray for him and us! Thanks! We feel so happy God set us a date for us to have a camp meeting, June 13, Saturday. We'll be praying for the outpouring of the Holy Spirit at this camp meeting God set the date for us to meet together where two or three are gathered together in God's name, there God will be in our midst. (Matt. 18:20.) We read in *Last Day Events* book by Sister White the chapters, "The Shaking", "The Latter Rain", and "The Loud Cry", pp. 172–214. Also, we read in *Testimonies to Ministers* and *Gospel Workers* by E. G. White, the chapter, "Pray for the Latter Rain", pp. 506–512. Also, we read in *The Crisis Ahead* book by Robert W. Olson, he quotes Spirit of Prophecy quotations by Sister White on "the Holy Spirit"; "The Latter Rain"; "The Loud Cry." (pp. 79–111) We pray God will pour His Spirit out on us at our camp meeting June 13! We pray we'll be emptied of self and sin. God is just waiting for us to be ready to receive the Holy Spirit and wrap things up and come for His people. On June 12, Friday, Mary sent five Don __ DVD's we got in the mail that day! We had been praying that God would please send, in the mail, some information for us to have for our camp meeting, June 13, Saturday! Mary knew nothing about us having a camp meeting June 13 at our home for David, and me, and our son, Jonathan. God answered our prayers, through Mary, for material for our camp meeting! God had set the date for us, June 13, Saturday. God even lined up the "guest speaker" He wanted us to have for our camp meeting, Don, a dear friend. This is now, June 15, and we're still having our camp meeting, and we've been so very blessed!!!! Thank you, God, and Bill and Mary, and Don for making this a very special camp meeting for us personally! Praise God! Our camp meeting texts: Hosea 6:3; Luke 21:7–8; Jer. 33:3; Jer. 29:11–14. Our camp meeting theme was: "Come and Find Jesus and Be Filled with His Holy Spirit." Our theme song was "Come Holy Spirit We Need Thee." We read in *Testimonies for the Church*, vol. 2, p. 594–597, by E. G. White, "An Impressive Dream"; also, we read on pp. 597–603, "Our camp meetings"; we, also, read, "A Solemn Dream" by E. G. White on pp. 604–609. We enjoyed sermons and health talks and music and Bible study time. We read some of my dreams and articles. We studied herbs and natural remedies. We enjoyed good healthy camp meeting meals together and took a picnic drive. We, also, had time for Questions and Answers and discussions. We prayed together for each other and for the outpouring of the Holy Spirit. We sang songs together and felt the Holy Spirit in our lives at our camp meeting. Praise God! We read in *Testimonies to Ministers* and *Gospel Workers* by E. G. White pp. 506–512, "Pray for the Latter Rain." On p. 508 Sister White says, "The convocations of the church, as in camp meeting, the assemblies of the home church and all occasions where there is personal labor for souls, are God's appointed opportunities for giving the early and latter rain." On June 18, we received a Jan Marcussen letter in the mail to read at our camp meeting. We, also, read in Sister White's book, *Acts of the Apostles*, pp. 25-56: "The Great Commission," "Pentecost," and "The Gift of the Spirit."

Also, on June 20, in the mail, we received, from Mary, my DVD of my dreams and articles and three of Don's DVD's. We had been having our own personal camp meeting in our home, me and David and our son, Jonathan. We've been praying for the forgiveness of our sins and to gain the victory over sin and praying for the outpouring of the Holy Spirit and for the conversion of our son, Jonathan. We were praying and asking for God to please send my DVD from Mary and more of Don's DVD's to have to hear for our camp meeting we were still having, since June 13. God used Mary, again, to answer our prayers! God bless her for all the ways she's a blessing to others and to us!

And during our camp meeting time, June 13 and on, one night I dreamed the song, "Redemption Draweth Nigh!" This is the same song I kept dreaming over and over again, some time back. The General Conference, 2015, I believe this was to be their theme song, too? But then they changed it. We've been praying for our General Conference, 2015, coming up, that the Lord would please be in control of things! We're now singing this song, "Redemption Draweth Nigh", for one of our theme songs for our camp meeting we're having in our home.

On June 23, 2015, David and Jonathan and I had been having our camp meeting in our home, the three of us, and we had been praying for the baptism of the Holy Spirit and on June 23, 2015, I dreamed that David and Jonathan and I wanted to be baptized with the Holy Spirit. There were other people who said they, too, wanted to be baptized, when they knew we were wanting to be baptized with the Holy Spirit.

More Stories

CHRISTMAS SURPRISES!

It was Christmastime of the year when we struggle to pay our taxes and be able to buy winter propane and still keep up with bills and still pay our expenses and money for gas in the car and food and building materials for the "Ark" of safety we're building for the crisis soon to break upon those of us when the Sunday Laws will be passed and if we're true to God's seventh day sabbath, and not go along with keeping the Sunday man-made Sabbath, then we won't be able to buy and sell and will be persecuted and oppressed and fined and imprisonment, etc., and will need to be in the country where we'll be able to eat from our gardens and fruit trees and drink from our own hand pumped wells, etc.

God's people need to be preparing for this crisis soon to come upon us with blinding force and as an overwhelming surprise, as *Selected Messages*, book 2, p. 142 and as *Testimonies for the Church*, vol. 8, p. 28 says. Read, also, Sister White's counsel in *Country Living*, p. 8, 9, 10–15, 20, 21, 24, 28, 29, 30, 31. Read *Testimonies for the Church*, vol. 5, pp. 132–137, "Laborers for God." God is impressing His people around the world to prepare their country homes as "little Arks" for God's people to flee to when they'll have to leave these large cities and have nowhere to go. Sister White writes in *Country Living*, pp. 20 & 29, "God means that we shall not locate in the cities for there are troublous and stormy times before us."

It was Christmastime and I knew it wasn't really the day Jesus was born. I wanted to give Jesus a thank offering for all He had done for us and for all the answered prayers we had received from Him like: The refrigerator we had been praying for to put in our dining hall on the "Ark," but we had no money to buy one. Then, one day on his way to town my husband saw out on our gravel road just less than 1/4 mile from our drive was a BIG refrigerator! My husband left it there to see if someone would pick it up, and on his way home, no one had gotten it, so he brought it on home and it worked! Praise God! Thank you, Jesus! Then, we were needing propane bought for the winter, our meter was down in the RED and snow and cold winds were coming in and we had no money to buy any propane! We kept praying and that night I dreamed: I was in need of money to pay for something and I didn't have the money, and I looked in my purse and there was the money I needed. (End of dream)

So, I thought I'd call the bank and see what they showed in our account and they showed $400 more than what I showed! So, I called the propane company and asked them to please deliver propane to us, and that our tank was showing in the Red! I thanked her and our propane man came that day and I said to him, "I only have $400 for you to fill it up." He filled it 85% for $400 and said, "That's as full as I can fill it and be safe." I thanked him for coming and taking care of our needs! I then thanked the good Lord for supplying us with money in our checking account for just the amount we needed! Praise God from whom all blessings flow!

Then, one day the mail truck drove up and surprised us with a Big box! When I opened it, to my happy surprise, it was a box of oranges, grapefruits, and tangerines from Florida freshly picked and sent from the citrus orchard straight to us from my dear cousin, Nancy, who lives in Florida. Yum! Yum! God again was supplying our need for food! Phil. 4:19, Matt. 6:25–34. Thank you, Nancy. May God richly bless you for the joy you brought us!

Like I had said earlier, I wanted to give a Christmas gift to Jesus but all we had was a $10 bill left, and that was all we had to last us until we got our small Social Security check about two weeks from now. But I wanted so much to send that $10 to 3ABN for our Christmas gift to Jesus in thanks to Him for all the answered prayers and for taking care of our needs! I looked at the $10 bill and I thought of all our needs and struggled to keep it! Then, I thought of how much Jesus gave up to save me! John 3:16 and Matt. 1:21 and I thought of Matt. 6:24–34. I prayed, as I dropped the money in the mail, that God would please impress my dear cousin Diane and her husband Larry in Florida, or my dear cousin Nancy in Florida, who had just sent me all those citrus fruits from Florida or someone God would please impress to send us some money to help keep us going till we could receive our Social Security check. I claimed Phil. 4:19. I knew God was testing my faith and I knew in Heb. 11:6 it says, "But without faith it is impossible to please Him," so I put God first and prayed He'd bless me in return and supply our needs at this time! The same day I gave my thank offering of $10 and dropped it in the mail to 3ABN, trusting the Lord to take care of us, the Lord let me receive in the mail that very day a $100 bill from my dear cousin Diane and her dear husband Larry from Florida! How grateful I was that they had listened to the Holy Spirit to send their Christmas money gift to me just in time for me to receive it on the very same day I had given all the money I had to Jesus in faith, trusting Him to care for my needs! I thought of Eph. 3:20, 21! Thank you, Jesus! Thank you, Diane and Larry, and may God richly bless you.

I remember another Christmas surprise came in the mail from a dear friend like a sister to me, Sandie, from New Jersey. She had sent $30 and a beautiful card! This money came in the mail just when we needed it to buy lots of quarts of transmission fluid for our old 1989 Chevy truck that sprang a leak in the transmission line and we lost all our transmission fluid from the truck and no money to buy any transmission fluid. We prayed for help from the Lord, and before we had even had the trouble with the truck, God was impressing Sandie to send us that Christmas money to use it to meet our needs, and Sandie knew nothing about our truck breaking down in our driveway and we couldn't drive it, because we had no money to buy the transmission fluid needed to get it going again!! The non-Seventh-day Adventist neighbor friend we have welded the transmission line for us, but we had no money to buy the transmission fluid it needed to get it running again. That day God let Sandie's money come to us in answer to our prayers for help to supply our need! Praise God! Isa. 65:24, "And it shall come to pass, that before they call, I will answer and while they are yet speaking, I will hear." God bless her for her love and kindness shown to us. What a happy surprise that money was and how very thankful we were to receive it for a Christmas love gift. We knew she was retired on a low fixed income like we were and didn't expect any money from her for Christmas. God bless her and all those who have blessed us with Christmas surprises with their money love gifts and all they've done to be a blessing and a help to us!

Oh! Yes! Another Christmas surprise came when God supplied us with money for some food and some gas for our car and to get our bills paid that were due! The way it happened was: When I figure our bills, I never know for sure how much our electric bill will be each month, so I always leave plenty of money in our bank account to cover the cost when the bill comes due. But this December when I thought our electric bill would be real high, because we had used a lot of electricity in December and even in November, but the bill was actually a lot lower than normal and that left us more money in our checking account to use for food and gas and money for paying some bills that were due. We have no savings account to fall back on. Receiving this extra money to use was a pleasant Christmas surprise and so thankful to God for hearing our prayers for help and to meet our many needs! Praise God again for all He has done! Thank you, Jesus, for all your "Christmas Surprises" and blessings from above! We love you!

As I went to close this "Christmas Surprise" article, we received in the mail two more money love gifts! One was from a dear friend in New York, Cynthia. God bless her for thinking of us in our time of need, without her even knowing we were in need! Her money helped us with things like lumber and propane parts for our propane cook stove we needed to get hooked up and working and other things that we needed to buy to help us keep working on the "Ark." God is so good to hear our prayers and answer through His people that will listen to His Holy Spirit to be a blessing to others in need. Thank you, Cynthia, for letting God use you and may God richly bless you! You're in our prayers!

The other Christmas surprise money love gift came in the mail from David's sister, Hilma, from Chicago! She has been such a blessing and a help to us through the years as we have been building on the "Ark." She plans on a visit to the "Ark" sometime next year, 2016. Thank you my dear sweet sister-in-law for letting God use you to help us meet our needs and to keep building on the "Ark"! We love you and pray for you and the family! God's richest blessings be upon you for sharing your money with us! We appreciate your kindness and unselfishness shown to us! We look forward to your visit to the "Ark."

God just kept pouring the blessings on us with all these many "Christmas Surprises" that came so unexpectedly! Praise God for doing "exceedingly abundantly above all that we ask or think…" Eph. 3:14–21.

This next experience I'm going to relate to you reminds me of a dream I had that explains why things happen like they do and you can't see or understand why they are happening the way they are. We can't see behind the scenes how God is working things out for our good, as Rom. 8:28 promises. God is in control of things and we must learn to have faith and trust in God when we're going through our trials and troubles and wonder why God doesn't seem to be answering our prayers like we want. But God is there hearing our prayers and orchestrating things the way He knows is best and for reasons He has in mind. Have faith in God! Heb. 11:6. Put God first in your life and He'll take care of things. Matt. 6:33. Jesus loves you and is with you to help.

Here's the dream I had: There was a man having all kinds of trouble and couldn't figure out why things were happening like they were. But God was working things out for his good behind the scenes, as Rom. 8:28 says. But at the time this man couldn't see this yet. (End of dream)

This dream reminds me of what my husband David went through when he had gone with our truck to pick up a big heavy propane cook stove to put in our dining hall. He was having a hard time getting it loaded onto the truck by himself. He'd almost get it up onto the truck, but not quite. He kept praying for help and trying and trying to get it lifted up and onto the truck, but he just couldn't do it. God put it in his mind to go out on the gravel road and ask for help from the next person who drove by. Within one minute a young husky man drove by and David asked him to please help him lift this big heavy propane cook stove up onto his truck. The young man and David just slid it into the truck with no problem. David was so happy and thankful for the help and thanked the man and shook his hand and the man was so happy he was able to help Dad with his problem. David gave the man a *National Sunday Law* book and explained to him about what's coming and that Jesus is soon to come. The man was so very happy to get the book and thanked David for it. Now David could see why he couldn't get the cook stove up on the truck by himself, even though he had prayed, but still he couldn't do it. Now he saw and understood it was because God wanted this young man to get this book that he needed! This trouble came to him because God was wanting him to come in touch with a man who could help him with his problem he was having and also, so David could get the *National Sunday Law* book in this man's hands. But David couldn't see all this yet, until the experience he was going through was over and he could look back and see how God was working it all out. This is what we call God's providential leading. Sister White writes in *Last Day Events*, p. 72, "In reviewing our past history, having traveled over every step of advance to our present standing, I can say, Praise God! As I see what the Lord has wrought, I am filled with astonishment, and with confidence in Christ as leader. We have nothing to fear for the future, except as we shall forget the way the Lord has led us, and His teaching in our past history." We need to learn to say like Jesus said, "Not my will but thine be done." Luke 22:42.

ANGEL TO THE RESCUE!

Ps. 34:1, 3, 4, 6, 7, 8, 9, 15, 17–19, "I will bless the Lord at all times: his praise shall continually be in my mouth… O magnify the Lord with me, and let us exalt his name together. I sought the Lord, and he heard me, and delivered me from all my fears… This poor man cried, and the Lord heard him, and saved him out of all his troubles. The angel of the Lord encampeth round about them that fear him and delivereth them. O taste and see that the Lord is good: blessed is the man that trusteth in him. O fear the Lord, ye his saints: for there is no want to them that fear him… The eyes of the Lord are upon the righteous, and his ears are open unto their cry… The righteous cry, and the Lord heareth, and delivereth them out of all their troubles. The Lord is nigh unto them that are of a broken heart; and saveth such as be of a contrite spirit. Many are the afflictions of the righteous; but the Lord delivereth him out of them all."

Now that we had received the money for more building materials to continue work on the "Ark's" 24' x 44' greenhouse, we had prayer together and David was ready to leave in our old 1989 Chevy truck for another load of building materials. I reminded him it was Friday, the preparation day, and to be sure and get home in time for us to get the truck unloaded before Sabbath, and that there was a rain storm supposed to come in and to be careful. It was around 10:15 a.m., and he had to make an hour's drive to where he gets our lumber we needed for the greenhouse. He arrived safe to the lumber store and had gotten the things we needed and had gotten it all loaded up and was getting into the truck and a man, walking by our truck, said to Daddy, "You have a big puddle under your truck." David thanked him and he checked it out and so he drove over to a car parts place to purchase a new water hose that ours was old and dry rot and cracked and pouring water out.

So David began to work on the problem. He couldn't reach his big hand in there to work on the problem and he kept trying and finally he had to go into the car parts place to buy a small tool he needed. He worked and worked and still couldn't get to the problem to fix it. While he worked, he noticed a young man in a real rich car putting something on his car there at the car parts place, parked right next to David. Finally, after some time, the young man came over and asked Daddy what the problem was and if he could help him. David explained to him his problem and the young man said he had the right tool size and he'd be glad to fix it for him. He spent over two hours fixing it and then he left David the tool he needed. He wouldn't accept anything for his help. Then he left after David thanked him over and over for all his time and help.

It was getting toward evening and David had no phone to call me to tell me what was happening, because he knew I'd be worried. But he realized, too, he couldn't reach me on my phone anyway, so he began the long journey home. Jonathan and I had been praying and praying for Daddy because it was so many hours ago since he left and he wasn't home yet. Finally, about ten minutes before the sun set we saw his truck lights coming into the driveway. We just prayed and thanked the good Lord that he was safely home! I ran out to meet him and asked what happened. He said, "I'll tell you all about it in the house." We just left the truck loaded and went on into the house to pray and thank the good Lord for his safe trip. Then, David told us the whole story what had happened and I said, "Daddy, that could have been an angel God sent to help you with your problem! Praise the Lord! I said, "We've really been praying for you and were so worried that maybe you had an accident, or truck trouble or your load fell out. We had no idea why you were so late. God is so good! Thank you, Jesus!" Satan has sure been attacking our truck, but God keeps overruling the devil!

GOD SENT AN ANGEL!

This experience happened several years ago, before we had our dog, we now have.

We had just moved out into the wilds in the Chippewa Hills, where we began to build the "Ark" and get our place set up for the time of trouble when you won't be able to buy and sell and will have to live out of your own gardens.

This was in the days before we had put in a yard light that would come on automatically as night comes on. It can really be pitch black at night out in the deep woods with no yard light to come on and lighten things up all around you, so you can see what's out there creeping around out there in the woods. I have a tendency to be afraid in the dark, and especially when my husband has to be gone at night and I'm left home all alone out in the deep dark woods, 3 1/2 miles from town. This experience happened, too, before we were able to get a telephone. This particular time, David, my husband was planning to attend a camp meeting for a few days and encourage and warn the people that they should be heeding the counsel of the Spirit of Prophecy and be getting out of the big wicked cities while they still could and get set up for the early time of trouble and have a garden to survive on, a place that has woods for firewood and water from a creek or hand well pump. While at camp meeting he was going to have to sleep and eat in his car because we didn't have the money to pay for the expense for his lodging and cafeteria meals, therefore, I wouldn't be able to go with him, and would have to be left home alone. This made me feel apprehensive knowing I'd have to spend the nights alone out in the deep dark woods with no telephone, no money and no night light to come on at night, so I could see what was going on around me. Even though I had all God's promises to care for me, I was still feeling scared to be left all alone, and I knew I needed to show faith in God while my husband felt impressed, by God, to go warn God's people to leave these big wicked cities before God's judgments fall on them and before the Sunday Laws are passed and get out and prepare a place of refuge to be able to go through the early time of trouble and keep God's seventh day Sabbath holy. He was going to encourage them to read their *The Great Controversy* book and *Country Living* book and *Last Day Events* book by E. G. White and show them pictures of how he was getting his little "Ark" ready for the crisis ahead.

I remembered one of the quotes he was going to share was taken from *Country Living*, p. 31, "Out of the cities; out of the cities!"—this is the message the Lord has been giving me. The earthquakes will come, the floods will come; and we are not to establish ourselves in the wicked cities, where the enemy is served in every way, and where God is so often forgotten. The Lord desires that we shall have clear spiritual eyesight. We must be quick to discern the peril that would attend the establishment of institutions in these wicked cities. We must make wise plans to warn the cities, and at the same time live where we can shield our children and ourselves from the contaminating and demoralizing influences so prevalent in these places."

Well, the day came when he was to leave and we had prayer together and prayed God would please take care of each of us while we were apart. David hated to leave me home alone, too, because he knew how frightened I would be at night, and I was concerned for him going so far from home in our old car, with not much money on him. But we both agreed God's dear people at camp meeting needed to be encouraged and warned to leave these large wicked cities and get ready for the crisis ahead of us when you won't be able to buy or sell and all earthy support will be cut off and you'll be without your utilities and not able to buy your food at the stores, or gas for your car, and no telephones and without the conveniences of life because you won't go along with the Sunday Laws passed and be told you'll have to give up keeping God's seventh day Sabbath.

We had to step out on faith and trust God that He would care for me home alone and care for Dad, as he sacrificed our gas and food money from our little Social Security check, to make this trip and do without the conveniences of a comfortable lodging and tasty cafeteria meals, so he could help God's people see the dangers of remaining in the large cities, unnecessarily, and the necessity of having a place in the country and a garden to live out of during the crisis soon to come like Sister White says in *Selected Messages*, book 2, p. 142, "The work of the people of God is to prepare for the events of the future, which will soon come upon them with blinding force." Also, *Testimonies for the Church*, vol. 8, p. 28, "Transgression has almost reached its limit. Confusion fills the world, and a great terror is soon to come upon human beings. The end is very near. We who know the truth should be preparing for what is soon to break upon the world as an overwhelming surprise."

We knew it was urgent that Daddy go to camp meeting and share this information with God's people. Like the quote in *The Desire of Ages*, pp. 121–122, "In the last great conflict in the controversy with Satan those who are loyal to God will see every earthly support cut off. Because they refuse to break His law in obedience to earthly powers, they will be forbidden to buy or sell."

While Daddy was packing the car, getting ready to leave, a strange big dog, we had never seen before, just came up to our house and laid on our front porch by the front door and was content to stay right there. He was very friendly and David said, Well, the good Lord heard our prayers and sent you a dog to be company to you while I'm gone and will help you feel safer out here in the woods at night all alone by yourself." We prayed and thanked the good Lord for sending the dog for me and we prayed he'd stay with me while Dad would be gone for a few days. We kissed goodbye and waved, and as he left, I went into the house and got the dog some water and some old cat food we had left from a stray cat that had come here sometime back, but then the coyotes in the woods got him. The dog was such a friendly dog and a lot of company to me while Daddy was gone and every night, like a guard at his post of duty, he remained laying outside in front of my door, making me feel safe and secure and protected. I knew the Angel of the Lord encamped round about me as I read and claimed Ps. 34:7 each night before I went to bed. The Lord took care of Daddy, too, while he was witnessing for Jesus at camp meeting.

When Daddy arrived safely home from camp meeting, the dog left and we never saw him again! I knew then for sure, that God had heard my prayers and had known my human fears and had sent an angel, in the form of a guard dog that I could see, to quiet my fears and make me feel safer being able to see a dog at my door each night. We both thanked the good Lord for His tender loving care to take care of us both while we were apart. This experience God gave us just reinforces our faith and trust in God and His Word to care for His own during the two times of trouble ahead, the early time of trouble, when we'll be eating from our own gardens and can't buy or sell, and the great time of trouble when we'll need to flee for our lives to desolate and solitary places, when the plagues will be falling, and God will protect us and send help to supply all our needs, Isa. 33:15, 16, and Phil. 4:19. Now is the time to memorize these precious Bible promises of God and claim them and learn to have faith in God and trust Him to get us safely through the trials and troubles we'll face ahead. Sister White says in *The Ministry of Healing*, p. 249, "We need never feel that we are alone. Angels are our companions." In *The Great Controversy*, p. 512, it says, "Angels are sent on missions of mercy to the children of God. To Abraham…Elijah…Elisha…Daniel…Peter…prisoners at Philippi…to Paul and his companions…thus holy angels have, in all ages, ministered to God's people." Also, in *The Great Controversy*, p. 630 it says, "Could men see with heavenly vision, they would behold companies of angels that excel in strength stationed about those who have kept the word of Christ's patience." In *The Great Controversy*, p. 629 is the comforting promise given, "The people of God will not be free from suffering; but while persecuted and distressed, while they endure privation and suffer for want of food they will not be left to perish… While the wicked are dying from hunger and pestilence, angels will shield the righteous and supply their wants. To him that 'walketh righteously' is the promise: 'Bread shall be given him; his waters shall be sure…' "Isa. 33:15, 16. Also, Ps. 91 and Ps. 46 are encouraging promises to memorize. Read in *The Great Controversy* the chapter, "The time of Trouble." Read Isa. 56 and Ps. 27.

THE POWER OF PRAYER

We had brought Jonathan, our son, home for a visit around Christmastime from the nursing home where he had been staying.

We had bought him a watch on sale from Walmart, since he had no watch. We prayed we'd be able to figure out how to set it. David couldn't do it and so we gave it to Jonathan to figure it out. He worked with it for a while and finally said, "I can't do it either." Then he said, "I got it!" I asked him how he did it. He said, I prayed and asked the Lord to please help me and it just fell into place." I said, "It didn't just fall into place, God heard your prayers and set it for you!" I said, "Jesus loves you and wants you to take time to talk to Him in prayer. He's always there to help you in all your problems and needs and wants you to spend time in prayer and Bible study so He can be your help and strength in time of need. Satan knows if he can get you to neglect prayer and Bible study you won't have the power and strength from Jesus to resist him and he'll get you to fall into sin and his traps he set for you. Claim God's promises like Phil. 4:13; Jude 24; James 4: 7, 8. Jesus is stronger than Satan and He can keep you from falling, just submit your will to Jesus and resist the devil. Jesus can do anything like Luke 1:37 says and Mark 10:27 promises." I said to Jonathan, "I'm so proud of you that you know to turn to the Lord in prayer to help you with your problems! Jesus wants you to know He's with you to help you, but Satan tries to make you think you're too sinful to talk to God in prayer and hopes to discourage you from turning to Jesus for your strength and help in resisting him. Satan knows all he can keep from prayer and Bible study he can overcome, so he'll try in every way to prevent you from spending time in prayer and Bible study and separate you from Christ so he can get you to fall into sin. He doesn't care what sin he gets you to commit, because he knows sin is what will separate you from your source of power to resist his temptations. So, I'm so glad you know where to turn for help when you're in need! Jesus will never fail you. Have faith and trust in Him and His power to save and in His promises. Heb. 13:5.

THE PARCEL

Several years ago on 1-21-10 I had a dream that had the words, "The Parcel." I didn't know what the word Parcel meant so I looked it up in the dictionary to find the meaning and it said: a tract or plot of land, a company, collection or group of persons, animals or things, a wrapped bundle, package, a unit of salable merchandise, to divide into parts, distribute, to make up into a parcel, wrap.

I had no idea what the words, "The Parcel" meant in my dream, so I just went on my way wondering what it could mean, if maybe I'd be getting some kind of a parcel in the mail? I thought of Parcel Post.

Anyway, in the last two or three years we've been ordering books for our school here in "The Ark" that we'll be using to train people as they come to learn the medical missionary work and gardening, etc.

It had been about two months now since my dream about "the Parcel." I was getting an order ready for books and materials from Laymen Ministries. I was ordering (1) *Foxe's Book of Martyrs*, (1) *Omega II* book, (4) *Bible Chain Reference Texts* sheets, and (4) *Bible Handbooks* by S. N. Haskell. I really was wanting to order more *Bible Chain Reference* sheets and S. N. Haskell's *Bible Handbook* but I couldn't afford to order any more so I sent in my money order with my order to Laymen Ministry.

After about four weeks I hadn't received my order yet so I called Laymen Ministries. The lady said the orders are sent Media Mail and that's a slower delivery and you should be receiving your order any day now.

Then a week later I still hadn't received my package of books and materials yet, so I called again and she looked it up on the computer and it showed the order hadn't even been sent out yet. So she said she'd send my order by Priority Mail so I'd get it right away.

So in a few days on the Sabbath I got my order sent by Priority Mail that I had ordered six weeks ago! Then the next Sabbath the mailman drove up again to the house with a little piece of brown cardboard package all wrapped up with a lot of clear tape all around it and I saw it was from Laymen Ministries and I opened it up wondering what they were sending me and found out it was the same order of books and materials I'd ordered six weeks ago, and this package had come by Media Mail, and was a duplicate order and they had said their computer showed they hadn't sent the order, but here it was six weeks later and I was holding the order of books and materials in my hands and it was dated February 11, 2010. I thought how can I be getting this package six weeks later when they said their computer showed they hadn't even sent it yet!

Then I remembered my dream I had back there on 1-21-10, "The Parcel." I thought, "Maybe God sent this to me, that this was the meaning of the dream?

Then I thought I better call and let them know I got a duplicate order and be honest even though they said their computer showed it was never sent six weeks ago!

So I figured I'd call them Monday morning when they opened up but then I thought, it's not even on their computer that it was sent six weeks ago, so why call? This must be the parcel from the Lord I dreamed about!

My husband and I discussed it and prayed about it and decided we should call them and let them know what had happened because we wanted to be honest and right with God and live to please Him.

So when I called Monday morning I let the lady know I got my order she had sent by priority mail and I thanked her. Then I added, "But just this Sabbath I received a duplicate order in a little brown piece of cardboard all wrapped up with a lot of clear tape wrapped around the package from Laymen Ministries dated February 11, 2010, and it had come Media Mail.

She was so surprised because she knew by her computer she had never sent that order six weeks ago, and that's why she sent me the order Priority Mail. She was just so surprised about the package by media mail that I had just received. She asked if I had opened it and I said, "Yes! That's why I know what's in it! But I don't know what to do? I wanted to be honest and let you know I received a duplicate order from Laymen Ministries."

She asked me, "Can you use the duplicate order?" I said, "Oh! Yes! But I can't afford to pay two times for the order because my husband and I are retired and on a fixed low income."

She answered and said, "If you can use the things sent then just keep them, because it's not even recorded on our computer that they were ever sent six weeks ago from us."

I thanked her and said, "It must be a parcel from Jesus, because awhile back I had a dream about a parcel and this must be the parcel mentioned in my dream and Jesus knows we needed those things but couldn't afford to order more.

(This truly was a miracle from God!)

I then asked her since Jeff Reich, her boss, trains people to be Bible workers and sends them out overseas, but if someone would want to stay in the USA and do Bible work, maybe you can let them know we'd love to have a Bible worker to work in our area and find and give Bible studies to interested people?

I explained that my husband and I have passed out A LOT of books all over these counties around us and we'd love to have someone come here and work this area. There's truly a harvest here! I said, "We're in the country and have a garden and they could stay in a cabin we have for them, but there's no running water to the cabins, only electricity and wood stove." I told her that we see Jeff Reich on 3ABN and we pray for him and each of you in the wonderful work you're doing for Jesus to hasten His coming! I said, "We're trying to train up as medical missionaries ourselves like the Lord wants us to do. Please pray for us," I said, and then I thanked her again for what she had done for us and said, "God bless each of you at Laymen Ministries.".

When I hung up from talking to her I was so happy and so excited and thankful for what God had done for us to bless our little "Ark" school with His donation of books and materials we needed to help in our training of medical missionaries in which I really wanted more of these books and materials but couldn't afford them. God knows our heart's desires. It is so thrilling and exciting to know God is in the work we're doing in building "the Ark" for His glory and for His people He'll send when He knows the time is right. We just praised the Lord and thanked Him for what He had done for us in giving us this donation for our little Ark school and to let us know He's right there to help us in our needs! Just that very Monday morning before I was going to call Laymen Ministry and let them know the truth about the duplicate order that we received, I had dreamed, "Jesus loves you!"

Being honest and wanting to please the Lord makes Him happy. In Heb. 11:5 it says, "…for before his translation he (Enoch) had this testimony, that he pleased God."

This experience of receiving "the Parcel" from Jesus encouraged us to keep on doing what we're doing for the Lord's work knowing that He's behind us and helping us and supplying our needs as He's promised in Phil. 4:19, "But my God shall supply all your need according to his riches in glory by Christ Jesus."

We just want to be faithful and keep living to please Jesus and do His will and keep receiving His blessings to us.

Praise God from whom all blessings flow!

David & Linda Clore

MATTHEW 21:22

"And all things, whatsoever ye shall ask in prayer, believing, ye shall receive."

Before we had gone to bed that night we had listened to the weather band station and they had said it was going down to -2 degrees that night. That night as we had our worship we prayed it wouldn't freeze up our cold water pipes. Our hot water line was already turned off some time ago from the bad freezing weather and had cracked and was leaking bad and we had been without hot water for some time and unable to enjoy our hot showers.

That night I had a dream, 12-24-13. It was Matt. 21:22. As I woke up from this dream, I was claiming Matt. 21:22 and praying the Lord would please keep our water line from freezing, and I was praying two other prayer requests, too, as I made my way in the dark to the bathroom to use the toilet. When I flushed the toilet and went to wash my hands, I noticed there was no sound of water running back into the toilet and the faucet wouldn't turn on. It dawned on me, the water line had frozen! I prayed, "Please, Lord, I believe you can do anything, please hear my prayers to not let our water line freeze up," and I reminded Him of my dream of Matt. 21:22 I just dreamed and claimed the promise. Then I heard the water coming back into the toilet and water began coming out of the faucet! I praised God and thanked Him for hearing my prayers and thanked Him for keeping His promise in Matt. 21:22. I then proceeded to go turn on the cold water in the kitchen and other bathroom to make sure they were running, too, and they were! The other two prayer requests I was claiming as I made my way to the bathroom I don't remember what they were, but I knew one had to do with my son, Jonathan. I prayed and asked the Lord to please hear my other two prayer requests I had made in the early hours of the morning and claimed Matt. 21:22 and said to the Lord, "I know you can do anything, so please grant me my other two prayer requests, too. Thank you! I have faith in you and your promise." I had fasted just that day by eating just a very little for breakfast and praying for God to please answer my prayers. Mark 10:27 and Luke 1:37.

During the same night I dreamed Matt. 21:22 again and saw it snowing in my dream. I woke up. I was praying it wouldn't snow anymore, because we had already had a bad ice and snow storm. I claimed Matt. 21:22 as I prayed.

We had our worship and listened to the weather band station and they were forecasting more snow. We prayed it wouldn't snow anymore and claimed Matt. 21:22. It didn't Snow*!* Praise God!

We prayed, too, that our propane would please last in our tank until we got our next Social Security check eleven days from now. I reminded the Lord of the promise in 1 Kings 17 where He kept the Zarephath widow woman's barrel of meal and cruse of oil from failing during the drought and we thanked the Lord for hearing these earnest prayers.

On December 30th I called to let the propane company know we wanted to order propane and they give us one week to pay it, when we pay cash. I told her we wouldn't have the cash until we got our Social Security check January 3. She said it wouldn't be for another week before they would deliver propane out our way. I thanked her and hung up the phone and prayed God would please supply all our needs as Phil. 4:19 promises and I left it in the Lord's hands to keep our propane going for another week. Then, that evening after dark, our propane man that delivers propane in our area came up our driveway in his big propane truck with his headlights on and with our propane! I thanked him for coming and he said, "I wanted to beat the big snows coming in and I was out your way and got the call you needed propane so I decided to come on out now and fill your tank for you." I thanked him again for thinking of us and for coming after dark and I asked him if he'd accept a predated check for January 3 when we'd get our money to pay him. He said, "Sure, that will be okay." I thanked him again and wished him a Happy New Year as he drove off in that big propane truck in the dark. I, also, thanked my heavenly Father for looking after us and supplying our needs like He had promised to do in Phil 4:19 and Eph. 3:20, 21. The next day the big snows and ice storms hit and lasted for several days with bitter cold winds! We were so thankful our propane tank was full! Praise God!

WHO WAS IT?

It was at the end of the month again and we were down to just what change we had left. We were needing gas in our car and we had only about $5 in change. As David got into line to buy gas, he laid the change out on the counter for the cashier to count out how much change he had to buy some gas with. Gas was running $3.42 a gallon. There was a middle-aged lady standing in line and was right behind David. She could see the predicament we were in, down to our last penny. She handed David a $10 bill. David thanked her over and over again for her help and kindness and how much he appreciated what she had done!

He hurried out to the car to get a book to give to her and in seconds he returned with the book and she was nowhere around. He looked all over inside and outside and at the pumps, but she had just vanished and was gone! He pumped the gas in and when he got back into the car he told me what had happened! I said, "It could have been an angel! Only God knew we were down to the last of our money! He must have sent an angel to supply our needs! Praise the Lord!

We prayed and thanked the Lord for supplying us with money for gas and asked God to bless the lady who gave us the money, if maybe it had been someone impressed to give us that $10 for gas, we needed so much, or if maybe God had used an angel in the form of a lady to get the $10 in our hands to supply our need for gas? However it happened to be, we were most grateful for God looking out for us and keeping His promise in Phil. 4:19.

God is so wonderful! He's always there when we need Him and never fails us! He watches over us and even knows the number of the hairs on our head. (Matt. 10:30)

God just keeps giving us experiences like this so our faith will stay strong in the Lord to care for us and meet our needs in the time of trouble ahead of us, when we'll have to show faith and trust in God to take care of us and supply all our needs when we can't buy or sell and every earthly support will be cut off. (Read *The Desire of Ages*, p. 121 & 122; Eph. 3:19, 20)

Soon the Sunday Laws will be upon us and we'll be so thankful then that we're out in the country and have our own garden to eat from when you won't be able to go to the store to get your food.

There are troublous times before us and we need to be preparing our country homes for the crisis ahead and preparing our hearts to learn to depend on God to be there with us and claim His promises to us as we endure the trials and troubles and hardships and burdens we'll be going through during the Sunday Laws that will be passed and everyone will have to decide which side they're going to be on. Either keeping God's seventh day Sabbath holy as God commands and being cared for by God and His holy angels and receive the seal of God and go safely through the early Time of Trouble and the Great Time of Trouble and the death decree and the seven last plagues and receive eternal life when Jesus comes to rescue us.

Or, choose to keep Sunday, man's sabbath, and receive the Mark of the Beast and the seven last plagues and be eternally lost.

Read Joshua 24:14, 15. Yes! We need to be choosing each day whom we will serve. So, when the final choice is made, we'll choose to serve and obey God and His seventh day Sabbath and keep all His Ten Commandments.

The choice is up to you and me which side we'll be on then, by the choices we're making day by day now. Learn now to trust and obey God and have faith in His promises to see you through each day and have faith that He loves you and will care for you and your every need. Have faith in God. Heb. 11.

THE ANGELS DID IT!

David and I had been working on our 12' x 20' concrete block basement for some time now, and God had been giving us the help and strength and wisdom and knowledge we needed in answer to our many prayers to be able to build this basement God had given me a dream to build, with all the tons of blocks He had supplied for us to do the job with.

This was something we had never done before and we had had to go to the library to get information to know how to construct such a project and we praised God at every step He had helped us and strengthened us as we prayed through every phase of this project.

We knew the weather was changing into colder weather and we'd had several freezes and we still had to get another layer of concrete blocks laid to make it seven feet high. We knew the freezing weather wasn't the best condition for laying concrete. We were in an extra big hurry to get finished before nightfall. We kept praying and asking God to please help us get the job done fast.

David had gotten a big pile of rocks he had gathered up so he could break them into pieces with a 20-pound sledge hammer and use the pieces to fill in the holes in the concrete blocks along with concrete and rebar to make the block walls stronger. He had chipped up a lot of pieces, but the remainder rocks were hard as granite and he was having a hard time cracking them and taking all his time away from laying the blocks.

So, I prayed and talked to the Lord about our situation we were in and that David needed help, that this really was a two-man job and I wanted to help him and get the job done before nightfall. I wanted to be able to crack up those hard rocks for him and save him time. I prayed and said to the Lord, "Lord, I can't do this, if David, as strong as he is can't crack them, I know I can't do it either, but Lord I know you can do anything, like Phil. 4:13 says and also, the promises in Mark 10:27; Luke 1:37; John 14:13; John 15:7; and Matt. 21:22, I claim all these promises in Your name! Please send angels to help me crack up these extra hard rocks into pieces, so I can help David get this layer of blocks finished. Please, Lord, when I hit the rocks with this 20-pound sledge hammer, would you please let the angels crack the rocks into pieces for me, I can't do this in my own strength? Thank you so much, Lord for hearing my prayer for help!"

I picked up the 20-pound sledge hammer and began slinging it down on the rocks and they were splitting up into pieces and with every blow of the 20-pound sledge hammer pieces were flying and in no time I had enough pieces of rock cracked up so David could hurry and finish up the job before nightfall. I just praised and thanked the good Lord for hearing my earnest prayers for help and for sending the angels to crack the rocks into pieces for me.

David was so amazed when he saw what I had done and said, "How did you do that??!! I could hardly crack them up, but with every blow of the sledge hammer, they're just falling apart for you!"

I said, "It's not me doing it, it's the angels Jesus sent in answer to my prayer for help! They are cracking them up as I hit them!"

We both thanked the good Lord for all the help He'd been to get the job done before nightfall and also, kept it from freezing, so our concrete could set up and dry okay. Praise God! He's so powerful and wonderful!

We're seeing and experiencing how God can do anything when we're in need of help.

We share this experience to encourage others and to show the power of God and His loving care in our time of need and stands behind His promises.

We have got to learn to let the Lord prove His promises in our lives and show His power to answer our prayers and learn to have faith and trust in Him to get us through the difficult times ahead of us during the early time of trouble when we'll have to walk by faith and trust in the Lord to hear our prayers for help and supply all our needs, as Phil. 4:19 promises.

God is getting us in condition now, as He allows us to go through our hard times and difficulties now and trusting in Him to help, so we'll be used to depending on Him to see us through the crisis ahead of us when every earthly support will be cut off and we won't be able to buy and sell and will be totally depending on the Lord to strengthen us through the hard times and trials and troubles that will come to those of us who will remain faithful and true to the Lord and His seventh day Sabbath and not give in to the pressures to go along with the Sunday Laws that will soon be passed.

In *The Desire of Ages*, pp. 121–122, Sister White gives us these words of counsel, "In the wilderness, when all means of sustenance failed, God sent His people manna from heaven; and a sufficient and constant supply was given. This provision was to teach them that while they trusted in God and walked in His ways He would not forsake them… Often the follower of Christ is brought where he cannot serve God and carry forward his worldly enterprises. Perhaps it appears that obedience to some plain requirement of God will cut off his means of support. Satan would make him believe that he must sacrifice his conscientious convictions. But the only thing in our world upon which we can rely is the Word of God… When we learn the power of His Word, we shall not follow the suggestions of Satan in order to obtain food or to save our lives. Our only question will be, What is God's command? and what His promise? Knowing these, we shall obey the one, and trust the other. In the last great conflict of the controversy with Satan those who are loyal to God will see every earthly support cut off. Because they refuse to break His law in obedience to earthly powers, they will be forbidden to buy or sell. It will finally be decreed that they shall be put to death. See Rev. 13:11–17. But to the obedient is given the promise, 'He shall dwell on high: his place of defense shall be the munitions of rocks: bread shall be given him; his waters shall be sure.' Isa. 33:16. By this promise the children of God will live."

Sister White in *Testimonies for the Church*, vol. 2, p. 579, says, "'Ye are the light of the world,' says the heavenly Teacher. All have not the same experience in their religious life. But those of diverse exercises come together and with simplicity and humbleness of mind talk out their experience. All who are pursuing the onward Christian course should have, and will have, an experience that is living, that is new and interesting. A living experience is made up of daily trials, conflicts, and temptations, strong efforts and victories, and great peace and joy gained through Jesus. A simple relation of such experiences gives light, strength, and knowledge that will aid others in their advancement in the divine life."

Listen to what Sister White has to say about prayer. In *The Great Controversy*, p. 525, "Again, worldly wisdom teaches that prayer is not essential. Men of science claim that there can be no real answer to prayer; that this would be a violation of law, a miracle, and that miracles have no existence… Such teaching is opposed to the testimony of Scriptures. Were not miracles wrought by Christ and His apostles? The same compassionate Saviour lives today, and He is as willing to listen to the prayer of faith as when He walked visibly among men. The natural co-operates with the supernatural. It is a part of God's plan to grant us, in answer to the prayer of faith, that which He would not bestow did we not thus ask."

There's a statement by Sister White found in *Acts of the Apostles*, p. 564, where she says, "Prayer is heaven's ordained means of success in the conflict with sin and the development of Christian character. The divine influences that come in answer to the prayer of faith will accomplish in the soul of the suppliant all for which he pleads. For the pardon of sin, for the Holy Spirit, for a Christlike temper, for wisdom and strength to do His work, for any gift He has promised, we may ask; and the promise is, 'Ye shall receive.'"

Sister White says in *My Life Today*, pp. 18, 19, "True prayer, offered in faith, is a power to the petitioner… But the prayer that comes from an earnest heart, when the simple wants of the soul are expressed just as we would ask an earthly friend for a favor, expecting that it would be granted—this is the prayer of faith… Divine help is to be combined with human effort, aspiration, and energy."

In *Testimonies for the Church*, vol. 6, pp. 404–410, the chapter entitled, "Preparation for the Final Crisis," Sister White has these solemn words of admonition to speak to those of us living today. "The great crisis is just before us. To meet its trials and temptations, and to perform its duties, will require persevering faith. But we may triumph gloriously; not one watching, praying, believing soul will be ensnared by the enemy… Brethren, to whom the truths of God's word have been opened, what part will you act in the closing scenes of this world's history? Are you awake to these solemn realities? Do you realize the grand work of preparation that is going on in heaven and on earth? Let all who have received the light, who have had the opportunity of reading and hearing the prophecy, take heed to those things that are written therein; 'for the time is at hand'… The return of Christ to our world will not be long delayed. Let this be the keynote of every message… The battle of Armageddon is soon to be fought… It is now but a short time till the witnesses for God will have done this work in preparing the way of the Lord… We are to throw aside our narrow, selfish plans, remembering that we have a work of the largest magnitude and highest importance. In doing this work we are sounding the first, second, and third angel's messages, and are thus being prepared for the coming of that other angel from heaven who is to lighten the earth with his glory… The watchman is to know the time of night. Everything is now clothed with a solemnity that all who believe the truth for this time should realize... The judgments of God are about to fall upon the world, and we need to be preparing for that great day. Our time is precious. We have but few, very few days of probation in which to make ready for the future, immortal life. We have no time to spend in haphazard movements. We should fear to skim the surface of the Word of God... The restraining Spirit of God is even now being withdrawn from the world. Hurricanes, storms, tempests, fire, and flood, disasters by sea and land, follow each other in quick succession... Men cannot discern the sentinel angels restraining the four winds that they shall not blow until the servants of God are sealed, but when God shall bid His angels loose the winds, there shall be such a scene of strife as no pen can picture..."

Joel 2:12–17; Luke 21:34; Mark 13:36.

"Prayer is heaven's ordained means of success in the conflict with sin and the development of Christian character..."

Acts of the Apostles, p. 564

THE DREAM

I was having a lot of dreams from the Lord and thanking Him for all the good dreams He was giving to me. Then I thought, "I think I'll pray and ask the Lord to please give me a dream this night and see what He says." This is what I dreamed in answer to my prayer for a dream that night: Someone was saying to me, "You need to get a refrigerator. Make this first on your list. Be watching for one!" I said to the person speaking to me, "Would you please watch the papers for me, too?"

We needed a refrigerator for our 12' x 20' cabin we're building over our basement. That way we won't have to take one out of our other cabins that all have a refrigerator in them. We wanted a BIG refrigerator for the cabin over the basement we're building on right now.

We began praying and asking God to please direct us to the right one. We checked different papers and bulletin boards in the stores, but no refrigerator. We had no money to buy one anyway, but knew God would somehow supply us with the money at the right time. We took the last of our money out of the bank, $40, and I called a used furniture place to see if they had a cheap used refrigerator for sale? They didn't have any, but the lady at the store said to call this other used furniture place and they might have one and she gave me their number to call. I called and explained we needed a big refrigerator and what was the cheapest one they might have? She said they had a cross-top for $175. I asked if she would take $40 down payment and then when we got our Social Security check on the 3rd we'd give her the other $135 and she said she would do that. We started to make the 45 mile trip there and back to give her the $40 to hold it for us. David said, "Why don't you call and see if she'll take a predated check?" So as we started off in the car to hurry over there with our down payment of $40, because they would close in about 1/2 hour. I reached her by phone and asked if we brought the $40 to her and wrote a pre-dated check for the other $135 if she'd do that until we got our Social Security the 3rd and could pay her then? I then said that we'd drive our truck over there the 3rd and pay her the rest of the money and pick up the refrigerator then. She said, "Why don't you just wait making the trip over here with your $40 and a predated check? We'll hold it for you and when you get your money the 3rd just drive your truck over then and pick up the refrigerator." I thanked her and then my husband asked me to ask her if it worked okay? I asked her and she said, "My service man works at Sears and he goes over everything real well checking it out; and we also will give you a 60 day guarantee and we'll hold it for you, so just come with your truck and pick it up the 3rd when you get your money then and not have to make two trips." I thanked her for being an answer to our prayers and that God would bless her for her help to us. I wished her a Happy New Year and told her we'd be there the 3rd. Then I said to her, "We're supposed to get a bad snow and freeze the 1st and we wouldn't be able to make it over there in the bad weather, shall I send you the check when we get our money the 3rd? She said, "Don't worry about anything, we'll hold it for you, and just come when you can make it." I thanked her again for doing this for us.

When I hung the phone up my husband and I thanked the good Lord for working this all out for us. We turned the car around and headed back home, which we were only about three miles from home. We were so happy for the dream and how God answered our prayers in only one week with a BIG refrigerator for our cabin. Praise the Lord!

But the bad snow and ice storms came and we weren't going anywhere in a storm like this one! Then we kept having one storm after another. Then when a few weeks had passed and we could safely make the trip and our yard had dried out so we could roll it on a dolly to our cabin, we called and found out she had sold the refrigerator. But she assured us she'd get others in and to keep checking.

We called other used appliance stores and dealers, but all the used refrigerators were from $300–$600. We knew we couldn't afford anything like that so we kept praying. About a few weeks later we checked back with the lady with the used refrigerators and she had gotten some in but they were all gone. Then we checked back again in a week or so and she said she had some but her service man had ordered parts for them and was waiting for parts to repair them and for me to check in another week.

When I checked again she said, her service man hadn't been in to repair them because his horse was ready to deliver the colt and he couldn't come in and work on the refrigerators. She said to check back in maybe another week and they'd be repaired.

So in a week I called and she said she didn't have any at the $175 price range she had quoted to me before, but she had a real good one that her service man put a lot of new parts on and made it like a brand new refrigerator and she'd sell it to me for $245. We thanked her and said we'd be right over to get it. When we got there we saw it was a BIG 20 cubit-size refrigerator, Kenmore, white and the freezer was on the bottom and the refrigerator on top. It was a nice beautiful refrigerator, too. She said to me, "I'm not going to charge you any tax on this sell since you've had to wait so long to get your refrigerator. We thanked her and wrote the check and as we were going out to back our pickup truck up to the door, a friend of hers drove in the drive and she said, "Well, he came just in time! He can load up the refrigerator for you and rope it down." We knew God let him come just in time to help us and we thanked the good Lord for His timing. When we were ready to leave we gave each of them literature and thanked them both for the help they'd been to us. She gave us a 60 day guarantee on the refrigerator.

When we reached home safely with our big refrigerator, we thanked the Lord for getting us such a nice refrigerator, like new! Then we prayed and asked the Lord to please send angels to get it unloaded off the truck and up the steep ramp into the cabin. It was a terrible struggle and it just barely fit through the cabin door! It worked really well and we were so happy God had gotten us the right refrigerator for our cabin and it was worth waiting for! Praise God from whom all blessings flow!

We thanked God for the dream and the answers to our prayers in being able to get such a BIG nice pretty refrigerator like new. God is good! God knew which refrigerator He wanted us to have! God, also, supplied us with the money to be able to purchase the refrigerator He wanted us to buy. I received birthday money from family and friends! Praise God! Phil. 4:19, "But my God shall supply all your need according to His riches in glory by Christ Jesus."

GOD SHOWED HIS POWER!

One day David was in Ottawa, Kansas, a town of almost 12,000 population, around twenty miles to Walmart there. He was shopping at the Walmart and he noticed a mammoth stack of used big-size concrete blocks, about 800–1,000 blocks that had been used at the Walmart for a construction project and they no longer needed the blocks. They had a BIG FOR SALE sign up. They were selling them at a very cheap price. He just couldn't pass up such a bargain price. He felt impressed by the Holy Spirit to go into Walmart and talk to the one responsible for selling the blocks. He paid for a load and brought them home in our little S10 Chevy truck. We unloaded them together and he then hurried back into Walmart to get another load before someone else came along and got them all before we could get them.

We kept praying God would please help us to get the blocks and that no one else would buy them and that God would please give us the strength to hold up and be able to work through the night bringing them home one small truckload at a time. We couldn't load too many at a time in our little Chevy truck, because it's all rusted out underneath the truck and the sides and fenders are all rusted out, so we couldn't put too many blocks in the truck at one time, it would be dangerously unsafe.

So, David worked all through the night loading up the truck by himself and then bringing them home one load after the other load at a time and I'd help him unload them at home. All through the night we worked. One load at a time. The Lord sent His angels, in answer to our prayers, to please help us to hold up and give us both strength to continue all through the night getting these blocks loaded and unloaded and praying, too, that no one else would come along and buy them.

In the morning as David went in to pay for the last load and give the man a book, he said to the man selling the blocks, "Thanks a lot for saving these blocks for me. I'm surprised no one else wanted them." The guy answered him and said, 'I didn't save them for you. I had several people come to me and say, "I'll be right back, I want those blocks.' But no one ever came back for them, except you."

We knew then that God had heard our prayers and had kept anyone else from getting those blocks, so we could have them. We knew, too, God had given us the strength to get them all safely home, working through the night and keeping our old 1989 rusted-out Chevy truck from breaking down. We praised and thanked the good Lord for doing this for us!

As we looked at the BIG stack of 800–1,000 concrete blocks, we thought, what are we going to do with so many blocks? What plans does God have for us to use so many blocks?

We have used those blocks for so very many projects working on the "ARK." They have been a big help and savings to us, since big concrete blocks are so expensive. We have used them as a foundation under the cabins we have built and bought for the "ARK."

But even after all the many uses we had made of those many concrete blocks, we still had a mammoth stack of blocks left and we wondered, "Why did God impress us of the urgency to hurry and buy up all those many blocks?"

It took several years of those tons of blocks staying stacked up there and unused and knowing by faith that God wouldn't have helped us get all those many blocks so cheap and the power and strength to move them all home all through the night, if He didn't have a purpose and a plan for us to make use of them. And He kept anyone else from buying them!

We thought maybe we'd make a root cellar to store our garden products in to preserve them in the winter. We kept praying and asking God for wisdom and knowledge to know what He wanted us to do with all these hundreds of concrete blocks!

Then, one night in a dream, God showed me a 12' x 20' basement made with the concrete blocks, and to put a 12' x 20' cabin on top of the basement. We thanked the good Lord for answering our prayers.

Then, David began to dig down by hand with a pick and shovel to clear the big hole for a 12' x 20' basement, which he had to dig even a bigger size than that so we'd have room to work down in the hole to be able to lay the concrete blocks up 7 feet high. With God's help and strength and wisdom and knowledge, He answered our payers to help us get it dug by hand and how to lay the concrete blocks to make a basement. We neither one are carpenters. We rely totally on God for building the "ARK" and all its projects! We have faith God will help us and we begin to build, praying all the time for God to send His angels to give us power and help and strength and wisdom and knowledge to do what God tells us to do in building the "ARK" for the Little Time of Trouble "that will come before the Great Time of Trouble when the Sunday Laws will be passed enforcing people to keep Sunday as Sabbath that man has set up, and we faithful Seventh-day Adventists won't go along with this Sunday Law sabbath, we'll then be unable to buy and sell like Rev 13:17 says. We'll be true to God's seventh day Sabbath and all His Ten Commandments.

This will be the "early or "little" time of trouble when we'll be living out of our own gardens out in the country where God has told His people they should be so they can survive the little time of trouble when we won't be able to buy anything or sell anything. We'll need to be able to exist during this period of time living in our little ARKS of safety we have prepared ahead of time, until we have to flee to the desolate and solitary places God has provided for us to be safe during the Great Time of Trouble when the seven last plagues are falling and the death decree has been passed, upon those of us who have remained loyal to God's true seventh day Sabbath and all His Ten Commandments. God promises our bread and water will be sure then in Isa. 33:15, 16. I like the promise God gave Sister White to write to those of us living during the death decree time and how angels will be sent to direct us to places of safety out in the forests and the clefts of mountains to preserve our life during the death decree and the seven last plagues. It's found in the book, *Maranatha*, p. 270 entitled, "Angelic Protection in the time of Trouble." Also, read *Testimonies for the Church*, vol. 5, pp. 454–467, "The Church the Light of the World."

God will also show His power through the Holy Spirit to parents who are praying to God for guidance and direction in their lives and who want to save themselves and their children from the soon coming crisis ahead in the near future and be able to get out of these BIG wicked cities as soon as possible, as God opens the way before them to do so. As they pray in faith and trust God through His Holy Spirit to give them wisdom and knowledge and power and strength and courage and faith to step out and make the move, trusting God's plans for their lives.

In the book, *Country Living*, by E. G. White she says this on pages 24–28, "Guided by God's Providences," on p. 24 it says, "The time has come, when, as God opens the way, families should move out of the cities. The children should be taken into the country. The parents should get as suitable a place as their means will allow. Though the dwelling may be small, yet there should be land in connection with it, that may be cultivated... Parents can secure small homes in the country with land for cultivation, where they can have orchards and where they can raise vegetables and small fruits to take the place of flesh meat, which is so corrupting to the life blood coursing through the veins. On such places the children will not be surrounded with the corrupting influences of city life. God will help His people to find such homes outside the city... More and more, as time advances, our people will have to leave the cities."

Also, read *The Great Controversy*, pp. 603–612, "The Final Warning." Joel 2:28, 29; Isa. 8:20. God will show His power also to pour out His Holy Spirit on those of us who are preparing our hearts and lives to receive this power.

Read in *The Desire of Ages*, the chapter "'Let Not Your Heart Be Troubled", pp. 662–680. On p. 672 Sister White gives this counsel, "Christ has promised the gift of the Holy Spirit to His church, and the promise belongs to us as much as to the first disciples. But like every other promise, it is given on conditions. There are many who believe and profess to claim the Lord's promises; they talk about Christ and about the Holy Spirit, yet receive no benefit. They do not surrender the soul to be guided and controlled by the divine agencies. We cannot use the Holy Spirit. The Holy Spirit is to use us. Through the Spirit God works in His people 'to will and to do of His good pleasure.' Phil. 2:13. But many will not submit to this. They want to manage themselves. This is why they do not receive the heavenly gift. Only to those who wait humbly upon God, who watch for His guidance and grace, is the Spirit given. The power of God awaits their demand and reception. This promised blessing, claimed by faith, brings all other blessings in its train. It is given according to the riches of the grace of Christ, and He is ready to supply every soul according to the capacity to receive."

It was by faith and the Holy Spirit's power that we felt the urgent need to buy up all those concrete blocks and hurry and get them bought and brought home before anyone else purchased them. And even though it was several years before we knew and understood why we were impressed to do this, God has His plans and we acted on faith and the Holy Spirit impressing us! Praise

God! He's always one step ahead of us preparing the way for His plans. Isa. 65:24, "And it shall come to pass, that before they call, I will answer; and while they are yet speaking, I will hear." Also in Jer. 33:3 we read God's promise, "Call unto me, and I will answer thee, and show thee great and mighty things which thou knowest not."

This was just another way we saw how God showed His power to supply our needs way in advance before we knew and understood what He was doing. We thank Him now that we can see what His plans were for all those tons of blocks, before we even knew for sure why we were getting them. Now the 12' x 20' basement is done and the 12' x 20' cabin on top. Praise God! Thank you, Jesus!

Sister White tells us how wise God is in managing things in our lives. In *Testimonies for the Church*, vol. 5, p. 348, she says, "He, God, is wise enough to manage the complications of our lives. He has skill and tact. We cannot always see His plans; we must wait patiently their unfolding and not mar and destroy them. He will reveal them to us in His own good time." Also, on p. 346 she writes, "Let us remember that Jesus knows us individually and is touched with the feeling of our infirmities. He knows the wants of each of His creatures and reads the hidden unspoken grief of every heart… Jesus cares for each one as though there were not another individual on the face of the earth."

We need to live and walk by faith and trust in God's guidance and direction in our lives through His Holy Spirit's power.

Heb. 10:37, 38, 39, "For yet a little while, and he that shall come will come, and will not tarry. Now the just shall live by faith: but if any man draw back, my soul shall have no pleasure in him. But we are not of them who draw back unto perdition; but of them that believe to the saving of the soul."

For those wanting to be led by God's Holy Spirit through His providential leading and who want to obey God's orders to get out of these large cities as soon as possible, will show faith and trust in God and let Him direct their paths as God opens and closes doors for them so they can be taken from their present circumstances and placed in a more favorable setting. Claim God's promises to you. Prov. 3:5–8; Ps. 37:3–5.

Sister White has these words of encouragement to all who are listening for God's orders, it's found in *Counsels to Parents, Teachers, and Students*, pp. 182, 183, "The shield of faith will be their defense and will enable them to be more than conquerors. Nothing else will avail but this—faith in the Lord of hosts, and obedience to His orders… Without faith, an angel host could not help. Living faith alone will make them invincible and enable them to stand in the evil day, steadfast, unmovable, holding the beginning of their confidence firm unto the end… True faith asks the Lord, "What wilt thou have me to do? And when the way is marked out by the Master, faith is ready to do His will, at whatever hardship or sacrifice."

I encourage you to seek wisdom from God and pray and fast over your plans and decisions made. Follow the counsel Sister White gives in her book, *Country Living*, p. 25, "Those who have felt at last to make a move, let it not be in a rush in an excitement, or in a rash manner, or in a way that hereafter they will deeply regret that they did move out… All that anyone can do is to advise and counsel, and then leave those who are convicted in regard to duty to move under divine guidance, and with their whole hearts open to learn and obey God."

GOD KEEPS HIS PROMISES!

Gen. 9:8–17, Prov. 22:6

On June 16, 2010, God put a double rainbow over the "ARK." I was out jogging around our circle driveway and it began to lightly rain. I looked up in the sky and saw a beautiful rainbow. I said to the Lord, "Lord, I know you've promised never to destroy the whole world again with a flood and you put your rainbow in the sky to show you'll keep your promise. But Lord, would you please put another rainbow in the sky to show me You'll keep your promise in Prov. 22:6 about my son, Jonathan?" Then, David and I both saw the second rainbow appear over the other one and I was able to get a picture of it! Dad and I both prayed and thanked God for the double rainbow! We know God has plans for our boy, Jonathan. Praise God! Please keep praying for him! Thanks! Prov. 22:6, "Train up a child in the way he should go: and when he is old, he will not depart from it." God has spared Jonathan's life over and over again! Praise God! God has plans for Jonathan.

> "Train up a child in the way he should go: and when he is old, he will not depart from it."
>
> Proverbs 22:6

GOD PUTS A DOUBLE RAINBOW OVER THE 'ARK' TWICE!

It was August 11, 2010, the weather station was warning of a severe storm headed toward Lyndon and Quenemo, Kansas, with 70 mile per hour winds and hail and heavy rains and telling the people to take cover *Now!* Dad and I prayed for God's protection over us and "the Ark" and over Jonathan in the nursing home. We prayed God would divert the storm from us. The storm went around us and went south and north of us and we were spared. Praise God! We prayed and thanked God! I went outside to ride my bike around our circle driveway and it was just lightly sprinkling rain and dark clouds in the sky and lightening some. The severe storm had parted and just a much-needed, gentle rain we were getting in answer to our prayers for rain on our garden that God had already blessed and spared us many other times from other bad storms that He had kept from hitting and destroying our garden and "the ARK" and us. I looked in the sky for God's rainbow and saw none, like I'd seen the double rainbow over our place on June 16, 2010, in answer to my prayer for God to send a double rainbow to show He'd keep His promise in Prov. 22:6 about our son, Jonathan, and He did! Praise God! Then I prayed God would please put another double rainbow in the sky over "the ARK" to show He'll protect "the ARK" and us and our son, Jonathan, during the storms and through the time of trouble ahead that we're preparing "the ARK" for. I said, "Lord, I know I'm not worthy to pray and ask this of you, and I don't mean to be presumptuous in asking you to please put two rainbows in the sky again over 'the ARK.' "

There was no rainbow present in the sky at the time I prayed and asked God to put a double rainbow over "the ARK" like He did on June 16, 2010. Then as I kept praying and watching in faith for the double rainbow to appear over "the ARK," I first saw a beautiful rainbow appear over "the ARK." Then I kept praying He'd please put the second one over the first one. I watched and waited and prayed and then the second rainbow appeared over the first one over "the ARK." I prayed and thanked God for hearing my prayers for a double rainbow over "the ARK" and praised Him for hearing my sincere and heartfelt prayers! I called David out to see God's double rainbow over "the ARK" and I took a picture of it to remind me that God heard my prayers to send a double rainbow over "the ARK" to keep His promise to protect "the ARK" and us and our son, Jonathan, during the time of trouble ahead of us. I know God has other people He'll be sending here, too. God is looking out for His ARK we're preparing for God's people and us to go through the time of trouble ahead when Sunday Laws are passed and you won't be able to buy or sell because you're keeping God's true seventh day Sabbath and all His commandments and not going along with the Mark of the Beast. Just like God protected Noah and his family in the flood. Heb. 11:7. Praise God!

THE TWO PRAYERS

Jonathan had been having trouble quitting smoking and his heart had been racing and skipping. The doctor had adjusted his medicines to try and help his problems. Jonathan knew smoking was one of the biggest problems and he knew he had to quit, no matter how much he enjoyed smoking! We had told him he'd end up in a nursing home if he wanted to keep on smoking and having all these complications and bad side effects from the drugs he was being put on. So Jonathan wanted us to take him to see his M.D. doctor and talk to her about a medicine to help him quit smoking.

We really didn't want him on that bad drug, but he was desperate to quit smoking! While in the doctor's waiting room we noticed two other guys in there about Jonathan's age. The one fellow had driven his friend in to see the doctor about his problem with kidney stones. We all were talking about the end of the world and the conditions of the world and how bad and wicked things were getting and how it is like Noah's day before the flood and talking about all the signs of Christ's soon coming. These two fellows were asking Jonathan why he was there to see the doctor. Jonathan explained about his heart acting up and wanting help to quit smoking.

One of the guys came over to Jonathan and asked if he could offer a prayer for him? Jonathan said, "Yes." The guy laid his right hand on Jonathan's right shoulder and began to pray a most beautiful touching prayer for Jonathan! In his prayer he mentioned that Jonathan's heart would feel better and that things would work out for Jonathan with the doctor's visit. He prayed the Holy Spirit would come upon Jonathan and that Jonathan would accomplish the purpose the Lord had for his life and that the Lord would go with Jonathan and help him get well. Jonathan thanked him and I did, too. I gave him a piece of literature.

As we all continued to talk, Jonathan said he thought the reason we don't see more miracles in our day, like in Bible times, was because the people are farther from the Lord in our day. The fellow, that had prayed for Jonathan said, "Yes, but God still works miracles in our day today, too. We need to show more faith in God."

Then, Jonathan asked the fellow that had the painful kidney stones if he could say a prayer for him? The fellow said, "Yes." Then Jonathan prayed a beautiful simple short prayer saying, "Dear Jesus, please give healing to this man, if it's Your will, and please take away his pain. We thank you and in Jesus name we pray. Amen." The man thanked him. Then, Jonathan was called into the doctor's office and everything went well. Jonathan checked out okay and got the medicine he wanted to help him stop smoking.

David told us that while we were in seeing the doctor he was able to talk to this guy who had prayed for Jonathan. David said he was telling him natural remedies and explaining to him about the seventh day Sabbath and how important it was to keep it holy and how urgent it is to get ready for Christ's soon coming. David was saying how things are like back in Noah's day before the flood. The man was very interested as he listened. I said to David, "I bet the two nurses behind the desk could hear what you were saying to that fellow." David said, "Yes, I was thinking that, too." David said he had gotten a book out of the car and gave to the fellow. I had already given him a piece of literature, too. I also had given Jonathan's doctor on another visit *The Ministry of Healing* book and the two nurse's books, too. All we can do is try and warn of the seriousness of the days we're living in and pray God will help them get ready!

Daddy and I were so proud of Jonathan offering a prayer for that hurting man in pain with his kidney stones. It strengthened our faith in our prayers for our son, Jonathan, to be converted and get well and walk and be a worker for Jesus. I said to Jonathan, "This is the work the Lord has for you to do and try to encourage and help others and pray with them and share your own personal testimony with others to help them and tell how God has helped you. Jonathan has come a long ways in the months he's been home. He's been working out with weights and working his legs on the stationary bike and swimming in Pomona Lake, just twelve miles from here and standing up on his feet in the sand under the water. And doing his leg exercises on the floor. He stood up on his feet for a couple seconds beside his exercise bike and looked down to the floor and said, "It seems so far down to the floor." I said, "No wonder, you're 6' 2" and that's a long ways looking down to the floor, and remember it's been so many, many years since you've stood up on your feet!" We just praised God for all the improvements we've seen in Jonathan and it gives us hope that he can walk again, with God's help.

I remarked to David when we left the doctor's office, I wonder if that could have been an angel in disguise, that fellow that prayed for Jonathan? His prayer covered all Jonathan's needs that only God knew. I believe Jonathan has been touched by an angel!" David said, "Maybe so. Who knows for sure when angels have been near to us and helped us without us knowing it."

Jonathan came out of the doctor's office with the stop smoking drug he wanted, but with the risks of it causing terribly dangerous side effects. The doctor really didn't want to prescribe it for him, but he was so desperate for help to stop smoking she went ahead and ordered it for him, against her better judgment. After three days on the drug he had such terribly dangerous side effects we took him to the emergency room and was hooked up to the EKG machine monitor and admitted for help. Praise the Lord, God saw him through that horrifying experience and spared his life!

The same thing happened when he bought the over-the-counter medicine to help him lose weight. That medicine was against our wishes. Then, again he was taken to the emergency room from the terribly dangerous side effects it caused and had to be admitted again to get well.

It's been one crisis after another that God has seen Jonathan through that could have been life threatening! Like the time they tried him on a new type medicine that sent him to the emergency room and then admitted to get straightened out. The devil is trying his best to destroy Jonathan and God keeps helping him through it all and healing him! I said, "Jonathan, God has a plan for your life. Praise God he's taking care of you through all these trials and troubles the devil puts you through! God is stronger than Satan!" Jonathan is seeing and experiencing firsthand God taking care of him and sparing his life. We just keep praying Jonathan will hang in there and let God make something beautiful of His life to be a help and encouragement to others of the power of God to save to the uttermost. Heb. 7:25.

ANGELS HELP!

Now that we've taken on the extra work of caring for our son, Jonathan, whom we brought home from the nursing home four months ago to get him well, with the Lord's help, and off his thirty-two drugs they had him on, we have really been overworked and run down and tired from all we've had to do to keep things going on the building of the "ARK" and helping Jonathan revive, and garden and yard work and housework!

I had often prayed to God for someone to please be able to help us care for Jonathan and also help with all the work there is around here to keep things going in the garden and in the yard and all the home duties of cooking, cleaning house, washing, and help us build on the "ARK." But we knew we had no way of paying someone to help us and no one would want to stay in a cabin that had no running water to it. So, we just kept praying God would help us and strengthen us two old people to keep up with all we had to do and trusted Him to help us get the job done He'd given us to do! We claimed promises like: Deut. 33:25; Ps. 55:22; Ps. 91:11; 1 Peter 5:7; Matt. 11:28–30; Isa. 41:10; Isa. 40:21–31.

Then one day I said to my husband, David, "Honey, have you noticed the front door screen that was broken down and dragging isn't dragging anymore?!" He said, "Yes! I have noticed that!" Then, I said, "Also, my bathroom sink faucet that was leaking and needed fixed isn't leaking and it shuts off now without any problems of any leaks! You won't have to fix that problem either or the front door screen. Also, the Lord has answered our prayers to fix our old 1992 car computer problems that would have cost us hundreds of dollars to fix! The Lord has sent His angels to help us get things done around here, saving us time and money and hard work! Praise the Lord!" We thanked the good Lord for sending angels to help us with our problems! What a help and blessing!

David then said, "Let's pray God will stop the water leaks under the house trailer so I don't have to go to all the trouble to crawl under there and fix the leaks! This will save me a lot of time and money and hard work." So we have begun to pray. God's will be done. The angels helped. David fixed the water leaks and it wasn't too bad! Praise God!

A TIRE, A SCREW, AND A PRAYER

David had to go into town for building materials in the truck. When he got home he noticed the tire on the driver's side was in shreds but not blown yet, but dry rotted. He said, "I'm going to have to find another used tire for our old 1989 Chevy S-10 truck. But they are so rare to find and expensive." So we prayed and he set out in search of another tire. We used this old truck for so many things.

He first stopped at a truck garage in Ottawa and the man said he had just taken one off his truck, but it's dry rotted but still holding air, you can have it if you want it he said. David thanked him and as he was going to pick up the tire the man said, "Well, I've got to get back to finding a little valuable screw I lost and I've been looking and looking for it with this big magnet." David said, "I'll say a little prayer for you to find it." Then as soon as he had prayed in his mind, the man said, "I found it!" David said, "Thank you, Jesus!" Then he gave the man a piece of literature. Then he left there and went to a big tire dealer that sells lots of used tires. When David told him the kind of truck tire he needed, the man said, "Just five minutes ago I changed a tire on a guy's truck and that's the exact size you need." He put it on our rim and didn't charge a whole lot. David thanked him and gave him a piece of literature.

When David got home we prayed together and thanked the Lord for supplying our need for a truck tire. God is so good to keep His promise in Phil. 4:19. We put the other tire away that the man gave us that was his old dry rot from his truck. Now we have a spare tire if we ever need another tire for our truck.

Praise God from whom all blessings flow!

ALL THINGS WORK TOGETHER FOR GOOD

David and I had wanted to go to Oklahoma camp meeting July 11–19, but Jonathan didn't want to go. So on July 11 we began having our own little camp meeting here at home, just the three of us. On July 15, at 8:30 p.m., while having our camp meeting here at home, Jonathan said he wanted to go to Oklahoma camp meeting. We were all happy and excited and prayed and thanked the Lord and started to make plans the next day, July 16, to pack and call for a rented tent on the camp meeting grounds. They said, "Yes, we have available tents."

Then we listened to the weather station and Oklahoma City was having bad rains and possible flooding. I said, "I don't think I want to be in a tent with all that rain. Why don't we call and make arrangements to stay in an air-conditioned motel close by the camp meeting grounds? It's always so unbearably hot down there during camp meeting time anyway and I won't have to go to all the time and trouble to pack for staying in a tent. So we called and made reservations at a motel, using our building material's money for the greenhouse we're building on. We felt this was more important right now to put our money on going to camp meeting where the Holy Spirit could work on our son's conversion.

We failed to pick up one of Jonathan's medicines that had been ordered and he was out of it, but the pharmacy was closed and we couldn't get it. Jonathan said he could do without it and just keep taking the medicine he was coming off of. So Jonathan took that medicine as we packed the car and left around 8:30 p.m. As we journeyed down I-35 highway to Oklahoma camp meeting, Jonathan took some more of his medicine he had been working off of. He didn't feel like it was helping him like his other medicine did, that we hadn't been able to pick up at the pharmacy, so he took a little more of the medicine he'd been working off of. We had no idea what he was doing, since he administers his own medications himself. Well, after about fifty miles down I-35 highway, Jonathan spoke up and said, "We can't go to camp meeting! I'm feeling terribly strange all over! You need to get me to the emergency room immediately!"

So as we turned the car around and headed for the emergency room, we prayed God would please be with our son and help him to get well. He then told us he had taken more and more of his medicine than he should have and was having a bad reaction from it! We hurried and rushed him to our regular hospital in Ottawa into the emergency room. We explained to them what had happened. Jonathan had gone into the bathroom to try and vomit it up, but nothing came up. When we checked him in around 10:30 p.m., they immediately took a urine sample and checked poison control center to know what to do. Then they hooked him up to the EKG machine to monitor his vital signs. They said he'd be there at least four to six hours being observed. We were there seven hours as Jonathan's vital signs kept going down more and more. They drew blood and hooked him up to an IV. They hooked him up to an EKG machine to check how his heart was doing. They gave him medicine to try and counteract the bad side effects he was having. I stayed up all night sitting beside him, praying God would please spare his life and for God to give the doctor and nurse's wisdom and knowledge to know what to do!

While in the emergency room all night, I could hear all the different patients come in with all their problems and I'd be praying for them, too, as I prayed for my own son. One young girl was brought in by her family. She had overdosed on drugs and she was screaming out and saying, "I'm afraid! I'm afraid." I prayed for her, too, as she went through the painful experience of having her stomach pumped out! Another patient was brought in by ambulance. This was an elderly man who couldn't get his breath and they had him on a breathing machine. They were trying to convince him that he needed to be cared for in a nursing home, because he could die if he went back home to try and stay there all alone and be unable to get his breath and that he'd die at home. I prayed for him, too, that he would get the care he needed and be able to breathe okay. On and on through the night they came in needing help. I kept praying for them, asking God to be their Great Physician and comfort and heal and help them like I was praying for my own son, as he hung in the balance that God would please spare his life and that he'd turn his life over to Jesus and be a worker for Jesus!

Finally, at 5:30 a.m., they said he could go on home and get his rest and return to the emergency room if things worsened for him. We thanked them for all their help taking care of our son and we really did appreciate it! We praised the Lord and thanked Him for sparing our son's life! We know God has a plan for Jonathan.

When we got home, we all three went to bed, feeling so exhausted from the whole experience! When Jonathan woke up and came out to the kitchen I had a prayer of thanks with him and I began to tell him what all happened through the night in the emergency room and how God had answered our prayers to save you and how angels must have been around you. We just praised the Lord for all He'd done for us!

We had all remarked why it all happened like this, to get all packed for Oklahoma camp meeting and then be stopped and ended up in the emergency room and Jonathan's life hanging in the balance and God showed His power to spare Jonathan's life.

I told David and Jonathan of the dream I had while sleeping after bringing Jonathan home from the emergency room. I dreamed these words, taken from my favorite text in Rom. 8:28, "ALL THINGS WORK TOGETHER FOR GOOD."

We know God is in control of things and He knows best and He can see the end from the beginning and we'd choose His way, if we could see things as God sees them. It gave us courage to realize God is always moving and working behind the scenes, always working things out for our good. We just need to have faith and trust in Him and His leading and guiding in all our affairs in life. God is in control as we ask Him to direct our paths, like Prov. 3:5, 6 says.

In Sister White's fabulous book, *The Ministry of Healing*, read the whole chapter on, "Help in Daily Living." What a wonderful and encouraging chapter! The whole book is such a blessing! Here's some excerpts. On pp. 471–482 we read, "It is because God is leading them that these things come upon them. Trials and obstacles are the Lord's chosen method of discipline and His appointed conditions of success... Often He permits the fires of affliction to assail them that they may be purified... Our plans are not always God's plans... Often our plans fail that God's plans for us may succeed... In the future life the mysteries that here have annoyed and disappointed us will be made plain. We shall see that our seemingly unanswered prayers and disappointed hopes have been among our greatest blessings... Every man has his place in the eternal plan of heaven. Whether we fill that place depends upon our own faithfulness in cooperating with God... Of all the gifts that heaven can bestow upon men, fellowship with Christ in His sufferings is the most weighty trust and the highest honor... Christ in his life on earth made no plans for Himself. He accepted God's plans for Him, and day by day the Father unfolded His plans. So should we depend upon God, that our lives may be the simple outworking of His will. As we commit our ways to Him, He will direct our steps... Let God plan for you... God never leads His children otherwise than they would choose to be led, if they could see the end from the beginning and discern the glory of the purpose which they are fulfilling as co-workers with Him... Worry is blind and cannot discern the future; but Jesus sees the end from the beginning. In every difficulty, He has His way prepared to bring relief...

Our heavenly Father has a thousand ways to provide for us of which we know nothing. Those who accept the one principle of making the service of God supreme, will find perplexities vanish and a plain path before their feet... The faithful discharge of today's duties is the best preparation for tomorrow's trials... Let us be hopeful and courageous. Despondency in God's service is sinful and unreasonable. He knows our every necessity... He has means for the removal of every difficulty, that those who serve Him and respect the means He employs may be sustained... He watches over His children with a love that is measureless and everlasting. In the darkest days, when appearances seem most forbidding, have faith in God. He is working out His will, doing all things well in behalf of His people. The strength of those who love and serve Him will be renewed day by day. He is able and willing to bestow upon His servants all the help they need. He will give them the wisdom which their varied necessities demand." 2 Cor. 12:9, 10.

Yes, we had thought in our own planning if we could just get Jonathan down to camp meeting he could be converted, possibly. But God can use other ways to convert our son, Jonathan. In the book, *Last Day Events*, p. 188, we have these words from Sister White, "The convocations of the church as in camp meeting, the assemblies of the home church, and all occasions where there is personal labor for souls, are God's appointed opportunities for giving the early and the latter rain." We just have to be patient and wait on the Lord. God has His way and His time for conversions to take place. In *Last Day Events*, p. 194, Sister White writes, "But God knows how and when to answer our prayers. It is our part of the work to put ourselves in connection with the divine channel. God is responsible for His part of the work."

AN EXCITING AND THRILLING EXPERIENCE!

This is an exciting and thrilling experience that happened on, July 3, 2014, that gives us hope of Jonathan's conversion:

When we had gotten our cabin over the basement built and done and all the things moved in and freshly painted and the rugs down, I wanted Jonathan, our son, to see it. So I rolled him down in his wheelchair and up the ramp into the cabin. He sat down on the little loveseat and looked all around and said, "I want to be your first missionary! I want to live in this cabin! I really do like it here!"

Right now he's living with us in our house trailer and we're trying to help him get well and converted and hopefully to walk again, with God's help.

Please keep praying for our son, Jonathan! Thanks!

> **Jonathan said, "I want to be your first missionary! I want to live in this cabin! I really like it here!"**

FIGHT THE ENEMY!

While writing on my articles for my book, ***Don't Be Trapped in the Cities!! Get Out Now!*** a BIG wasp darted right at me and I ran and got my flyswatter to kill him. I know Satan hates my book and he's constantly trying to stop me from writing it! This time he was working through a wasp to get to me to harm me. I swatted at the wasp and I missed him.

He flew into the bathroom. I hurriedly pursued after him with my flyswatter in position to hit him. I swatted again at him in the air, as he darted toward me again, right in my face. I quickly swung my flyswatter at him and hit him and he fell somewhere, but I didn't know where. I looked in the tub and he wasn't there. I could hear him buzzing but couldn't see him. So, I jumped into the tub to look around the window to see if he was there, so I could finish killing him off. Then I heard him buzzing and jumping and flying around my bare feet and landing on my bare feet while I stood there in the tub! I quickly prayed, "Jesus protect me!" as I quickly made a leap out of the tub and slipped on the rug and went sprawling head first across the bathroom floor banging my foot and knee on the tub as I was flying out of the tub to get away from the mad wasp! I hurried and grabbed my flyswatter weapon and went back to the tub to finish killing off the wasp enemy. Jesus heard my short quickly-prayed prayer for protection and the angels watched over me! I was so thankful I was okay and thanked the Lord I had no broken bones or sprains or stings, and no hurt back. He had heard my sincere cry for help! Praise God!

I thought of Peter's quick short prayer he prayed when he took his eyes off Jesus and was sinking in the water and cried out, "Lord, save me!" (Matt. 14:30) The Lord, too, will hear our sincere and desperate cries for help during the little time of trouble before probation closes and also, during the Great Time of Trouble after probation closes and during the seven last plagues.

This experience with the wasp makes me think of the battles we're each having with the devil trying to attack us and harm us and destroy us. We're not safe a moment without Jesus to fight our battles for us! We need to stay close to Jesus so He can protect our lives from Satan when we'll be fleeing to desolate and solitary places when the death decree will be passed on those of us who have remained faithful to Jesus and His seventh day Sabbath and all His Ten Commandments. We need to have faith and trust in Jesus to hear our prayers for help during the trying days ahead of us. These are real battles being fought over our salvation between Christ and Satan. We need to heed the counsel found in Rom. 8:35–39; Eph. 6:10–18; James 4:7, 8.

David wanted me to mention the dream I had some time back, when the Lord said to us, "Train up like the military soldiers (like the Green Berets.) We need to stay in shape for the days ahead of us. David and I lift weights, ride bikes, run and jog and walk, chin-ups, push-ups and sit-ups. We try and watch our diet and eat more raw foods and practice the eight natural laws Sister White mentions in *The Ministry of Healing*, p. 127, "Pure air, sunlight, abstemiousness, rest, exercise, proper diet, the use of water, trust in divine power—these are the true remedies." Also, read in *Testimonies for the Church*, vol. 3, pp. 161–165, "The Health Reform."

We are called to be Christ's soldiers and representatives of Him and His church and bring glory to God in our lives and our bodies. We are Christ's property. We are admonished by Christ's prophet, E. G. White in *Review and Herald*, pp. 3–9, 1905, "Let us strive with all the power God has given us to be among the 144,000." Read in *The Great Controversy*, by E. G. White, pp. 648–650 about the 144,000. Read the whole chapter 40, "God's People Delivered" in *The Great Controversy*. We not only need to stay in shape physically but, also, spiritually and be filled with God's Holy Spirit power as we hasten from place to place to proclaim the "Loud Cry" message from heaven. Read about it in *The Great Controversy*, pp. 611–612. Read the whole chapter 38, "The Final Warning." We'll, also, need to know our Bibles and what we believe. Read in *The Great Controversy*, the chapter, "The Scriptures a Safeguard", pp. 593–602.

Another dream, I had some time ago, David wanted me to share it with others. This is the dream: We were practicing marching, how to do attention and then about face and then dress right dress, like line up your line straight, then attention and about face. I noticed a lady having a hard time in doing the about face right and I helped her and showed her how to do it right. We were like soldiers in an army, drilling, practicing and lining up. God is getting His army trained and ready for the final showdown! Sister White says in the book, *Sons and Daughters of God*, p. 269, "The soldiers of Christ should stand shoulder to shoulder, loyal to truth, vindicators of the law of Jehovah."

On p. 166 of *Counsels to Parents, Teachers, and Students*, Sister White writes, "If ever we are to work in earnest, it is now. The enemy is pressing in on all sides, like a flood… to train the young to become true soldiers of the Lord Jesus Christ is the most noble work ever given to man." Sister White tells us in the book, *Fundamentals of Christian Education*, p. 217, "The Lord will accept of thousands to labor in His great harvest field, but many have failed to fit themselves for the work. But everyone who has espoused the cause of Christ, who has offered himself as a soldier in the Lord's army, should place himself where he may have faithful drill."

In *Selected Messages*, book 2, p. 124, Sister White says, "Every follower of Christ stands pledged to dedicate all his powers of mind, soul, and body to Him who has paid the ransom money for our souls. We engaged to be soldiers, to enter into active service, to endure trials, shame, reproach, to fight the fight of faith, following the Captain of our salvation."

It reminds me of the song, "Onward, Christian Soldiers!"

In *Last Day Events*, p. 58, Sister White says, "There seemed to be a great movement—a work of revival—going forward in many places. Our people were moving into line, responding to God's call." Also, on p. 62 she continues, "The work is soon to close. The members of the church militant who have proved faithful will become the church triumphant… Compassion beamed from His countenance and His conduct was characterized by grace, humility, truth, and love. Every member of His church militant must manifest the same qualities, if he would join the church triumphant."

Linda's Dream: "WARFARE." (The dictionary says, Military operations between enemies, war, struggle between competing entities, conflict.) There is a Great Controversy, a real battle being fought over us going on between Christ and Satan over us and also those souls out there that God has to bring the knowledge of the truth to. Satan wants us lost and destroyed. Jesus wants us saved and healthy and happy. The choice is ours. Which side will we choose to be on?!

Sister White says in *Testimonies for the Church*, vol. 9, pp. 28–29, "An Impressive Dream," "In the visions of the night a very impressive scene passed before me. I saw an immense ball of fire fall among some beautiful mansions, causing their instant destruction. I heard someone say: "We knew that the judgments of God were coming upon the earth, but we did not know that they would come so soon." Others, with agonized voices said: "You knew! Why then did you not tell us? We did not know." On every side I heard similar words of reproach spoken… If every soldier of Christ had done his duty, if every watchman on the walls of Zion had given the trumpet a certain sound, the world might ere this have heard the message of warning. But the work is years behind. While men have slept, Satan has stolen a march upon us."

In *Last Day Events*, p. 152, Sister White gives this counsel, "When the storm of persecution really breaks upon us, the true sheep will hear the true Shepherd's voice. Self-denying efforts will be put forth to save the lost, and many who have strayed from the fold will come back to follow the great Shepherd. The people of God will draw together and present to the enemy a united front. In view of the common peril, strife for supremacy will cease, there will be no disputing as to who shall be accounted greatest…" Also on p. 154, Sister White goes on to say, "Afflictions, crosses, temptations, adversity, and varied trials are God's workmen to refine us, sanctify us, and fit us for the heavenly garner." In the book, *The Crisis Ahead*, by Robert W. Olson, he quotes on p. 41, Sister White saying, "Before the warfare shall be ended and the victory won, we as a people are to experience trials similar to those of Paul… God would have His people prepared for the soon-coming crisis."

This is why I've been writing my experiences to encourage people to pray and put their faith and trust in God to see them through.

GOD WROTE US A PERSONAL MESSAGE!

One day while we had been building on the "ARK," David had to make a trip into town for some building materials. On his way home, when he was about a mile from home, David saw something strange that caught his eye. He hurried on home to tell me what he had seen. He said, "I saw the strangest thing on the way home! It was a Bible text written with green spray paint in real BIG LETTERS on the railing on the concrete bridge over the river! You couldn't help but see it!" I said, "A Bible text? What did the Bible text say that's written among all that vulgar stuff written in black spray paint written on the railing on the bridge, too?" He said, "I wrote it down so I wouldn't forget it." It said, "And the word of the Lord was published throughout all the region."

I looked up the text and found it came from Acts 13:49 KJV. David had been doing some canvassing in different towns around us and selling and giving away books here and there to those who were interested but couldn't afford to buy the book. I said to David, "Drive me down the road to the bridge so I can see the text, too!" We drove down to the bridge and I saw the text, too. I said to David, "I feel God is trying to tell us something! I feel God is wanting us, like Noah, to not only build the "ARK," but preach while we're building." David said, "But we're not preachers." I said, "No, we're not, I know that. What I mean is to preach through these E. G. White paperback books that we have that we use for canvassing. We're trying to hurry and build the "ARK" for God's people to come to when the Sunday Laws are passed and people will have a place of refuge to come who want to keep God's seventh day Sabbath holy and not go along with the Sunday Law. It takes us so much time to go door to door and try and find people home and people who are interested in the books we have, and the way the economy is now, most people can't afford to buy them, even though we offer them for just a donation and we end up giving away more than we sell. So, why don't we just take these hundreds and hundreds of books we have for canvassing and just hurry and spread them out like the leaves of autumn, like Sister White says to do and just go door to door around all these towns around us and give the light to the people like the Lord said to do in this text in Acts 13:49. God has promised us in Isa. 55:11 that His word would not return unto Him void." So, we prayed about it and felt this message, God wrote on the bridge railing and just one mile from our home, was meant for us, personally. It was our marching orders from God to hurry and spread the truth far and near! We felt the Spirit of the Lord upon us like Isa. 61:1–4 says. So when we weren't building on the "ARK," David and I would drive from city to city and town to town going door to door passing out our truth-filled books by E. G. White like: *The Great Controversy*; *The Desire of Ages*; *Steps to Christ*; *The Ministry of Healing*; *Christ's Object Lessons*; and Jan M. book, *National Sunday Law*, etc. We would pray as we hurried from door to door that God would please be with these little preachers as we left them at each door and bless the people as they read the truth and would let the Holy Spirit lead them to see the light and accept it and be saved. We felt like we were doing Joel chapters 1–3, like soldiers for Christ as Joel 2:7 says, "They shall run like mighty men; they shall climb the wall like men of war; and they shall march everyone on his ways, and they shall not break their ranks."

Finally, after a few weeks of doing this we were down to our last few books and had about ten left. So we prayed and asked the Lord where we should pass these last few books out. So we decided as we prayed and drove our car along, that whenever we saw a red bird fly across our road we'd stop at that house and give them a free book. So we started down the highway and there went a red bird right across our path! We stopped and left a book there at that house. Then we drove on and we saw a red bird go across in front of us and down a gravel road, so we turned down the gravel road and followed the red bird who directed us to a house where we left them a book. We continued on down that gravel road and one red bird after another kept flying across in front of us and that's where we'd stop and leave a book. I kept watching for red birds to cross our path, as we drove on and on and I'd say to David, "Honey, stop! I just saw a red bird cross our path!" Then we'd turn around and go to the house where we saw the red bird fly out of their driveway, and give them a book, until our books were all gone. We knew God knew where His people were who needed to know the truth and receive a book that would guide them into the truth. We were so joyful and praising God for the privilege and joy to have a part in spreading His love and truth all around the region like He had commissioned us Seventh-day Adventists to do in Matt. 28:18–20. And, also, like God's personal message He gave us written on our bridge railing, Acts 13:49, "And the word of the Lord was published throughout all the region."

Oh yes! After we had obeyed God's personal message written to us on the concrete bridge railing in big letters written in green spray paint, and we had finished passing out all our books door to door from town to town, then as mysteriously as the text appeared, it just as mysteriously disappeared and was no longer there and no proof that it had ever been there! It was no longer there, but the vulgar stuff, written in black spray paint, was still there! We had done what we felt God wanted us to do, then the message was completely erased and gone, as if it had never been there, even though it had been written in BIG LETTERS with green spray paint!! We continue to pray for these dear people who received these books and we claim God's promises in Isa. chapter 55; Isa. 60:1–4; Isa. 52:7; Joel 3:14, "Multitude, multitudes in the valley of decision: for the day of the Lord is near in the valley of decision."

So many times we have prayed and wished there was a Bible worker that could follow-up on these hundreds and hundreds of truth-filled books that have gone out in all the regions around us. But we're kept so busy building the "ARK," we just don't have the time to do the follow-up on these books, like a Bible worker could do. We just pray and leave the results in God's hands how He'll work all this out!

Today, God is sending His people a message of warning to get out of the cities, as soon as possible. Are we listening and heeding the sobering warnings God is trying to send us through His messages, like the one found in *Country Living*, by E. G. White saying, "Out of the cities; out of the cities!"—this is the message the Lord has been giving me." It reminds me of the Titanic back in 1912. Warnings were given of "Iceberg ahead!" but no one heeded the warnings! The warnings were ignored until it was too late and lives were needlessly lost because of it! The same is true of us today, in these last days. There's so many signs and warnings for us to be getting ready for the crisis ahead of us and to be getting out of these large cities, as soon as possible, but God's people aren't responding to the urgent warnings being given to them over and over again! They think they have plenty of time and develop a false sense of security and feel things are going along okay not realizing there's a serious time of trouble rapidly stealing upon them, and disasters are soon to strike! This is no time now to be a sleeping foolish virgin. (Matt. 25) Now is the time to put our priorities straight! Sister White writes, "Let the children no longer be exposed to the temptations of the cities that are ripe for destruction. The Lord has sent us warning and counsel to get out of the cities. Then let us make no more investments in the city."—taken from *Country Living*, pp. 12, 13 & 31.

Our dear prophet, Sister White, our prophet for our day gives these warning words, given from God to her to speak and warn God's people to rally and heed the warnings given to them to save them! In *Country Living*, pp. 8–12, she says, "There are reasons why we should not build in the cities. On these cities, God's judgments are soon to fall… The time is near when the large cities will be swept away, and all should be warned of these coming judgments… O that God's people had a sense of the impending destruction of the thousands of cities, now almost given to idolatry… The time is fast coming when the controlling power of the labor unions will be very oppressive. Again and again the Lord has instructed that our people are to take their families away from the cities, into the country, where they can raise their own provision, for in the future the problem of buying and selling will be a very serious one. We should now begin to heed the instruction given us over and over again: Get out of the cities into rural districts, where the houses are not crowded closely together and where you will be free from the interference of enemies…

The trade unions will be one of the agencies that will bring upon this earth a time of trouble such as has not been since the world began… The work of the people of God is to prepare for the events of the future, which will soon come upon them with blinding force… Trade unions will be formed, and those who refuse to join these unions will be marked men… The trade unions and confederacies of the world are a snare. Keep out of them, and away from them, brethren. Have nothing to do with them… But erelong there will be such strife and confusion in the cities, that those who wish to leave them will not be able. We must be preparing for these issues. This is the light that is given me…

We are not to unite with secret societies or with trade unions. We are to stand free in GOD, looking constantly to Christ for instruction… These unions are one of the signs of the last days. Men are binding up in bundles ready to be burned. They may be church members, but while they belong to these unions, they cannot possibly keep the commandments of God; for to belong to these unions means to disregard the entire Decalogue… Those who claim to be children of God are in no case to bind up with the labor unions that are formed or that shall be formed. This the Lord forbids. Cannot those who study the prophecies see and understand what is before us?"

I sometimes feel like John the Baptist, "The voice of one crying in the wilderness, prepare ye the way of the Lord, make his paths straight." (Matt. 3:1–3) May God help us and our loved ones to be ready and prepared and to help others be ready for the crisis that is soon to be upon us! This is my earnest prayer in Jesus' name. Amen.

What personal message and work has God given to you to share with others? Luke 2:49, Now is the time to be about our Father's business!

> "What personal message and work has God given to you to share with others?"
>
> Luke 2:49

THE LOST WAS FOUND!

I know we've all lost something from time to time or misplaced something and we're so happy and thankful when we've found what was lost and praise the Lord!

This is what happened to us: David was busy cutting the high weeds down in his garden, not knowing that he had lost the gas cap off his lawn mower. When he was through, he parked the lawnmower under the carport and went on his way. The next day he went to gas up the lawnmower to cut more weeds and he noticed the gas cap was missing. He looked and looked for it and he finally came in and got me to help him look. I said, "Let's pray! This is next to impossible to find a small gas cap in all these weeds and not having any idea where you lost it!" So, we prayed that God would please help us find it! David went out to the garden and started looking. I looked around the carport and finally I was going up the driveway and my foot stepped on the gas cap in the driveway! I called to David that I had found the lost gas cap and we prayed and thanked the good Lord for helping us do the impossible, to find a small gas cap lost and not having any idea where it could be. We praised the good Lord and thanked Him for hearing our prayers for help! I think of that text in Luke 1:37, "For with God nothing shall be impossible." Also, Mark 10:27, "And Jesus looking upon them saith, With men it is impossible, but not with God: for with God all things are possible." Matt. 21:22, "And all things whatsoever ye shall ask in prayer, believing, ye shall receive." Mark 9:23, "Jesus said unto him, If thou canst believe, all things are possible to him that believeth." I had a dream that said, "God can do anything."

I think of us who are parents and have lost our children to Satan and it seems like an impossible situation to ever see them come back to Jesus and be delivered from their life of sin. Jesus gives His promise to bring our lost children back to Him and to the fold. Read Luke chapter 15. Prov. 22:6, "Train up a child in the way he should go: and when he is old, he will not depart from it." We must pray in faith and claim God's promises, like Jer. 31:15–17.

In *Testimonies for the Church*, vol. 6, p. 401, Sister White gives this encouraging statement, "Self-denying efforts will be put forth to save the lost, and many who have strayed from the fold will come back to follow the great Shepherd." Praise the Lord!

WHY, LORD?

David, one day, took off in our old 1987 Ford van to get a load of lumber. He stopped by the post office to pick up our mail on his way into the city of Ottawa. When he came out of the post office he tried to start the old van and it wouldn't start. He checked over everything he thought could be the problem and he just couldn't figure out what to do. Finally, he decided he better start walking the 3 1/2 miles home to get me and our old 1989 Chevy pickup truck so we could pull it home with the big chain we had. He knew our truck bumper was cracked and could break off trying to pull the big heavy van, and the brakes on the truck were bad but we had no other way to get it home and no money for paying for a tow truck. When he got home we had prayer together asking for God's help in our time of need.

We tried to jump the battery on the van, when we drove back into town, but nothing happened. We began to hook up the chain to pull the van on home. A man came out of the beer joint that was close by and as he walked over to his truck, he saw what we were doing and he noticed our broken bumper and he said, "That little truck with that broken bumper will never pull that big heavy van! How far are you going to pull it?" I said, "We're 3 ½ miles from home." He said, "I'll be glad to help you and pull your big van with my truck." We were so thankful God had heard our prayers for help! We thanked him for his help and kindness as he was finishing up hooking up our van to his truck. We could smell beer on his breath, but we breathed a prayer God would get us safely home as I drove our truck for him to follow me and David steered the old van as the drunken man drove his truck pulling our big van home.

Praise the Lord we got safely home with no trouble! We offered to pay the man for his help. He said, "No, I'm just glad to help you out." I then gave him *The Great Controversy* book and David explained what the book was all about and he said, "I'm interested in things like that!" He thanked us for the book and started up his truck to leave and put it in reverse and banged into our van. He said he was sorry. He hadn't hurt our van or his truck, but he was drunk and not thinking clear. He finally made it safely out of our driveway. We prayed again and thanked the good Lord for protecting us and our van and his truck, too. We were so happy to get *The Great Controversy* book in his hands. Sometimes things have to happen to get a truth-filled book into certain people's hands.

We found out our old 1987 Ford van was junk and we had to drop the insurance because we couldn't afford to have it repaired. So, we were down to just having our old 1992 Honda and our 1989 Chevy truck with a lot wrong with it, too, but we still needed it for hauling our building materials to keep building on the "ARK" and pray God will keep it going!

Then, one day, Jonathan, our son, and David and I took off in our old 1992 Honda, which has been falling apart on us and costing us a lot of money in repairs, and we had decided to go into Ottawa for groceries and then on to Lawrence, 45 miles from our home, to go to the health food store to get Jonathan's herbs he takes. It was getting toward late afternoon and we figured we'd be home before dark. We don't like to be out late in our old car that has so much wrong with it, especially with Jonathan in a wheelchair. So, we had gotten a few things in Ottawa and were on I-35 highway headed out of town to go to Lawrence, Kansas, health food store. We had just filled up with gas and then, all of a sudden the car died and we had to pull over onto the shoulder on I-35. It was during rush hour and cars and semi-trucks were flying by us at high speed. We prayed God would please start our car! But it wouldn't start. David got out and looked under the hood and checked over different things he thought it could be, while we kept praying for the Lord to please help us with our car problem. It was getting late and dark out. A policeman came by and stopped to see what was wrong. We explained to him our car wouldn't start and he said for us to get a tow truck to get the car off the Interstate, it was too dangerous for us to be in the car at night. We explained our insurance doesn't cover the cost of a tow truck and we had no money to pay for one to come and tow us home 20 miles. He called in another cop to come and help him get me and David and Jonathan and Jonathan's big wheelchair home, 20 miles from where we were. They were so kind and nice and thoughtful to help us in our predicament. We thanked them for their help and told them they were an answer to our prayers. When we got home we gave each cop a piece of literature and they thanked us for it. The cop had told us we had 48 hours to get the car off the Interstate.

The next day David and I prayed God would please help us be able to pull our car home safely using our old Chevy pickup truck with the broken bumper and the bad brakes it had, and that our big chain we had would hold okay. God helped us get it hooked up out there on the busy Interstate with cars and big semi-trucks whizzing by us at fast speed. I drove the truck pulling the car with David steering the car. We prayed all the way God would please help us get safely home and the chain wouldn't come loose or break the bumper and our brakes on the old truck would hold up and no cops would stop us! Praise God! We made it safely home with no problems!

As we prayed and thanked the good Lord for seeing us through this terrible ordeal, we asked ourselves the question, "Why, Lord?" Did this have to happen to us so we could get literature to these two cops?!

Sister White says in the book, *My Life Today*, p. 93, "…In every affliction God has a purpose to work out for our good…. The very trial that taxes our faith the most severely and makes it seem as though God had forsaken us is to lead us more closely to Him, that we may lay all our burdens at the feet of Christ and experience the peace which He will give us in exchange… God loves and cares for the feeblest of His creatures, and we cannot dishonor Him more than by doubting His love to us. O let us cultivate that living faith that will trust Him in the hour of darkness and trial." (Read 1 Peter 4:12, 13)

Also, on p. 94 of *My Life Today*, Sister White tells us, "We are coming to a crisis. Let us stand the test manfully, grasping the hand of Infinite Power. God will work for us. We have only to live one day at a time, and if we get acquainted with God, He will give us strength for what is coming tomorrow, grace sufficient for each day, and every day will find its own victories, just as it finds its trials… As the trials come, the power of God will come with them. God will help us to stand in faith on His word, and when we are united, He will work with special power in our behalf." (Read 1 Cor. 10:13)

Sister White makes this beautiful comment in *The Ministry of Healing*, p. 479, "God never leads His children otherwise than they would choose to be led, if they could see the end from the beginning and discern the glory of the purpose which they are fulfilling as co-workers with Him." On p. 481 she continues saying, "…In every difficulty He (God) has His way prepared to bring relief." On p. 482 she writes, "In the darkest day when appearances seem most forbidding, have faith in God. He is working out His will, doing all things well in behalf of His people. The strength of those who love and serve Him will be renewed day by day." I love the quote of Sister White in *The Ministry of Healing*, p. 474, "In the future life the mysteries that have annoyed and disappointed us will be made plain. We shall see that our seemingly unanswered prayers and disappointed hopes have been among our greatest blessings."

Right now we don't know what the outcome will be for our old 1992 Honda, that we've had to park until we can see what the problem will be and if it's worth fixing. It's all in God's hands as we trust Him to care for our needs as Phil. 4:19 promises. We have faith that God will work all things for our good, as Rom. 8:28 promises. God is in control of all we do. His will be done. If we have to buy another car, so be it. God will help us through that problem, too, as God says in Ps. 50:12, "For the world is mine, and the fullness thereof." He also promises in Phil. 4:19 that He'll supply all our need. I also claim Matt. 21:22. When David and I had gotten safely home pulling the car with a junky truck with a badly cracked bumper and bad brakes and an old chain that could break or come loose, I laughed and said to my husband, "We're getting too old for excitement like this!" And I'm sure the Lord must have smiled and said to Himself, "It doesn't matter how old you get, I can handle it. Have faith in God and trust Me to work all things for your good, as Rom. 8:28 promises."

STRANDED!

We had all three of us, me, David, and Jonathan had gone into Walmart and when we came out and tried to start the car, it wouldn't start up, but start and run for a couple seconds and then it would turn off. We prayed God would please help us with our car problem and we claimed James 1:5.

It was 104 degrees and we were under a high heat index warning and we have no air conditioning in our car either, so we hadn't planned on remaining long in town. We knew we'd be stranded in town, 20 miles from home, unless the Lord saw fit to help us figure out our car problem and help us fix it, because we sure didn't have the money to pay to have our car towed in and repaired. We earnestly prayed, as Daddy got out and lifted the hood and wiggled some wires on the ignition going to the distributor. Then he got back into the car, and we prayed again, and God let the car start right up and we were able to finish our errands. We just praised the Lord and thanked Him for hearing our plea for help!

When we arrived safely home, David checked over the car and got things straightened out and cleaned the corrosion off the battery terminals. We were so thankful God had again helped us in our time of trouble and answered our prayers for help. We know God will do the same for us during the early time of trouble when we won't be able to buy and sell, because we'll choose to keep God's seventh day Sabbath and not go along with the Sunday Laws passed, and we'll remain faithful to God and they'll cast us out of the system and we'll need to depend on God to supply all our needs, as we're learning to do right now through all our difficulties we go through now. God is allowing our faith and trust to grow in Jesus to care for us and see us through our troubles and trials now, so we'll be true to Jesus then when we'll have to make our choice, which day we'll keep then, when everyone will have to decide who they will serve and obey, Jesus or man. The decisions we're making now will determine what we'll do then. These are very serious and solemn times we're living in now. And it demands serious thinking and planning with God's help.

I remember another time we were stranded. We had pulled into the gas station to get gas and had shut the engine off. When we got back into the car, the car wouldn't start. Again we cried out to the Lord to please hear our prayers for help! We had no idea what was wrong. Daddy again got out and lifted the hood as I continued to pray and claim James 1:5. The Lord directed my eyes to a place by the gear shift that had a place to put a key in a lock. I took my key to the car, from my purse and placed it in the key lock and pushed down on it and prayed it would help me get the car started by turning the other key in the ignition. I told David what I was going to do and it worked! The car started and we weren't stranded anymore! We praised and thanked God for again seeing us through another problem He helped us solve in answer to prayer!

We need to learn to pray more now and have faith in God to hear our prayers for help. The time is soon coming when we'll have to endure trials and troubles and hardships during the little time of trouble and the Great time of trouble and the seven last plagues, and we need to be preparing now and getting ready for this time ahead of us! We have to let ourselves get in the condition like the little flowers, which naturally turn to the sun, so we'll just naturally turn to Jesus in prayer when we're faced with the crisis ahead of us during the times of trouble in the near future.

While Jonathan is living at home with us, he's seeing all the ways and times God is helping us in our troublesome times in answer to our prayers for help and showing and teaching him where to turn in his time of need, to the all wise and powerful God who loves His children and cares for them in any situation. We need to learn to trust in God's promises to us now. Ps. 56:3, "What time I am afraid, I will trust in thee." *Last Day Events*, p. 149 Sister White says, "Now is the time to cultivate faith in God."

Growing Faith for the Time of Trouble

Part 1

I had this experience happen and then I dreamed it in my dream: I was in my dream telling two ladies about this experience I had gone through. I was telling them about how God had safely watched over my $100 bill birthday money from my cousin, Nancy, in Florida, that she had hurriedly sent in the mail to me, but in her haste she had forgotten to lick the envelope shut, but God sent an angel to watch over that money all the way from Florida to Kansas, so no one would steal it, and kept it from falling out. She had also, sent a little message pass it on card with the birthday card that read, "RELAX! It's all in God's Hands, "and also, the text, Ps. 3:5. (End of dream)

I had put the envelope and little message card in a frame and hung it on the wall to remind me to have "faith" in God, that He can do anything and that nothing is too hard for God. Mark 10:27 and Luke 1:37. Again, I was praying for money for more building materials, so we could get building on our 24' x 44' greenhouse. Again, I began fasting and praying for money, because we had put all our money on bills and some building materials and we had put "faith" in God to supply all our needs, like Phil. 4:19 promises, "But my God shall supply all your need according to his riches in glory by Christ Jesus." We were in need of food and gas money and money to buy telephone time. We only had 25 cents in the bank and a couple of dollars on us. We earnestly prayed God would honor our "faith" in Him and His promises to please help us get some money to keep us going through the rest of the month, since we had stepped out on "faith" and used our telephone and food and gas money for the month to buy building materials, so we could hurry and get started on our greenhouse.

There were some secondhand windows, in good condition, we wanted to buy at a secondhand store, so we could use them in building our greenhouse, but we had no money to get them and we didn't want anyone else to get them before we could get the money to buy them. We asked the Lord to please hold them for us until we got the money to buy them and also, enough money to buy some food and gas for our car and gas for our truck to go get the windows we wanted to buy for the greenhouse. We reminded the Lord that we were using all our money to build the "Ark" that He had told us to build for us and for His people during the time of trouble, when you won't be able to buy and sell, because we wouldn't go along with the Sunday Laws passed, and we wouldn't break God's true seventh day Sabbath found in His Ten Commandments in Ex. 20:1–17. We also, reminded God to please honor our "faith" in Him to supply us with our needs, since we were faithful tithe payers. We claimed God's promise in Mal. 3:10, "Bring ye all the tithes into the storehouse, that there may be meat in mine house, and prove me now herewith, saith the Lord of hosts, if I will not open you the windows of heaven and pour you out a blessing, that there shall not be room enough to receive it."

So, in "faith," we began to watch the mail for money that we just knew would come in answer to our prayers of "faith" and our fasting. We just knew God wouldn't fail us, like He'd promised in Deut. 31:6, 8: "Be strong and of a good courage, fear not, nor be afraid of them; for the Lord thy God, he it is that doth go with thee; he will not fail thee, nor forsake thee… And the Lord, he it is that doth go before thee; he will be with thee, he will not fail thee, neither forsake thee: fear not, neither be dismayed." Also, we read Josh. 1:5, 9 to encourage our "faith" to grow in God's presence and power and His promises. So, we began thanking and praising God for hearing and answering our prayers for help, and we claimed promises like: Ps. 37:3–5; Prov. 3:5–8; and Ps. 9:1, 2, "I will praise thee, O Lord, with my whole heart; I will show forth all thy marvelous works. I will be glad and rejoice in thee: I will sing praise to thy name. O thou most High." Ps. 100:4, "Enter into his gates with thanksgiving, and into his courts with praise: be thankful unto him, and bless his name."

We knew to be able to stand up through the time of trouble ahead of us, when every earthly support will be cut off and our "faith" severely tested, we knew we had to let our "faith" in God and His promises to care for us grow NOW, so we'll have "faith" then, to know God will be with us and our bread and water will be sure, as Isa. 33:15, 16 promises. In *The Desire of Ages*, pp. 121 & 122, by E. G. White, are these encouraging words to God's "faithful children," "In the last great conflict of the controversy with Satan those who are loyal to God will see every earthly support cut off. Because they refuse to break His law in obedience to earthly powers, they will be forbidden to buy or sell. It will finally be decreed that they shall be put to death. See Rev. 13:11–17. But to the obedient is given the promise, "He shall dwell on high: his place of defense shall be the munitions of rocks: bread shall be given him; his waters shall be sure." Isa. 33:16. By this promise the children of God will live. When the earth shall be wasted with famine, they shall be fed."

We'll be living by "faith" at this time. That's why it's so important to let our "faith" in God grow now. Even Jesus said in Luke 18:8, "…Nevertheless when the Son of man cometh, shall he find faith on the earth?"

Heb. 11:5, 6 tells how Enoch pleased God before his translation, and we, too, before we're translated to heaven must have the "faith" Enoch had, so we can live to please God, too.

One morning for my worship I asked the Lord to please give me words from Him that would be encouraging words for that day. And as if the Lord wrote me a personal love note message to calm my fears for where and when we'll be able to have money for our food and gas and building materials money, etc., I prayed and turned to Sister White's book, "*Thoughts from the Mount of Blessings*, pp. 99, and these words were underlined, "All these things,' said Jesus, 'do the nations of the world seek after.' 'Your heavenly Father knoweth that ye have need of all these things. But seek ye first the kingdom of God, and His righteousness; and all these things shall be added unto you.' Luke 12:30; Matt. 6:33. I have come to open to you the kingdom of love and righteousness and peace. Open your hearts to receive this kingdom, and make its service your highest interest. Though it is a spiritual kingdom, fear not that your needs for this life will be uncared for. If you give yourself to God's service, He who has all power in heaven and earth will provide for your needs." Praise the Lord!

This personal message of Jesus to me, in answer to my prayer for something to help me that day, helped to calm my worries about money to meet my needs and these words calmed my fears and I trusted Jesus to supply all our needs, as Phil. 4:19 promises and trusted Him in His own way and in His own time to answer my prayers for money. I stopped worrying about getting money to get us through this hard time we were going through. So, I continued to pray for money but showed "faith" in God to stand behind His promises. It made me think of God's promise found in *The Ministry of Healing*, by E. G. White, on p. 481, 482, "Worry is blind and cannot discern the future; but Jesus sees the end from the beginning. In every difficulty He has His way prepared to bring relief. No good thing will He withhold from them that walk uprightly… Matt. 11:30; Ps. 84:11. Our heavenly

Father has a thousand ways to provide for us of which we know nothing. Those who accept the one principle of making the service of God supreme, will find perplexities vanish and a plain path before their feet. The faithful discharge of today's duties is the best preparation for tomorrow's trials. Do not gather together all tomorrow's liabilities and care and add them to the burden of today, 'sufficient unto the day is the evil thereof.' Matt. 6:34. Let us be hopeful and courageous. Despondency in God's service is sinful and unreasonable. He knows our every necessity. To the omnipotence of the King of Kings our covenant keeping God unites the gentleness and care of the tender shepherd. His power is absolute, it is the pledge of the sure fulfillment of His promises to all who trust in Him. He has means for the removal of every difficulty, that those who serve Him and respect the means He employs may be sustained. His love is as far above all other love as the heavens are above the earth. He watches over His children with a love that is measureless and everlasting. In the darkest days, when appearances seem most forbidding, have faith in God. He is working out His will, doing all things well in behalf of His people. The strength of those who love and serve Him will be renewed day by day. He is able and willing to bestow upon His servants all the help they need. He will give them the wisdom which their varied necessities demand. Said the tried apostle Paul: 'He said unto me, my grace is sufficient for thee: for my strength is made perfect in weakness. Most gladly therefore will I rather glory in my infirmities, that the power of Christ may rest upon me. Therefore, I take pleasure in infirmities, in reproaches, in necessities, in persecutions, in distresses for Christ's sake: for when I am weak, then am I strong." 2 Cor. 12:9, 10

While praying and watching the mail day after day for money to come to meet our needs, and trying to show "faith" in God to keep our food supply going week after week and our little bit of gas in the car and truck going, and not able to use our telephone, since we had no money to buy telephone time for it, we kept praying in "faith" that God would please help our "faith" to grow in this crisis we were in. We had begun to work on the 24' x 44' greenhouse that we had purchased materials with our food and gas and telephone money, showing "faith" in God to work on the heart of someone to send us money to meet our needs through the month, while we kept building on the "Ark," trying to hurry and get this much needed greenhouse completed before the pope made his visit to congress in September 2015, to appeal possibly for a Sunday Law. We realized we didn't have much time to get things ready on the "Ark," before everything started breaking loose and we wouldn't be able to buy and sell. And we would need this greenhouse to grow our food in during the winter months, since we couldn't go to the store to buy our food, because we would be cut off from buying and selling because we wouldn't go along with the Sunday Law and we'd be true to God's seventh day Sabbath. We knew we had to hurry and buy these greenhouse materials while we could! We desperately needed money to buy more building materials and also, our food was going fast. We earnestly kept praying in "faith" for God to please send us money. Then the truck's motor to the wipers went out. We needed our truck to go get the materials for the greenhouse, when God supplied us with the money. But they were forecasting rain for several days and we couldn't drive the truck in the rain without wipers, even if the money came that day, so we could go get our building materials we needed to keep building. So, we prayed in "faith" that our junk car mechanic, that works on our vehicles, would be able to fix the problem for us right away and that he'd wait for us to pay him when we got our Social Security check on the third of the next month. He said, "Sure, bring it on over and I'll fix it for you and won't charge you but for the motor. I have one I can get out of the junk truck I have and I'll put it in your truck." We thanked him and took our truck over to him to be fixed. We just praised the Lord for helping us through our difficulties, the devil kept trying to stop our work on the "Ark" and discourage us, but God is always there to see us through Satan's attacks on us, as we do the work of Jesus in preparing the "Ark" for God's people to have a place of refuge to come to during the storms ahead of us during the early time of trouble. Now the truck is fixed and ready to go get more building materials that we need, but we're just waiting in "faith" for God to please send us the money we need to keep going. We're, also, praying in "faith" that God will keep giving us two old people the help and strength we need to build this big greenhouse and also, to keep up the gardening and everything else we have to do to keep things going around here.

Today is March 24 and I haven't checked the mail yet. I had a prayer before I opened the mailbox and when I opened it, there was a letter from my dear friend, Sandie, in New Jersey, who is like a sister to me! I praised the Lord for her letter and hoped and prayed as I opened it up and looked in there, there would be money in it. There was the "Ark" jar money in it, that she had said she'd send sometime! She saves money in a jar to help build the "Ark." I called to David out in the garden and he came running when he saw me waving the letter in the air! We prayed together, praising God, as we opened it and thanked God for sending the "Ark" jar money in it, that we so much needed! Praise God! There was $48 enclosed! God bless her for answering our prayers for money to keep on going through the month! I sat right down and wrote her a letter thanking her for remembering us with her money love gift. We praised and thanked God, too!

The following is the letter I sent in answer to her letter sent to me

March 24, 2015

My dear sweet Sister Sandie,

    Thank you so very much for your sweet letter and your love money gift!!! God bless you!! Sandie, you'll never know what an answer to prayer your money was to us!!!! We are so anxious to get the greenhouse started while we were having good weather and needed building materials to get started, and like you said, Yes! They are very expensive! So we prayed about it and stepped out on "faith" and used our telephone and food and gas money for the month of March to buy materials for the greenhouse and trusting the good Lord to please supply our needs and impress someone to please feel impressed, by the Holy Spirit, to send us some money to help keep us going with some food and gas money and telephone money so we could not waste any time building the greenhouse on the "ARK." We put God's work first and trusted the Lord to supply our needs as He promised in Phil. 4:19. All through the month of March no money came to help us out! I fasted and prayed! Still no money came! I thought maybe my cousin, Diane, in Florida would remember my birthday with some money, but she never did. Our food supply was going FAST—the cupboards and refrigerator and freezer was almost bare. Still no money came. Our gas in our car was almost on an empty tank. We had no money for buying telephone time, so we had no phone. I prayed and asked God to please impress you to send the "Ark" jar money, you had said a long time ago you'd send. Still no money in the mail came, as I checked the mail each day, trusting God to see us through the crisis we were going through. I said to the Lord 3-24-15, the day your money came, "Lord, before I check the mail today for money I'm going to show "faith" in your promise in Phil 4:19 and make out my grocery list of things I absolutely need to keep us going and then, I'll check the mail and trust you to please help us get money in the mail today, March 24! We never get money from anyone except my cousin, Nancy, in Florida. On my birthday she sent me $100. And once in a while, through the year, she'll send $100. Diane, my other cousin in Florida, has a few times, sent us some money. You're the only one who sends us money now and then and how very much we appreciate all you've shared with us! God has certainly used you to be a blessing and a help to us through the years to help keep us going! God bless you richly! I love you my dear sweet Sister! Thank you for coming to our rescue by listening to the Holy Spirit to help meet our needs! Praise the Lord for you, Sis!! I wish I could give you a hug!! Someday, the good Lord willing I will. If not here, it will be in heaven! We've just got to be there! Let nothing keep us from making it to heaven! Always put God FIRST!!! Matt. 6:33.

    I enjoyed reading your letter! You're always in my prayers and thoughts. Thanks so very very much for your prayers for us! God is hearing your prayers for us and looking out for us! Just like He'll do in the time of trouble ahead of us! May the good Lord get you here with us, on the "Ark," so we can make it through the hard times together! God knows each of our future. We can trust in God to care for us! Just like in our worship this morning, we three were talking about how God even keeps track of the numbers of the hairs we have on our head, and every time a hair falls out, He takes notice! Matt. 10:28-33. What a wonderful and loving God we serve! We can trust our life in His hands! I love you and miss you! I'm so glad you and your family are all doing okay.

We're all hanging in there! God is good! He helped us get the center wall built on the 24' x 44' greenhouse, now we have to get it lifted up and dropped down in the holes prepared for it. It's 12' high and 44' long! We're praying God will help us get it lifted and put in place!! We pray God will send angels to give us wisdom and knowledge and strength and help to get this BIG HEAVY wall picked up and dropped into the holes prepared for it! We're just two old people trying to build an "Ark" for God's people to have a refuge to come to when the Sunday Laws will be passed and we can't buy or sell. This could happen sooner than we think with the pope going in September of this year to congress to appeal possibly for the Sunday Law. The last movements will be rapid ones, Sister White says. That's why we're so URGENT to get this greenhouse built, so we'll be able to grow our own food, even through the winter, when you can't buy and sell and we'll eat from our own gardens, because we can't go to the store and buy anything. God has let us get our garden things out for in the spring. We have other things to plant for later on and the ground to get ready yet. David is rototilling right now, as I write. We're supposed to have hail, heavy rains, and strong winds coming in today! 50 percent chance. I hear thunder and see black heavy clouds! God directed the storm away. We pray God will protect our garden and our fruit blossoms that are in full bloom on all our trees because Thursday, snow and freezing temperatures are coming in! Satan is sure active, knowing that he has but a short time to do his damage! (John 10:10) God is stronger than Satan!

Glad you'll get to talk to Mary on the phone. She's a sweet lady! Glad you got her written and she wrote back to you. Glad you are enjoying my DVDs and being helped and blessed by them! That's why I spend all my time writing out my dreams, hoping God can use them for His glory! Please, keep praying for me, because I'm terribly busy trying to keep up with the load God has given me to bear! God will never give us more than we can bear! (1 Cor. 10:13) God is so good to keep us all going each day, one day at a time! Praise God!! You asked if I do a lot of cooking now that Jonathan's home with us from the nursing home. I do more than I used to, before he came home, trying to make him happy. David and I cook and do dishes. We work together since there's so much to do around here with just the two of us! You said you wished you could be here to help us out—Wow! That would be GREAT!! Yes, we have our water fixed and running. Yes, we can have HOT water when we turn the hot water heater on, but right now we're bathing with heating the water on the electric cook stove to save propane, because it's sooo expensive and we're trying to save all the money we can to put on building materials, so we can HURRY and build it before you can't buy materials. Yes, it is a BIG project building a 24' x 44' greenhouse, but we're depending on God to help us, James 1:5 and supply our needs, Phil. 4:13, 19. Sandie, you're always welcome to come here whenever you want! You mentioned you'd like to go to "Wellness Secrets" in Arkansas and learn the medical missionary course, hands on. Like I told you, they had one years ago, and I attended it, and was so helped and blessed. You would be so blessed and helped going there and getting cared for and while you were getting the help and attention you needed, you'd get professional help learning "hands on things, they could show you. Sherry, Franklin, and Ann Marie were there when I took the medical missionary course. I don't know if they're all three there now? But they were really good at what they did! Sherry did the cooking when I was there. Franklin worked in the health food store and cooked there. You can check it out on your computer? You might like to go and get medical help there? They're very reasonable. Ann Marie does the treatments and Sherry does the massages.

Yes, our car and truck are both fixed! Praise the Lord!! God is good! Yes, our weather is warming up, but spring is tornado time! Ugh! God will have to send angels to protect us! We have faith in His loving care! Ps. 34:6-7.

David and Jonathan say Hi and thanks for the love money gift! They love you, and so do I. You said you'll try and call me sometime? You can't reach us on the phone where we live out here in the country, because the telephone tower isn't strong enough in power to reach way out here. So, we have to go to town, 3 1/2 miles from here, before we can make phone calls. No one can call us and we can't call anyone, until we go to town, where the telephone tower is. It's a bad situation, but that's how it is. We'll give you a call sometime when we buy telephone time again. We have plenty of minutes but after thirty days they turn off the phone and you can't use your minutes till you pay $27 for another thirty days to use your phone again.

Sandie, you're a great medical missionary already! You have the love and compassion of Jesus in your heart and a tender, and kind and thoughtful and helpful spirit, where God can work through you to be a help and a blessing to others. God can use your voice, and hands, and feet, and ears to be a blessing and a help to those in need. You have Jesus in your heart and God, through His Holy Spirit, can work through you to reach hearts.

In book, "Ministry of Healing" by Sister White we read on p. 37, "In choosing men and women for His service, God does not ask whether they possess worldly wealth, learning, or eloquence. He asks, 'Do they walk in such humility that I can teach them my way? Can I put my words into their lips? Will they represent me?' God can use every person just in proportion as He can put His spirit into the soul temple." Also, on pp. 105-106 of "Ministry of Healing," Sister White says, "He who becomes a child of God should henceforth look upon himself as a link in the chain let down to save the world, one with Christ in His plan of mercy, going forth with Him to seek and save the lost. Many feel that it would be a great privilege to visit the scenes of Christ's life on earth, to walk where He trod, to look upon the lake beside which He loved to teach, and the hills and valleys on which His eyes so often rested. But we need not go to Nazareth, to Capernaum, or to Bethany, in order to walk in the steps of Jesus. We shall find His footprints beside the sickbed, in the hovels of poverty, in the crowded alleys of the great cities, and in every place where there are human hearts in need of consolation. We are to feed the hungry, clothe the naked, and comfort the suffering and afflicted. We are to minister to the despairing, and to inspire hope in the hopeless."

Sandie, you're just the kind of person I'd love to have here to help me with all I have to do and also, to help with our son, Jonathan! You have a sweet and loving and meek and quiet spirit about you that draws people to Jesus. You're a very valuable medical missionary for Jesus, and your kind is in great demand! One of the gifts God has given you is the gift of "helps." You're gifted in a lot of ways! God can use you.

In your letter you asked how I remember where all the Bible texts are to be found and all the book references are to be found and you felt I had such an amazing mind and the DVD of my book, was so interesting! But Sandie, it's not me, it's God doing all this! I give God all the glory! I earnestly and constantly pray, as I write, that God will be with me and help me find the texts and book references that go along with what I'm writing. He'll put thoughts in my mind as to what to write and I, then, pray He'll help me find the quotes I need. I don't have a computer or Internet, but I have access to God, through prayer to show me where to find the quotes I need in the Bible and the Spirit of Prophecy books. Just like the reference I quoted to you from, "Ministry of Healing" by Sister White, pp. 105-106, I remembered the reference, but couldn't remember where to find it, and I knelt down and prayed God would please help me find it, and He did! Praise the Lord! I pray about everything, and depend on God for everything! Just as naturally as the flower turns to the sun, so I just naturally turn to God for all my needs and claim His promises and believe God will stand behind His words He's promised. It's just like building the "Ark," it's not our strength and our wisdom and knowledge doing the work, it's God, in answer to our earnest prayers for help and guidance. (James 1:5.)

We just praise and thank the good Lord for seeing us through our "test of "faith" in Him to care for our needs and hear our prayers for help. We knew God wouldn't fail us! We thank God for you, Sandie, for helping to answer our prayers for money to help keep us going! Praise God! May God richly bless you for thinking of us and sacrificing your hard earned money you shared with us!

We love you! Hang in there!

Please keep praying for us! We pray for you!

Love ya,

David, Linda, and Jonathan

Remember, Jesus loves you and He's soon to come! Let's be ready!

Part 2

Eph. 3:20, "Now unto him that is able to do exceeding abundantly above all that we ask or think, according to the power that worketh in us." Praise God from whom all blessings flow!

In Part 1 of this story, we saw how God stepped in and supplied our needs with Sandie's $48 she sent from New Jersey to help us through our hard time we were going through, needing food and gas and telephone money for the month of March, because we had decided to use this money for building materials we needed so much to get started on our 24' x 44' greenhouse, we were building for the early time of trouble, when those who won't go along with the Sunday Law passed, because they'll be true to God's seventh day Sabbath and all God's Ten Commandments, and they won't be able to buy or sell. That's why we were so eager to get building our greenhouse so we could grow our own food when you won't be able to buy your food from the stores.

We had been praying and fasting for money in the mail to keep us going through the month of March till our Social Security check came April 3. We had wanted to get windows from a secondhand store for our greenhouse, but we needed the money. We had prayed and fasted for God to please hold the windows for us till we got the money. We had hoped my cousin, Diane, and her husband, Larry, in Florida would remember my birthday, the last of February, with some money that we so much needed. But when I wrote Part 1 of this story, we still hadn't heard from Diane and Larry and it was near the end of March. But on March 28, when I went to get the mail, there was Diane and Larry's letter and money! How happy and excited and thankful I was when I prayed and asked God to please let money be in the envelope and when I opened it up, there was $123. In her letter she wrote and explained how she came about sending $123. We were so very thankful and grateful to God for doing this for us in answer to our prayers for help in our time of need.

Here's what she wrote:

"I felt like I needed to get this in the mail today... You're not going to believe this but I found $3 on the grass (I think Jesus is dropping this money in front of me so I can send it to you.) (ha). The $20 is because we had it in a Christmas card to give to a special waiter and when we went *there at Christmastime with the card, he wasn't there. The next time we went there he was there, and we forgot the card and then we haven't seen him for a long time so I'm thinking maybe I am supposed to send it to you so that's how we arrived at a strange amount, $123. Need to go, so I can go to the post office.*

Love to all,

Diane and Larry

God is so good to hear our prayers of "faith" to meet our needs! Praise God! Thank you, Jesus! Thank you, Diane and Larry! May God richly bless you for thinking of us and listening to the Holy Spirit to help meet our needs! We'll be able to get our windows we wanted for the greenhouse, now that we got your money! On the date, 3-30, we got the five windows we wanted. God saved them for us. Praise God! You're in our prayers! Please keep praying for us! We love you! Thank you for letting God use you to be such a blessing and a help to us in our time of need! Matt. 25:40, "And the king shall answer and say unto them, Verily I say unto you, Inasmuch as ye have done it unto one of the least of these my brethren, ye have done it unto me."

I know Jesus loves you and is proud of you for letting Him use you to supply our needs! David and Jonathan say, "Thank you!" They love you, too. We'll be praying for God to see you through your trip to California and meet your needs there! Have "faith" in God! God can do anything! Luke 1:37, "For with God nothing shall be impossible." Claim Eph. 3:20. Thank you for seeing us through our "faith test" and helping our "faith" to grow, trusting God to meet our needs and care for us during the time of trouble ahead of us.

Part 3

Praise God, from whom all blessings flow; Praise Him, all creatures here below; Praise Him above, ye heavenly host; Praise Father, Son, and Holy Ghost.

Read in *Early Writings*, by E. G. White, chapter on "Prayer and Faith," pp. 72 & 73. When God blesses, He really blesses! God honored our "faith" in Him by us trusting Him to take care of our needs when we stepped out in "faith" in March and did without our gas and food and telephone money, so we could buy building materials, so we could get working on the "ARK" by building on the 24' x 44' greenhouse. We put God's work first and claimed Matt. 6:33 and Phil. 4:19. And we put "faith" in Him and His promises to see us through our hard times and prayed God would impress someone, through His Holy Spirit, to send us some money in the mail and help meet our needs, as we worked on God's "Ark," His refuge prepared for His faithful ones He'll impress to come here during the early time of trouble. We're trying to get the greenhouse ready so we'll be able to eat what we grow during the winter months, since we won't be able to buy food at the store, and all those who are here with us will be able to eat from the greenhouse. So we began building the middle wall to the greenhouse with our food and gas and telephone money for March. God has been letting our "faith" grow and God has let Sandie from New Jersey send us $48. Then, my cousin, Diane, from Florida sent us $123. My cousin, Nancy, from Florida had already sent me a $100 bill in the mail for my birthday in February. David's sister, Hilma Sue, and her husband, Tom, from Chicago have, through the years, have been a real blessing to us, too, as we've been building on the "Ark." We're so thankful to all who have been a help and a blessing to us through the years! Praise God! God bless each one! They've been helping our "faith" to grow in trusting God to hear our prayers for help and meet our needs!

Sister White, in *The Desire of Ages*, says on p. 371, "The means in our possession may not seem to be sufficient for the work; but if we will move forward in faith, believing in the all-sufficient power of God, abundant resources will open before us. If the work be of God, He Himself will provide the means for its accomplishment. He will reward honest, simple reliance upon Him. The little that is wisely and economically used in the service of the Lord of heaven will increase in the very act of imparting. In the hand of Christ the small supply of food remained undiminished until the famished multitude were satisfied. If we go to the Source of all strength, with our hands of faith outstretched to receive, we shall be sustained in our work, even under the most forbidding circumstances, and shall be enabled to give to others the bread of life." Sister White, also, says in *Last Day Events*, p. 149, "Now is the time to cultivate faith." Also, read in *Early Writings*, pp. 78–81, "Mrs. Whites Dreams."

When David went to buy our five windows we had wanted for our greenhouse, but hadn't had the money to get them, we had prayed God would please hold them and save them for us and please supply us with the money to be able to purchase them before someone else got them! Then, Diane and Larry's $123 came in the mail on 3-28-15. David went on a Monday, 3-30-15, with the money to buy them. We had prayed no one would have bought them. David said when he went in to buy the windows there was a lady there looking at them and measuring them, and so he kept praying she wouldn't buy them. Then, the lady left and David paid for them and loaded them up and brought them on home. We just praised the Lord for hearing our prayers!

Then, as we built on the greenhouse, we had used up the lumber we had purchased and we needed so much more to keep us being able to build on the greenhouse. We had no idea how we were going to purchase more expensive lumber to keep trying to finish this BIG expensive project we had stepped out on "faith" to build. But we kept praying in "faith" that God would supply our needs to keep us going. We knew God could do anything as Luke 1:37 promises, "For with God nothing shall be impossible." Also, we claimed the promise in Mark 10:27 for God to do the impossible to supply us with more money somehow, some way so we could keep hurrying to build our 24' x 44' greenhouse before everything broke loose and the Sunday Laws could be passed any time and we wouldn't be able to buy and sell and our work on the "Ark" would come to an end.

Then, on April 2, a Thursday, I prayed before I went out to check the mail praying there would please be money in the mail. I found a card in the mail from Sandi from New Jersey. I figured she wouldn't be sending me any more money, since it hadn't been long ago that she had sent us $48 that had been such a help and a blessing to us in answer to our prayers for help.

I opened it up and read her letter inside the pretty Easter card:

She wrote:

Linda, Dave, and Jonathan,

As I ponder on the Easter season, and what it really means, about our Lord and Saviour dying, resting, and rising from the grave my heart is very thankful for the sacrifice He made for us! Praise God! And He's coming soon to take us with Him, to be with him wheresoever He goes! Talk about pure gratification and satisfaction that's it! God's blessings be upon you Linda, and David, and Jonathan now and forever more.

I love you!

Sister Sandie, Joe, Chris, Val, and Lexie

Then, on a card she wrote:

I felt so cheap just sending you $48. I'm going to be sending you $500 in a few days. Just pray the money gets there safely, which I'm sure it will! Praise God from whom all blessings flow!! God bless you both as you build your greenhouse! I hope the $500 helps with building supplies or if you already got all you need, it will reimburse you and help with your needs or whatever you need it for."

God is sooo good! How very thankful we were for God's answer to our prayers for money to keep building on the greenhouse and also, so very thankful to Sandie sacrificing her hard-earned money to be such a help and a blessing to us in our time of need to do the Lord's work on the "Ark." I knew this was a Big sacrifice on her part since she drives a school bus and doesn't make all that much money. We certainly do thank her and ask God's richest blessings on her for being an answer to our prayers for money to meet our needs and for her listening to the Holy Spirit to send us all that money. She had no idea how very much we needed that money. Only God knew what we were going through!

We had the two outer walls built some time ago. Recently, we had completed the center wall, 12' high and 44' long. We weren't sure how we were going to get that BIG HEAVY wall picked up and dropped into the holes prepared for it. Then, we prayed and claimed James 1:5 and we were impressed to cut the 44' long wall into half and put it in place, making two 12' x 22' walls, easier to pick up and put the 22' wall down into the holes and then bring the two 12' x 22' walls together and re-enforce them together. Praise God! He helped us! Thank you Jesus! God is helping our "faith" to keep growing as we keep trusting Him to supply our needs and give us two old people the wisdom and knowledge and "faith" and strength to build this Big greenhouse. We have "faith" in God to help us do the job He's asked us to do for Him and His people He will soon be bringing here when the Sunday Law will be passed and people, who need a place of refuge, will be able to come to the "Ark" for safety.

Friends, what are you needing "faith" for in your life to be able to step out in "faith" and do what God is asking you to do for Him? Won't you, right now, show "faith" in God and His promises and let your "faith" grow for the time of trouble ahead of you? God will honor your "faith." Have FAITH in God; Heb. chapter 11.

Part 4

"Now Faith is the substance of things hoped for, the evidence of things not seen… but without faith it is impossible to please him: for he that cometh to God must believe that he is, and that he is a rewarder of them that diligently seek him." Heb. 11:1, 6; also, read verse 7, "By faith Noah, being warned of God of things not seen as yet, moved with fear, prepared an ark to the saving of his house; by the which he condemned the world, and became heir of the righteousness which is by faith.

God let Sandie's $500 she sent get safely to us! Praise God! We went to the lumber store and bought more lumber we needed. I called her on the phone to thank her for her great sacrifice of money for us to continue building on the "ARK." I let her know how very much we appreciated her gift of money given to us in answer to our prayers for money to keep building on the "ARK." Sandie answered me and said, "You'll be getting another $500 in the mail in a few days! Watch for it!" I was so very shocked and thankful and grateful to her for doing this for us, I just kept saying, "Thank you, Sandie! Thank you!" She then totally blew my socks off when she said, "Linda, we sold my husband's parent's old home and I'm going to be sending you $500 more, making it a total of $1,500 I'm sending you to put on materials for your greenhouse. I want to share some with you!" I was just so happy and excited I could hardly believe my ears! God was doing exceedingly abundantly above all that we ask or think! All I could do was say, "Praise God from whom all blessings flow! Thank you! Thank you! Thank you! Sandie! God bless you!! You're truly an answer to our prayers for money we needed to build the greenhouse!"

We had stepped out on "faith," knowing it would be thousands of dollars to build this big 24' x 44' green house, but we were trusting God to supply all our needs, as Phil. 4:19 promised. We had stepped out on "faith" and used our March food and gas and telephone money to buy building materials with that money showing "faith" in God to show His power to provide our needs! And God never failed us! We got along just fine without being able to use our phone all the month of March and our food and gas never ran out, even though they got low, but that's how God tests our "faith" so it will grow, so we'll show "faith" in Him to come through and keep all His promises. We had been praying each day that God would please work on the hearts of someone to please send us money we so much needed to finish this building on the "ARK" before the time of trouble began and we couldn't buy or sell. I thanked Sandie for listening to the Holy Spirit to answer our prayers for money! I just praised the Lord and thanked her again and again for her love and kindness and unselfishness shown to us in our time of need! I had prayer with her on the phone and asked God's richest blessings on her and her dear family for sharing their means with us. We were just so happy and excited and praising God for all He was doing to honor our "faith" in Him for supplying all our needs, as He had promised. We were going around singing the Doxology: Praise God from whom all blessings flow…"

Then, the next day when I went out to the mail I was so excited and happy to find a pretty card from my cousin "Nancy" in Florida. I prayed as I opened her card, that there would be money in it and there was a $100 bill and she had written in her letter, "I'm sending this $100 bill so you can keep building on the "ARK"! God bless all of you!" She quoted on her card, Deut. 4:29; and also, Ps. 37:7. She said on the card she sent, "Trust in God's timing. It's always right." Her card also said, "Thinking of you…as I often do!" She further wrote on her card… "God has been good to me. Pray that we will all stay faithful to Him, because I want to spend eternity with Him. God bless you and give you the health and strength to work on the "Ark." P.S. This time I hope I remember to seal the envelope. I always pray over your letter with the money that angels will protect it. And they did! Praise God!"

We were just so happy and on Cloud 9 as we praised and thanked the good Lord for hearing our prayers for all this money coming in and now Nancy's $100 bill! I hurried and wrote her and let her know we got her money safely and that we were buying some more windows we needed for the greenhouse and I'll call her later. I thanked her for letting God use her to answer our prayers for money to meet our needs and that we pray for God to richly bless her for her sacrifice made for us! We really did appreciate her thinking of us and we love her and thankful for her prayers for us. God just keeps pouring out His blessings on us and now we're singing, "There shall be showers of blessings!" Praise God! As we faithfully pay tithe on all this money we've received, we claim Mal. 3:10, and 2 Peter 1:4–8.

Then, one day David came home from talking to a builder professional and he was figuring up all it will cost us to build a 24' x 44' greenhouse and he figured $8,000 approximately. David was ready to cut down on the size, because he felt we'd never get that much money to complete this BIG project we had started in faith. I quoted to David Mark 11:22, "And Jesus answering saith unto them, have faith in God." Also, I quoted Luke 18:8, "… Nevertheless, when the Son of man cometh, shall he find faith on the earth?" Then, I quoted *The Ministry of Healing*, by Sister White, on p 481, "Our heavenly Father has a thousand ways to provide for us of which we know nothing. Those who accept the one principle of making the service of God supreme, will find perplexities vanish and a plain path before their feet. The faithful discharge of today's duties is the best preparation for tomorrow's trials."

I said, "David, this is a "FAITH" project we've started on building this BIG greenhouse trusting God to be with us and help us and strengthen us and supply all our needs. We must show "faith" in God and let our "faith" grow for the time of trouble ahead of us. God will see us through any problem. We just have to work by "faith" and let God show what He will do! I have "faith" that it won't cost that much. Let's just show "faith" in God and keep building and let God supply our needs. You just wait and see what God will do as we put our "faith" and trust in Him. Just look what He's done already to help us build and meet our needs. God has plans for the "Ark." Just keep building and buying the materials we need as the money comes in and work by "faith" and God will honor our "faith" and will see us through building the big greenhouse on "faith." Have "FAITH" in God!

So, he went to get more materials in the truck, after we had prayer together. But when he got in the truck the wipers wouldn't turn on, the electric switch on the steering wheel had gone bad. It was supposed to rain that day, so he hurried over to our mechanic friend to see if he could put a toggle switch on the truck to operate the wipers, since we couldn't afford an electrical switch to be bought and put on. He just had to ground the wire for a better connection and it worked and he charged us nothing. Praise God! After that was done, we were ready to continue getting our building materials in the truck. We knew God was testing our "faith." We were fighting Satan trying to stop us, too.

I was out in the building where we store our building materials and I went to hit a wasp and a snake, all curled up just about 1" from me dropped down in front of me and almost hit my arm and fell at my feet all curled up and I took off running and praying, "Oh!! Jesus, please protect me!!!" I was afraid the snake was going to chase after me! But God protected me from being bit! Praise the Lord! Thank you, Jesus! Satan is constantly trying to get to us, because he's wroth with what we're doing, preparing an "Ark" of safety for God's people to find refuge here when the Sunday Laws will be passed. We have to be getting used to living in the country and with what we'll have to contend with like: snakes, ticks, mosquitoes, wasps, chiggers, and also ants, etc.

Even now, as I'm sitting at my writing desk, there's a wasp buzzing all around me, trying to attack me. God will protect us through whatever happens to us during the early time of trouble and into the Great Time of Trouble. We now, need to be having "faith" in God and learn to live by His promises. We'll be going through all kinds of inconveniences when we can't buy or sell when the Sunday Law is passed. We will have to grow our own food, can't buy from the store. Our utilities will be cut off, because we'll keep God's seventh day Sabbath and not go along with the Sunday man-made Sabbath. Then, when persecution and fines and imprisonment comes upon us, and finally the death decree, we'll need a strong "faith" in Jesus to care for us then and see us through the experiences we'll be going through. NOW is the time to let our "faith" grow, so we will be able to stand through the trials and troubles we'll be having then. It's like soldiers in boot camp training. They're taught to be strong and courageous and to be tough and fearless to meet the enemy. They're put through rigorous training, so they'll be ready and able to stand when they're in battle and they won't retreat when the enemy comes in strong upon them, but they will be in a condition to stand and fight to the finish. Jesus will strengthen us for the days ahead of us and prepare us for that time. This is how we are to grow our "faith" for the time of trouble, by each day claiming God's promises and believing in His Word and develop "faith" in Jesus that He'll take care of us and meet all our needs when every earthly support is cut off. We will naturally turn to Jesus in "faith", as the little flower naturally turns to the sun. Jesus is giving us, each one of us, tests to go through right now so our "faith" will grow in Jesus.

In the book *Maranatha*, by Sister White, she says on p. 57, "This world is a training school for the higher school, this life a preparation for the life to come. Here we are to be prepared for entrance into the heavenly courts. Here we are to receive and believe and practice the truth until we are made ready for a home with the saints in light." 2 Cor. 13:5 tells us to examine ourselves. We must be watchful and pray because Satan is on our track to destroy us and our "faith" in Jesus. God knows what's ahead for each one of us, and He knows what He has to do to get us ready to stand at the time of the Sunday Law crisis. Some of us may be martyrs, some of us may be treated as slaves or exiled, or put into prison and some of us will have to go before courts to give a reason for our "faith." (*Last Day Events*, p. 149)

Sister White writes in *Last Day Events*, p. 153, "Soon there is to be trouble all over the world. It becomes everyone to seek to know God. We have no time to delay…"

Also, she writes on p. 145, *Last Day Events* book, "Those religious bodies who refuse to hear God's messages of warning will be under strong deception and will unite with the civil power to persecute the saints. The Protestant churches will unite with the papal power in persecuting the commandment-keeping people of God… This lamb-like power unites with the dragon in making war upon those who keep the commandments of God and have the testimony of Jesus Christ." (And read Rev. 13)

Sister White goes on to say on pp. 150 & 151 in *Last Day Events* book, "Many will be imprisoned, many will flee for their lives from cities and towns, and many will be martyrs for Christ's sake in standing in defense of the truth… Men will be required to render obedience to human edicts in violation of the divine law. Those who are true to God will be menaced, denounced, proscribed. They will be 'betrayed both by parents, and brethren, and kinfolks, and friends' even unto death… We shall find that one must let loose of all hands except the hand of Jesus Christ. Friends, will prove treacherous and will betray us. Relatives, deceived by the enemy, will think they do God service in opposing us and putting forth the utmost efforts to bring us into hard places, hoping we will deny our faith. But we may trust our hand in the hand of Christ amid darkness and peril… The only way in which men will be able to stand firm in the conflict is to be rooted and grounded in Christ. They must receive the truth as it is in Jesus. And it is only as the truth is presented thus that it can meet the wants of the soul. The preaching of Christ crucified, Christ our righteousness, is what satisfies the soul's hunger. When we secure the interest of the people in this great central truth, faith and hope and courage come to the heart… Many, because of their faith will be cut off from house and heritage here, but if they will give their hearts to Christ, receiving the message of His grace, and resting upon their Substitute and Surety, even the Son of God, they may still be filled with joy… As enmity is aroused in various places against those who observe the Sabbath of the Lord, it may become necessary for God's people to move from those places to places where they will not be so bitterly opposed."

Read Ps. 91 and Ps. 27 and Ps. 40 and Ps. 46.

A quote from *Maranatha*, p. 277, by E. G. White, has this to say, "The people of God will not be free from suffering; but while persecuted and stressed, while they endure privation and suffer for want of food they will not be left to perish."

Read what Sister White says Satan will say, on p. 149 of *Last Day Events*, "Satan says …" For fear of wanting food and clothing they will join with the world in transgressing God's law. The earth will be wholly under my dominion."

Also, read in *Maranatha* book by E. G. White on pp. 274 & 275, "The season of distress and anguish before us will require a faith that can endure weariness, delay, and hunger—a faith that will not faint though severely tried. The period of probation is granted to all to prepare for that time… All who will lay hold of God's promises, as he [Jacob] did, and be as earnest and persevering as he was, will succeed as he succeeded… The time of trouble such as never was is soon to open upon us; and we shall need an experience which we do not now possess, and which many are too indolent to obtain… God's providence is the school in which we are to learn the meekness and lowliness of Jesus. The Lord is ever setting before us, not the way we would choose, which is easier and pleasanter to us, but the true aims of life. None can neglect or defer this work but at the most fearful peril to their souls… In the midst of the time of trouble—trouble such as has not been since there was a nation—His [God's] chosen ones will stand unmoved. Satan with all the hosts of evil cannot destroy the weakest of God's saints."

Friends, I pray you're letting God develop "faith" in Him and His Word now, so you'll stand true to God then. Jesus loves you and wants to get us all ready and prepared to stand in the Sunday Law crisis soon to come upon us as an overwhelming surprise. Read about it in *Testimonies for the Church*, vol. 8, p. 28, by E. G. White. She also, writes in *Selected Messages*, book 2, p. 142, "The work of the people of God is to prepare for the events of the future, which will soon come upon them with blinding force."

Friends, please pray for us as we continue, in "faith," to build this big 24' x 44' greenhouse on the "Ark." Thank you! And we pray for you, that you and your loved ones will prepare to meet God and the crisis ahead of us all. Have "faith" in God! Please read Matt. 6:19–34. God bless you! May you show "faith" and courage and trust in Jesus to step out in "faith" and follow in Jesus' footsteps and be willing to go where He leads the way and obey His counsel given to His church, His bride. Put your hand in Jesus' Hand and begin now to do God's will in your life and He'll be with you all the way and strengthen you and care for you and supply all your needs and direct your path on your journey to new adventures with God! You can do it! I'll be praying for you!

READY TO COMMIT SUICIDE!

This is an experience I had many years ago when I and my husband were out taking up donations, going door to door, for Harvest Ingathering for our church, to raise their goal to help missions around the world to have money to work with to help those less fortunate and in need of help.

It was a cold winter night and we had been out in the cold snow and north winds going door to door for several hours. My husband would work on one side of the street while I worked on the other side and he could look across the street and see where I was at. My feet were freezing and my hands were frozen as I clung to the money donations in my hand that I had received going door to door. Not too many people would let you in their homes, as you stood outside waiting for them to go get their donation to give me. Finally, I arrived at a dark house but I knocked anyway, and was planning on leaving a pamphlet in the door handle explaining the work our Seventh-day Adventist church was doing to help people in need and also so they could enroll in a free Bible Study correspondence course advertised on the pamphlet. As I stood there knocking at the door and freezing I looked around and it just seemed so eerie and spooky at this dark house with bushes and trees all around it. As I was getting ready to leave and leave a pamphlet in the door, all of a sudden the door slowly opened and a man standing beside the door said, "Come in." I was so terribly cold I stepped in to try and get some warmth on my feet and hands. When I stepped in I noticed there were no lights on in the house. It was dark. I stood by the open door and gave my little speech as to what I was out doing and as I spoke I could see in the dark a knife in the man's hand. I kept praying as he walked into another room to get me a donation. He came back and handed me some money and I handed him a pamphlet and thanked him and said, "God bless you! There's a free Bible Study correspondence course inside." I then left and wondered if he was maybe ready to commit suicide with that knife in his hand and the house lights all out. I wonder what might have happened if I hadn't knocked on his door that night? Only God knows. God certainly cared for me, too, that night as I went from door to door with all that money I carried in my hand, trying to encourage people to give large donations by seeing all the money others had given. I had people say to me as I was going door to door with around $70 in my hand, "Aren't you afraid to be going around at night to peoples' doors with all that money in your hands?!" I would answer and say, "No, I'm out here doing the Lord's work of helping people in need and God takes care of me!"

One time someone said to me, "Aren't you afraid to be out at night with all that money, knowing there's been a murder here in town?!" I said, "No, I have a guardian angel watching over me and I'm doing the Lord's work and He takes care of me!"

The police would follow us around keeping track of us, but never stopped us. We had a permit with the police station to be doing this soliciting and we had on our authorized badges. I'm sure God was using the policemen to watch over us, too.

I think back on that man, in that dark house, with a knife in his hand, possibly depressed or discouraged, just ready to end it all and put himself out of the misery he may have been going through, not knowing that Jesus could help him and give him hope and a reason for living.

So many people today are in the same condition feeling despair and hopelessness and trapped with no way out! This is why Jesus calls His church, His people to let him use their hands and feet and voice and ears to hear the cry of His lost sheep out there in the world not knowing that Jesus loves them and has a plan for their life and wants to save them from Satan's hold on them and give them freedom from their sins and addictions. Time is running out, we must be about our Father's business of saving souls and rescuing them from Satan's traps and snares. Jesus loves them and died to save them and asks us Seventh-day Adventists to go in search of His lost sheep and find them and bring them into God's fold. (John 10:10, 16).

God wants to use us so He can place us in the right place, at the right time, crossing our path with the right people He's trying to help and save. It's so important to stay in tune with Jesus and be filled with His Holy Spirit so He can direct our steps like Prov. 3:5 & 6 says, "Trust in the Lord with all thine heart; and lean not unto thine own understanding. In all thy ways acknowledge him, and he shall direct thy paths."

Also, Ps. 32:7 & 8, "Thou art my hiding place, thou shalt preserve me from trouble; thou shalt compass me about with songs of deliverance. Selah. I will instruct thee and teach thee in the way which thou shalt go: I will guide thee with mine eye."

Sister White says in *Last Day Events*, p. 45 "The Lord has made us the depositories of His law; He has committed to us sacred and eternal truth which is to be given to others in faithful warnings, reproofs and encouragements... Seventh-day Adventists have been chosen of God as a peculiar people separate from the world. By the great cleaver of truth He has cut them out from the quarry of the world and brought them into connection with Himself. He has made them His representatives and has called them to be ambassadors for Him in the last work of salvation. The greatest wealth of truth ever entrusted to mortals, the most solemn and fearful warnings ever sent by God to man, have been committed to them to be given to the world... In a special sense Seventh-day Adventists have been set in the world as watchmen and light bearers. To them has been entrusted the last warning for a perishing world. On them is shining wonderful light from the Word of God. They have been given a work of the most solemn import—the proclamation of the first, second, and third angels' messages. There is no other work of so great importance. They are to allow nothing else to absorb their attention..."

Continuing on pp. 72–74, Sister White writes, "We have nothing to fear for the future, except as we shall forget the way the Lord has led us, and His teaching in our past history... If there ever was a time when serious reflection becomes everyone who fears God, it is now, when personal piety is essential. The inquiry should be made, 'What am I, and what is my work and mission in this time? On which side am I working—Christ's side or the enemy's side?' Let every soul now humble himself or herself before God, for now we are surely living in the great Day of Atonement. The cases even now of many are passing in review before God, for they are to sleep in their graves a little season. Your profession of faith is not your guarantee in that day, but the state of your affections. Is the soul-temple cleansed of its defilement? Are my sins confessed and am I repenting of them before God that they may be blotted out? Do I esteem myself too lightly? Am I willing to make any and every sacrifice for the excellency of the knowledge of Jesus Christ? Do I feel every moment I am not my own, but Christ's property, that my service belongs to God, whose I am...?

We should ask ourselves, 'For what are we living and working? And what will be the outcome of it all...?' I have questioned in my mind, as I have seen the people in our cities hurrying to and fro with business, whether they ever thought of the day of God that is just upon us. Every one of us should be living with reference to the great day which is soon to come upon us... We cannot afford to live with no reference to the day of judgment; for though long delayed, it is now near, even at the door, and hasteth greatly. The trumpet of the Archangel will soon startle the living and wake the dead... If we find no pleasure now in the contemplation of heavenly things, if we have no interest in seeking the knowledge of God, no delight in beholding the character of Christ; if holiness has no attraction for us—then we may be sure that our hope of heaven is vain. Perfect conformity to the will of God is the high aim to be constantly before the Christian. He will love to talk of God, of Jesus, of the home of bliss and purity which Christ has prepared for them that love Him. The contemplation of these themes, when the soul feasts upon the blessed assurances of God, the apostle represents as tasting 'the powers of the world to come...' If you are right with God today, you are ready if Christ should come today."

THE MYSTERIOUS DATE: 1-22-16

On 11-11-15 I saw this date: 1-22-16 in my dream. Nothing was said about it in my dream. It just showed the date: 1-22-16. When I told my dream to Daddy and Jonathan, we all wondered what it could mean. We prayed and asked God to help us know what the date 1-22-16 could mean! Naturally we wondered what was going to happen on 1-22-16, as we waited and watched the days go by on the calendar. With apprehension we kept praying and asking God to let us know what was going to happen on 1-22-16. For several months I had been in touch with a publisher, about them publishing my book, ***Don't Be Trapped in the Cities!! Get Out Now!***

We had been trying to come up with the money needed to complete the process. We had been praying and asking God to please help us know what to do to be able to get the money needed! We decided to sell our old tractor, plow, disc, and brush cutter to a neighbor who said he'd like to buy it. He said he'd only be able to give us $1,000 for it. We were desperate for any money we could get to hurry and have enough money to get our book started! God had given me a dream on 1-7-16 that said: I was saying to some people, "People need to know what is coming! They need to be warned, so they can prepare!" This is how I felt about my book.

Our neighbor had to go through the bank to get the loan to pay us the $1,000. We kept praying he'd hurry up and get us the money, but he kept saying, "I'm waiting on the bank." We kept praying and asking God what could be going to happen on 1-22-16. We thought, could one of us be going to become sick, or injured or have a car accident, or die?"

Then, as we kept nearing the date 1-22-16, we got to thinking, "Maybe we'll get our $1,000 on that date and be able to send in my contract and the money to the publisher so they can get started on my book?!" We wanted so much for our book to get published and out to the people to warn them as to what's coming with these Sunday Laws soon to be passed and what could happen to God's faithful people who remain true to God's seventh day Sabbath and not go along with the Sunday sabbath. They need to know not to remain in these wicked cities where calamities and God's judgments are going to be destroying these wicked cities!

Finally, on 1-22-16, the neighbor came and got his tractor and the accessories and gave us the $1,000! We hurried to the bank and deposited it and wrote a check for $2,000 to the publisher. We used the $1,000 we had in the bank to buy our winter propane for February and March, so we could send them $2,000 to begin doing all they had to do to type it up and have me go over it and then they could begin publishing it, while they waited for the rest of their money from us. The whole staff were so patient and kind to us waiting to get their money, God bless them! But we wanted to hurry and get this debt paid! So, on 1-22-16 we were so very excited as we sent the $2,000 and my signed contract to them and prayed God would protect it.

Now we could see how God, way back on 11-11-15 already knew that on 1-22-16 everything would work out for us to be able to have the money and get it sent to the publisher on that very day! God is so good! It helped us realize how God knows our future of each one of us and has things under His control and He's working things out behind the scenes always for our good! Rom. 8:28. It strengthened our faith in God and His promises that we can rest in His tender loving care, knowing that it's all in His Hands and He neither hastens nor delays, but He's always right on time! Praise God! How we prayed and thanked the good Lord for seeing us through this experience and supplying our needs as He's promised to do in Phil. 4:19. We know God will work it out for us to come up with the rest of the money needed to complete this project, of getting my book published and out to the people! Thank you, Jesus! Luke 1:37; Mark 10:27; Mark 11:22–24; Matt. 21:22.

PANIC ATTACK!

I would like to close my book with this final story I've entitled, "Panic Attack," because this is one of the things it took to get Jonathan's attention to make some serious decisions for the Lord.

Jonathan's life journey through the years has been a series of in and out of the emergency rooms and hospitals, depressed and suicidal on drugs and alcohol and trying to live out on his own and in and out of care centers and back and forth living at home, but never really going all the way with Jesus and living to please the Lord, but always living to gratify and please self in his sinful pleasures. Those of us who are living at this time in earth's history should have the testimony that Enoch had, found in Heb. 11:5, 6, that he lived to please God.

Jonathan had moved back home, to live with us, his parents, on April 1, 2014. We have always tried to encourage Jonathan to give up his old lifestyle and sinful pleasures and get ready for Christ's soon return. We kept claiming Prov. 22:6, "Train up a child in the way he should go and when he is old, he will not depart from it." Through the years we kept praying for him, but really no real lasting change would occur, only at times our hopes would rise, only to be let down again and again, as we kept praying for Jonathan's conversion.

When we brought him home to live with us this time, he had lots of time to listen to 3ABN and speakers like Kenny Shelton and Doug Batchelor from Amazing Facts, etc. As he listened to all these sermons and pretty music on 3ABN radio and DVDs from Bill and Mary from Idaho and Don and speakers like Hal Mayer and Pastor John, he began to think more serious thoughts and listen to us tell him about the Sunday Laws soon to be passed and how we need to be preparing our hearts for that time and be ready spiritually as well as physically for what's coming and to take his stand now and be true to Jesus and all His Ten Commandments and God's seventh day Bible Sabbath and not follow the beast, the papacy, and his man-made Sunday sabbath. We couldn't read his thoughts, but we knew the Holy Spirit was working on his heart. We just kept praying. Then when the pope made his visit to the U.S.A. on September 2015, this got him really thinking more seriously. Then in October 2015, he received his official Blessing is on the "Go"! Evangelistic Team member certificate by sending 3ABN a monthly donation. He was happy about that and hung it up in his room. I said, "God is wanting to use you as His witness! This is what we've always wanted for your life, to win souls for Jesus! God will help you! You can do it!"

Then on October 19, Jonathan had a panic attack and wanted to be taken to the emergency room. They gave him some medicine to calm him down, but he felt himself becoming very depressed and feeling suicidal and asked the doctor to please admit him to the hospital in Topeka, Kansas for help. So, at 3:00 a.m., October 20, we drove Jonathan to the hospital in Topeka to be admitted. While there, he refused to eat anything for two days. He just stayed in bed and slept. The third day he ate a meal, brought on a tray to his room. He would read and study his Bible and pray, but he wanted to just remain in his room. He continued to study and read his Bible and pray and eat only one meal a day. We encouraged him to drink water at least while he was fasting.

Finally, on October 24, 2015, he was dismissed to come home. When we went to pick him up, I looked over his discharge papers and noticed on the sheet they sent home with him was a question they had asked him, which was, "What is the one thing that is most important to you?" Jonathan answered, "THE LORD." I was so proud of him and he said to me, "The Lord wants me to keep His seventh day Sabbath holy and not Sunday. And the Lord wants me to keep all ten of his Commandments. And He wants me to quit this nicotine."

I said, "Praise the Lord, Jonathan! This panic attack that sent you to the emergency room, and then on to the hospital has been like your 'Damascus Road' experience where you have had days of fasting and praying and studying your Bible and being alone with the Lord and listening to His Holy Spirit speak to your heart, and you have responded and want to be ready for this Sunday Law coming and be true and loyal to Jesus and not go along with the Beast, the papacy, and his mark. I'm so very proud of you and I know Jesus is too! God will help you and see you through your decisions made for Him! Have faith in God and trust and rely on His promises like: Jude 24, 25, 'Now unto him that is able to keep you from falling and to present you faultless before the presence of his glory with exceeding joy, to the only wise God our Saviour, be glory and majesty, dominion and power, both now and ever. Amen.' Also, Phil. 4:13, 19, 'I can do all things through Christ which strengtheneth me.' Also, verse 19, 'But my God shall supply all your need according to his riches in glory by Christ Jesus.' Also, 1 Cor. 15:57, 58, 'But thanks be to God, which giveth us the victory through our Lord Jesus Christ. Therefore, my beloved brethren, be ye stedfast, unmoveable, always abounding in the word of the Lord, forasmuch as ye know that your labour is not in vain in the Lord.' Jonathan, this is what we've been praying for so long! Praise God that we're getting to see and witness our son coming back to Jesus! Jonathan, I have prayed and prayed and asked God to please let you come to the Lord before I sent my book to be published so I could write about your conversion and let the reader know you had taken your stand for Jesus and that you want to love and obey Him and not self! God bless you, Jonathan, as you continue your journey to heaven! I love you! Dad loves you! Jesus loves you! Hang in there and be strong in the Lord and let God use your life now to be a witness for Him and what He's done in your life! You've been our investment project for years and years as we've prayed God would make something beautiful of your life for God's glory! God has answered our earnest prayers for you and He has plans for your life as you stay close to Jesus and faithful to Him and His cause! Never give up!"

Please keep us and our son, Jonathan, in your prayers, as we'll be praying for each of you, dear reader, to make your decision to follow and obey Jesus and His counsel and love Him enough to leave these large cities as soon as possible and prepare for the crisis soon to come upon these cities and God's people, and be able to go through the storms and calamities coming and the crisis of the Sunday Law soon to come as an overwhelming surprise, as Sister White says in *Testimonies for the Church*, vol. 8, p. 28, "Transgression has almost reached its limit. Confusion fills the world, and a great terror is soon to come upon human beings. The end is very near. We who know the truth should be preparing for what is soon to break upon the world as an overwhelming surprise." Also, in *Selected Messages*, book 2, by E. G. White on p. 142 she writes, "The work of the people of God is to prepare for the events of the future, which will soon come upon them with blinding force."

We have not time to lose! Sister White says in *Last Day Events*, p. 11, "The calamities by land and sea, the unsettled state of society, the alarms of war, are portentous. They forecast approaching events of the greatest magnitude. The agencies of evil are combining their forces and consolidating. They are strengthening for the last great crisis. Great changes are soon to take place in our world, and the final movements will be rapid ones."

Sister White writes in her book, *Country Living*, p. 27, 28, "Let there be much praying done, and even with fasting, that not one shall move in darkness, but move in the light as God is in the light… If everyone will come to Jesus in a teachable spirit, with contrition of heart, then he is in a condition of mind to be instructed and to learn of Jesus and obey His orders… We cannot have a weak faith now, we cannot be safe in a listless, indolent, slothful attitude. Every jot of ability is to be used, and sharp, calm, deep thinking is to be done. The wisdom of any human agent is not sufficient for the planning and devising in this time. Spread every plan before God with fasting, [and] with the humbling of the soul before the Lord Jesus, and commit thy ways unto the Lord. The sure promise is, He will direct thy paths. He is infinite in resources. The Holy One of Israel, who calls the host of heaven by name, and holds the stars of heaven in position, has you individually in His keeping."

May God help us all to be ready and found faithful and move under the guidance of a wise, unseen Counselor, which is God. Remember, God is in control of things. None of us know what our future holds, but we're safe as we remain in God's hands and under His tender, loving care and continue to have faith in Him and His promises like: Ps. 46:1, "God is our refuge and strength, a very present help in trouble." Also, Ps. 34:7, "The angel of the Lord encampeth round about them that fear him, and delivereth them." Also, read: Ps. 91; Prov. 3:5, 6; Ps. 37:3–5; Ps. 32:8; 1 Pet. 5:7.

In closing, I just want to say to my dear readers, "May this book, God helped me to write, be an encouragement and a help to you, to do what God is calling you to do, so we all can meet at the feet of Jesus and walk on the Sea of Glass and the streets of gold and enjoy heaven together with our loved ones and friends, where there'll be no more tears, death, nor sorrow, nor crying, and no more pain: for the former things are passed away as Rev. 21:4 promises. This is my prayer for each of you!

"Maranatha!" The Lord is coming! God bless each of you!

OUR SON, JONATHAN

Our dear son, Jonathan Paul Clore,
Stand up and be accounted for.
Show the Lord that you love Him more,
And to your sins, you've closed the door.
And have put God first in your life,
And want to live the Christian life.
Mom and Dad are so proud of you.
Please Christ and do what He would do.
You've decided to follow Christ,
And do those things you know are right.
You're always in our prayers each day,
That you'll stay on the narrow way.
Keep your eyes on Christ and your goal,
And go to heaven winning souls.
You'll have many stars in your crown,
The smile of God, and not His frown.
You'll have joy, you lived to please Him.
With God's help, you got rid of sin.
And overcame the devil's wiles,
To be like Jesus, all the while.
Be a champion for Jesus.
Stand up for Christ and in Him trust.
Stand true to Jesus and His Word,
And share with those who have not heard,
Of God's great love and sacrifice,
And gives to us, Eternal Life.
Then, let God have control of you,
To help in all you have to do.
Then, if faithful, we'll meet up there.
Then, we'll look on Christ's face so fair.
To be there with God and His Son,
And to hear God's voice say, "Well Done!"
Let's keep busy doing God's will,
And His Word we will soon fulfill.
We'll see Him coming soon for us.
Don't let anything hinder us.
Stay close to Jesus and don't sin.
We'll cross the finish line and win!
Jonathan, "Let go and let God,"
And choose to walk on heaven's sod.
You've joined the 3ABN team.
You're now part of the "Go" Team.
So, let your light shine before men.
Be an evangelist for Him.
So, don't look back, just carry on,
Together we'll sing that "New Song!"
So, never give up, just "Hang on!"
My son, to God you now belong!

Written by Linda Clore

We invite you to view the complete
selection of titles we publish at:

www.ASPECTBooks.com

scan with your mobile
device to go directly
to our website

Please write or email us your praises, reactions, or
thoughts about this or any other book we publish at:

info@ASPECTBooks.com

11 Quartermaster Circle
Fort Oglethorpe, GA 30743

ASPECT Books, titles may be purchased in bulk for
educational, business, fund-raising, or sales promotional use.
For information, please e-mail:

BulkSales@ASPECTBooks.com

Finally if you are interested in seeing
your own book in print, please contact us at

publishing@ASPECTBooks.com

We would be happy to review your manuscript for free.

www.ingramcontent.com/pod-product-compliance
Lightning Source LLC
Chambersburg PA
CBHW080941300426

44115CB00017B/2903